Commonwealth Public Address

Essays in Criticism

"And what is the duty of a statesman? To watch the inception of events, to descry their tendency, and to forewarn his countrymen."

Demosthenes, "On the Crown."

"Eloquence, which speaks to the passions, is a species of oratory almost unknown in England. At the bar it is quite discontinued, and I think with justice. In the senate, it is used but sparingly, as the orator speaks to enlightened judges. But in the pulpit, in which the orator should chiefly address the vulgar, it seems strange, that it should be entirely laid aside."

Goldsmith, "On Eloquence."

Commonwealth Public Address

Essays in Criticism

Marian B. McLeod

STERLING PUBLISHERS PRIVATE LIMITED

STERLING PUBLISHERS PRIVATE LIMITED
A-59, Okhla Industrial Area, Phase-II, New Delhi-110020.
Tel: 26387070, 26386209; Fax: 91-11-26383788
E-mail: sterlingpublishers@airtelbroadband.in
ghai@nde.vsnl.net.in
www.sterlingpublishers.com

Commonwealth Public Address: Essays in Criticism
© 2007 Marian B. McLeod
ISBN 978-81-207-3349-7

All rights are reserved. No part of this publication may be reproduced, stored in a retrieval system or transmitted, in any form or by any means, mechanical, photocopying, recording or otherwise, without prior written permission of the publisher.

PRINTED IN INDIA
―――――――――――――――――――――――――――――――――――
Printed and Published by Sterling Publishers Pvt. Ltd., New Delhi-110 020.

In Memoriam

R. T. Oliver and Ilene Fife

Acknowledgments

The author wishes to thank the publishers of the following journals and books for permission to reprint materials of which they hold the copyright: *Actes du 16e Congrès de la Société des Anglicistes de l'Enseignement Supérieur; African Literature in English; Awakened Conscience,* ed. C. D. Narasimhaiah; *Bharat Darshan; The Canon of Commonwealth Literature,* ed. A. L. McLeod; *Caribbean Quarterly; Hindu Vishwa; Indian Horizons; Individual and Community in Commonwealth Literature,* ed. Daniel Massa; *Journal of Caribbean Studies; Literary Half-Yearly; Scan: The Australian Journal of Human Communication; Subjects Worthy Fame: Essays on Commonwealth Literature in Honour of H. H. Anniah Gowda; Tradition and Change: Proceedings of the 1980 Conference of the African Studies Association,* ed. Edna Steeves; *Westerly.*

Contents

	Preface	ix
1.	Gopal Krishna Gokhale: Spokesman for Indian Nationalism	1
2.	Ethical Proof in Three Speeches of R. G. Menzies	26
3.	Norman Manley and Eric Williams: Speaking for the West Indies	46
4.	R. G. Menzies as Parliamentary Speaker	62
5.	Speeches as an Artifact of Historiography	80
6.	B. G. Tilak and G. K. Gokhale: Advocates and Adversaries	90
7.	Public Address and Caribbean Studies	100
8.	African Speeches in English	114
9.	The Rhetoric of Cheddi Jagan and Forbes Burnham	133
10.	Race and Colour in Caribbean Protestant Sermons	149
11.	Thomas P. Callender: Presbyterian Preacher in Jamaica	170
12.	Public Address and Commonwealth Literature	185
13.	Maurice Bishop: The Voice of the Grenada Revolution	202
14.	Jessie Street and the Rhetoric of Australian Feminism	214
15.	Establishing a Canon of Commonwealth Public Address	228

Preface

As recently as fifty years ago the study of literature included several genres that have since been relegated to other disciplines or been deemed inferior to poetry, prose fiction, and drama, and so denigrated critically. Whereas biographies and autobiographies, letters and diaries, essays and journals, travelogues and histories, sermons and political orations—even pornography and philosophy—were considered legitimate components of literature as an academic discipline, they have been largely expunged and replaced by such subjects as children's and juvenile fiction, myths and legends, and film and television studies. However, a glance at the Acknowledgments page indicates that a number of highly regarded publications are again receptive to articles devoted to the study of speeches (public address, or oratory). No longer is rhetorical criticism restricted to the *Quarterly Journal of Speech, Speech Monographs,* and the several regional professional publications.

During the past half-century Commonwealth literature has developed as a subject of study and is sometimes subsumed under the rubric of Postcolonial literature (which somehow manages to exclude British and American literatures). And while the published literature of the former colonies and dependencies is sometimes sparse, the quantity of "oral literature" in the form of public speeches is impressive.

Alfred Harbage, the celebrated Harvard Elizabethan scholar, writing in *William Shakespeare: A Reader's Guide* about the few plays of the era that managed to get into print, might well have been speaking about speeches in the newer and smaller Commonwealth countries when he said, "those which happened to get into print were considered not 'literature' but popular ephemera, chiefly useful as mementos of or substitutes for" being there.

And then he reminded us that "no matter what the style of a speech or succession of speeches, each will seem to have been brought into being by something in the immediate context" (73). It is this consideration of audience and occasion that differentiates literary criticism per se and rhetorical criticism, a distinction clearly enunciated by Lord Curzon in his *Modern Parliamentary Eloquence*:

> In dealing with the parliamentary speakers of our time I shall ... not regard them as prose writers or literary men, still less as purveyors of instruction to their own or to future generations, but as men who produced, by the exercise of certain talents of speech, a definite impression upon contemporary audiences, and a whole reputation for eloquence must be judged by that test, and that test alone. (7)

Accordingly, in several of the sections that follow, considerable space is devoted to a presentation of audience and situation. Perhaps the best statement on the bases of speech criticism is that made many years ago by Herbert A. Wichelns in his essay "The Literary Criticism of Oratory":

> Rhetorical criticism is necessarily analytical. The scheme of a rhetorical study includes the element of the speaker's personality as a conditioning factor; it includes also the public character of the man—not what he was, but what he was thought to be. It requires a description of the speaker's audience, and of the leading ideas with which he plied his hearers—his topics, the motives to which he appealed, the nature of the proofs he offered. These will reveal his own judgment of human nature in his audiences, and also his judgment on the questions which he discussed. Attention must be paid, too, to the relation of the surviving texts to what was actually uttered: in case the nature of the changes is known, there may be occasion to consider adaptation to two audiences—that which heard and that which read. Nor can rhetorical criticism omit the speaker's mode of arrangement and his mode of expression, nor his habit of preparation and his manner of delivery from the platform; though the last two are perhaps less significant. "Style"—in the sense which corresponds to diction and sentence movement—must receive attention, but only as one among various means that secure for the speaker ready access to the minds of his auditors. Finally, the effect of the discourse on ... its immediate hearers is not to be ignored, either in the testimony of witnesses, nor in the record of events. And throughout such a study one must conceive of the public man as influencing the men of his own times by the power of his discourse. (212-13)

Preface

Notwithstanding this detailed list of considerations that should help determine a defensible evaluation of a speech or a speaker—or of a whole body of public addresses—the individual listener (or reader) is never relieved of the obligation to form his own opinion. The reader of the transcript of a speech must remember that he is of necessity at a disadvantage, since he is deprived of the atmosphere created by the ambience of the occasion, body language, gesture, applause, interruptions, repetitions, pauses. Reading a speech is really analogous to reading a play, which is not the same as being present in a theatre during an actual performance.

Notwithstanding, both Curzon and Wichelns essentially reiterate the continuing importance of the criteria for adjudicating speeches that were first clearly enunciated by the classical rhetoricians: *inventio* (content, ideas); *dispositio* (organization, arrangement); *elocutio* (style, language); *pronuntiatio* (delivery, voice, body language); *memoria* (spontaneity, familiarity with material). Each of these elements can be assessed by the audience members, but the effect of a speech may not always be apparent immediately and is often difficult to determine.

There has always been a ready reception for public address (whether in the form of inspirational sermons, deliberative arguments, forensic analyses, or epideictic evaluations), for people have an insatiable desire to hear what others have to say on subjects of importance to their lives. Today, however, the succinct statement is generally preferred to the detailed analysis or the extended harangue; the plain style is more favoured than the florid, the fustian, the literary, the sententious—though the memorable quip, slogan, or aphorism is welcomed as a substitute for the flight of fancy of an earlier age; the simple chronological or problem-solution organizational patterns appear to have supplanted the syllogistic, enthymematic, or convoluted (except, perhaps, in the courtroom); and argument from example, authority, or even anecdote is readily accepted as proof. Eloquence, in the traditional sense, is increasingly rare—and even suspect, being thought of as a substitute for sincerity, simplicity, and straightforwardness.

The vast erudition, skillful invention, careful adaptation, and ready wit of past orators are seldom encountered in our contemporary speakers, as leadership has shifted from an educated elite to more representative, proletarian men and women; and the occasional recourse to an adviser, authority, or speech consultant has given way to the employment of full-time, professional speech-writers, speech-writing committees—or even, in the case of President George W. Bush, well-staffed speech-writing departments.

Of course, when two or three major speeches are to be delivered in a single day, often on quite different topics, it is impossible for an individual to prepare them without assistance; and semiotics and semantics have become as important as style. Every trope has to be examined, every gesture has to be considered, every joke or allusion has to be pre-tested on a focus group. Accordingly, the extemporaneous or impromptu address by a major speaker has become a rarity; *memoria* has been eliminated by the omnipresence of the TelePrompTer, declamation has been modified by the ubiquitous microphone.

The length of the following essays has been determined by the journals in which they first appeared or by the time constraints of the academic conferences at which they were presented. Spelling has been made uniform, conforming to British usage; punctuation, capitalization, and documentation follow the Modern Language Association style; a few minor changes have been made in order to provide better transitions, to remove repetitions, or to add elucidating details. The papers appear in the order in which they were first published.

Trenton, N.J.   M.B.M.

WORKS CITED

Curzon, George N. *Modern Parliamentary Eloquence*. London: Macmillan, 1913.

Harbage, Alfred. *William Shakespeare: A Reader's Guide*. New York: Noonday, 1963.

Wichelns, Herbert A. "The Literary Criticism of Oratory." *Studies in Rhetoric and Public Speaking in Honor of James Albert Winans*. New York: Century, 1925.

1. Gopal Krishna Gokhale: Spokesman for Indian Nationalism

When Gopal Krishna Gokhale died on 19 February 1915, his contributions to the Indian Nationalist Movement were widely acclaimed by both Indians and Britons. This is remarkable when one considers that he lived during a period of great unrest, as Indians struggled to achieve equality and a representative government.

Sir Verney Lovett, who spent thirty-five years in the Indian service and who made careful appraisal of the Indian Nationalist Movement, had this to say of Gokhale: "There can be no doubt that his death was a serious loss to Indian politics. He had shown himself able to adjust idealism to circumstances, and bold enough to preach common sense. At the same time, up to the day of his death, he maintained his widespread influence. His place remained empty" (35).

Gandhi, coming from South Africa in 1896, had been instantly drawn to Gokhale and spoke of him in terms of admiration to the Indian National Congress at Lahore on 29 December 1909: "He seemed to me all I wanted as a political leader: pure as crystal, gentle as a lamb, brave as a lion, and chivalrous to a fault.... It was enough for me that I could discover no fault in him to cavil at. He was and remains for me the most perfect man on the political field" (55).

This esteem was reciprocated by Gokhale, who commented that there could be no mention of Gandhi's name "without deep emotion and pride," and called Gandhi "a patriot amongst patriots" (Gokhale 420). The two men shared similar interpretations of India's needs, and both were markedly righteous in their approach to problems of Indian nationalism. Both Gandhi and Gokhale stand in marked contrast to their fiery revolutionist contemporary, B. G. Tilak. A noteworthy feature of the early Indian Nationalist Movement is the apparent ease with which it accommodated, and emphasized from time to time, the views represented by both Gandhi and Gokhale, on the one hand, and Tilak on the other.

The purpose of this paper is to determine what influence the speaking of Gopal Krishna Gokhale had on the Indian Nationalist Movement. The inquiry is in the form of a biographical-rhetorical study. It includes an examination of the pertinent biographical facts, the problems Gokhale faced in his speeches, and the audience which he addressed.

Gopalrao Krishna Gokhale was born on 6 May 1866 in the Maharathi village of Kotaluk, located in the Ratnagiri district. He was a Brahmin and a descendant of the Chitpavan clan. Historically, this middle-class clan took the role of leading social reformation, some members advocating reform within the framework of British rule and others viewing such reform only as a necessary prelude to the time when British rule would be abolished.

Gokhale's father was a tax collector in his village and a minor clerk in the local government, so the family's position was superior to that of the average Indian peasant. As a younger son, however, he received little more than his college tuition and a meagre income after his father's death (Wolpert 22). Not many details are available concerning his college life at Deccan College and later at Elphinstone College in Bombay. He is pictured as a shy, diligent student, extremely proficient in English, and with a keen interest in English literature. He enjoyed poetry, and in his own poetry he seems to have been influenced by the work of Tennyson and Browning. The characteristics of his prose style have been said to show the influence of Burke, Mill, Bright, and Morley (Wolpert).

In 1885 Gokhale studied law at Deccan College and joined the faculty of the New English School at Poona as an assistant master. While at this Jesuit school he joined with its founders and supporters, including B. G. Tilak, in establishing the Deccan Education Society, whose aim was to promote education by founding schools and colleges under native Indian management. In 1885 the society founded Fergusson College, named after the retiring governor of Bombay, Sir James Fergusson, and which continues to this day.

In the period immediately preceding the formation of the Indian National Congress the Deccan Education Society became an important political force. Its members viewed education as an effective instrument of national regeneration, and the members were encouraged to participate in political activities. Gokhale became secretary of the Bombay Provincial Congress in 1888, beginning his career as a public figure with this appointment. During the same year he edited the English columns of the Sudharak, an Anglo-Marathi weekly. This secular journal emphasized freedom and equality among all men as necessary conditions for reform and pointed to the role of education in India's struggle. Education, it was felt, would allow Indians to "qualify" for equal treatment.

Gokhale's first public speech was probably delivered on 1 September 1889, at Poona, on the subject of the Crawford dismissal.[1] Protesting the dismissal of Indian magistrates implicated in the scandal, Gokhale exhorted both sides to reasonableness:

> In the interest of India and England alike, the Government of this country ought to be carried on with absolute impartiality.... if our English friends will kindly disabuse their minds of all bias against us, if they will take a calm and dispassionate view of everything, if sentiment will give way to reason, then they will find that in treating the natives of this country with courtesy, consideration, and equality, consists the best safe-guard of the British Rule. (142)

This approach to the problem typified Gokhale's view that ill-feeling on both sides could only be increased if violence, rather than reason, were permitted to dictate policy. He was unwilling to believe that an inherent hatred could exist between

Indians and Britons; his revolt against English rule was largely a moral one, for he felt that Indians should be treated with equality. (And his use of doubled elements and triads indicated his mastery of one element of formal prose style.)

Gokhale's political activities became more important, and in 1889 he participated in the Indian National Congress. The first Congress had been called in 1885 at the inspiration of Allan Octavian Hume, a retired English civil servant who felt that the British raj had largely failed to improve Indian conditions and that there would be no improvement for the masses until Indian government became truly representative. Delegates from all parts of British India were invited to attend the Congress in order to become acquainted with each other and to decide what political action might be taken during the coming year. In the words of the announcement: "Indirectly this Conference will form the germ of a Native Parliament, and if properly conducted will constitute in a few years an unanswerable reply to the assertion that India is still wholly unfit for any form of representative institution" (qtd. in Lovett 35).

At its inception the movement was Hindu-oriented and attracted middle-class intellectuals and members of the rising commercial class. The members of the Congress believed that by presenting a fair and reasonable case, and by conducting themselves according to parliamentary precedent, they could get the most pressing problems corrected and win freedom for themselves. The first Congress was conducted in English; in fact, the tradition of conducting everything in English was so strong that it was not until 1905 that Rabindranath Tagore, presiding at a provincial conference in Bengal, broke this custom by delivering a speech in Bengali (Andrews and Mookerjee 181). (Initially, the organizers of the first Congress had seriously considered asking Lord Reay, the Governor of Bombay, to preside over the meeting.)

Outwardly at least, the British seemed to attach little significance to the nationalist movement, and membership in the Congress was not considered incompatible with loyalty to the British Crown. Despite the Sepoy Mutiny of 1857, the British were not apprehensive that their administration of India would be shaken, for, as one lieutenant-governor expressed the British attitude, "good administration was like good digestion. It did its work and you heard no more about it" (qtd. in Lovett 18). In 1888 Lord Dufferin remarked, at a farewell dinner marking his retirement from the vice-royalty, that the Congress party was a "microscopic minority"; even so, he did send home confidential recommendations for liberalizing the legislative councils, "which is all that the reasonable leaders even of the most advanced section of Young India dream of" (42).

Actually, much more than this was at stake. The Congress members sought reform and broadening of the powers of existing local legislative councils, but on a much larger scale than the English considered appropriate, and with the appointment of a standing committee of the House of Commons to prevent the Crown executive overruling the council's majority decisions.

When Gokhale delivered his maiden speech to the Congress at Bombay on 27 December 1889, he rose to support an amendment by B. G. Tilak that would have given provincial councils the privilege of electing members of their own bodies to the supreme legislative councils. The amendment was lost, but his participation in debate the following day (on holding simultaneous public civil service examinations) was more favourably received. This resolution, based on the Queen's Proclamation of racial equality, and intended to assure equal treatment for Indian candidates, was a recurring theme at every Congress meeting. It had to wait for nearly forty years before it could overcome official opposition.

A good example of Gokhale's style may be found in a speech that he delivered on this problem at the 1894 Madras Congress:

> We have had this question in every shape. We have examined it from every point of view. Our invention has been exhausted. Reason is fatigued. Experience has given judgment. But Anglo-Indian obstinacy is not yet conquered. (Cheers.) And remember, Gentlemen, this that we have to conquer is perhaps the worst kind of obstinacy, for it is not based so much on wrong judgment; it is not based even so much on prejudice; it is obstinacy based on the strong foundations of self-interest and love of domination. (qtd. in Wolpert 106)

Here we find the initial parallel simple declaratives followed by a series of similar structures before the inevitable conclusion, "But...." And there is a growing intensity in the development from *had* to *examined*, to *exhausted, fatigued, obstinacy,* and *conquered* – with both *obstinacy* and *conquered* (in a cognate) repeated for effect. Further, the emotional words *wrong judgment* and *prejudice* are introduced in conjunction with *self-interest* and *love of domination*, applied to the "enemy," the whole section becoming a most effective use of emotional proof, of persuasive rhetoric. In many ways the composition replicates the prose of Patrick Henry's famous "Give Me Liberty" speech.

In addition to his association with the Indian Congress, Gokhale assumed other activities. He was secretary of the Sarvajanik Sabha, an association for political work, and edited its quarterly journal; he became a Fellow at the University of Bombay (1895) and secretary of the Deccan Education Society (1892). His work brought him into contact with many of the influential political minds of the day. Many of his ideas about economic questions came from his contacts with Mahadev Govind Ranade, the man who had been his guru since his teaching days at Fergusson College. Gokhale's idea of government initiative in economic development is hardly new to us, but at the time it was considered radical when he said,

> Is it not the duty of Government to see that the subject population is properly fed and clothed and housed?.... Does not the security of the country lie in the real prosperity of its teeming millions?.... But 'Let alone' is the policy of Government. Free-trade, or rather political economy, is working out her laws, say they. Well! We think the laws of political economy are largely amenable to human control. The Government must take the initiative here. They should support the falling industries of the land, if they want India to be prosperous. (qtd. in Wolpert 104-105)

In 1896 such were the divergent views within the Sarvajanik Sabha that Gokhale, along with Ganade and other moderates, broke away from that group and formed another organization, the Deccan Sabha, which they felt more adequately reflected their views of "giving to the rulers the loyalty that is due to the law they are bound to administer, but securing at the same time to the ruled the equality which is their right under law" (Gokhale xiv).

Gokhale was given the opportunity to explain his economic ideas directly to a royal commission appointed in 1897 to consider the state of Indian finance. He traveled to London on behalf of the Deccan Sabha, and his testimony before the Welby Commission gave him an opportunity to meet British politicians and to learn first hand the realities of English life. This was an experience not given to many of his countrymen, and Gokhale made the most of it to diminish the gap between Indians and the British. While there he had a cordial meeting with John Morley, who was later to serve as Secretary of State for India. (It is commonly asserted that Morley's favourable impressions of Gokhale were influential in his acceptance of the Indian portfolio.) The meeting also served to give Gokhale confidence in Morley and the Liberal Party.

From his stimulating and successful contacts abroad Gokhale returned to an atmosphere of hostility in India. While he was in England complaints had reached him of the conduct of British soldiers in enforcing anti-plague measures in Poona[2]: it seems to have been what we would call police brutality. Two Indian women had committed suicide after being raped by British soldiers. Gokhale described his informants as men "whose word I can trust absolutely," and in an interview in the *Manchester Guardian* he criticized the soldiers' conduct. When challenged to produce evidence of his charges Gokhale found his correspondents unwilling to support the charges publicly, and he was driven to make an embarrassing public apology. The ostracism of the Chitpavan community and the criticism from all sides depressed him for some time. He wrote that "recent events ... have distracted me so far that my mental equipment has been for the present seriously impaired.... it will be some time before my mind will be able to return to its normal condition" (qtd. in Wolpert 118).

Despite his humiliation, however, Gokhale immediately took part in organizing relief for the victims of the plague. In political affairs he gradually resumed his active role and was elected to the Bombay Legislative Council in 1899. During the two years that he spent as a member of the Council he was elected to represent its non-official members in the Viceregal Legislature. During both of these appointments he found himself involved in much committee work, and he delivered numerous speeches on the presentation of bills. He spoke for tax reform and vigorously opposed a bill to reform the universities, which he said would increase enormously the control of the Government over university matters and make the universities virtually a government department.

His fight against an amendment to the Indian Official Secrets Act won the support of his countrymen. The amendment would have made civil as well as military matters official secrets and their publication an offense. Gokhale charged that the bill would "Russianize the Indian Administration," and offered the following cogent defense of freedom of the press:

> The responsibility of the Government to the people in this country is merely moral, it is not legal, as in the West. There is no machinery here, as in Western countries, to secure that the interests of the general public will not be sacrificed in favour of a class. The criticism of the Indian Press is the only outward check operating continuously upon the conduct of a bureaucracy possessing absolute and uncontrolled power. (Gokhale 6)

Gokhale's work with legislative bodies convinced him that politicians could not be amateurs—they must view politics as a profession and become dedicated to it. He sought to provide India with such skilled men by founding the Servants of India Society in 1905. The inspiration for the organization came from the Society of Jesus, but the missionary seal was devoted to political and social matters rather than religious matters. The members' vows of lifelong service to India, pledging to promote their country's interests *by constitutional means*, did not necessarily mean rejection or acceptance of foreign ideas. Emphasis was placed on purity of personal example, responsible criticism of ongoing programs, women's emancipation, elevation of backward classes, industrial development, and political equality within the Empire: complete independence was not their goal. Gandhi became an apprentice in the society during the last year of Gokhale's life and Rajendra Prasad, who became the first president of the Republic of India, was also an early member.

Gokhale maintained his connection with the Indian National Congress and was elected president for its session at Benares in December 1905. It was a critical time. The British had announced the partition of Bengal in October, and a wave of nationalist feeling swept over India. Tilak headed a movement to conduct a boycott of British goods as a new agitational technique. The boycott idea was not the same as Gandhi's non-cooperation, for the boycott permitted violence, which was countered by extreme repression from Lord Curzon's government, but the notion of rebellion and revolution was firmly planted in the Indians' minds. The concept of *swaraj* (self-government) spread beyond the cities to remote districts where it had never before been contemplated.

In the midst of growing trouble Gokhale went to London on 16 September 1905 to represent the Congress in an attempt to explain to the British the state of Indian public feeling over Lord Curzon's repressive acts, particularly the partition of Bengal. One of his most challenging speeches was delivered on 6 October in Manchester, where he faced an audience of textile manufacturers and workers who were distinctly hostile to the Indian boycott of their cloth. The speech emphasized that his faith in Britain had not abated, despite Lord Curzon's policies, and that "when the whole position is brought home to you, you will rise as one man and put an end to these Russian methods of administration." In London he appealed personally to Liberal leaders, particularly John Morley; his speeches seem to have been received well and mark the beginning of a change in Liberal attitudes toward India.

En route to London Gokhale occupied himself with the preparation of the speech he was to give at the opening of the Benares Congress. It was a statement that would be closely scrutinized by all sides, and he felt weighed down by the responsibility: "God knows how it will be discharged in the end," he was reported to have said. When he returned to

Bombay the speech was still unfinished. The departure of Lord Curzon as viceroy made his task somewhat easier, for it permitted him to criticize administrative policies without having to face the viceroy himself in the Viceregal Legislature at Calcutta. The speech is doubtless one of the most important of Gokhale's career, for he managed to hold the Congress together in refusing to invoke the boycott. It was a narrow victory, but the same issue split the Congress the following year and set Gokhale and Tilak irretrievably apart.

The next five years were significant ones, with extremists and moderates struggling for control of Congress. John Morley had become secretary of state for India and Lord Minto was made viceroy. Gokhale traveled again to London in April 1906 to work through Morley in gaining reforms for India. Viewed in the light of history the Morley-Minto reforms were too much of the old pattern, but they had the effect of retaining the moderate element uppermost in the Congress and of delaying the time when more radical views prevailed. The difficulties of the situation were summed up by Morley in a letter to Lord Minto:

> Your way of putting this helps me to realise how intensely artificial and unnatural is our mighty *Raj*, and it sets one wondering whether it can possibly last.... Will your Reform Policy, Natives on my Council, Decentralisation, Economising of Taxation, and the rest of our virtuous deeds really make a pin of difference in their feelings about British rule? (qtd. in Gopal 303)

Gokhale found himself in the difficult position of trying to work with both the English and the Indians. To the British the idea of a recognized opposition point of view hardly existed; the viceroy saw Gokhale as the instrument of British authority in the Indian National Congress and was petulent when Gokhale did not play this role. As he wrote to Morley,

> As to Gokhale, if he chooses to play with fire he must take the consequences. We can't afford to let him tamper with the Army, and if he says anything to me... I shall tell him straight to his face. I am thoroughly disappointed in Gokhale; I had liked what I had seen of him and believed that he was honest at heart, but the part he has

played of late has disgusted me. ... he is as big a revolutionist as the rest of them. (Gokhale xxxi-xxxii)

Gokhale persisted in his own view of his role, despite the viceroy's disappointment and the criticism of extremist elements in the Congress. In 1910 he became a member of the enlarged Viceregal Legislature, where he continued to act as a critic of the government. Indians had expected improved conditions in the wake of Lord Minto's reforms; instead, repressions seemed to increase. The atmosphere of the times can be clearly seen in the issues which occupied Gokhale's attention: the Press Bill of 1910 (which imposed a heavy tax on operators of printing presses) and the Seditious Meetings Bill of 1911 (which limited freedom of speech).

While on the Legislative Council Gokhale used his position to present the annual Congress resolutions directly to the council. In the reforms that he urged upon them he gave great weight to education, and in 1911 he presented a bill enabling qualified districts to make education compulsory for boys between the ages of six and ten, the central government to provide at least two-thirds of the cost. Indian public opinion was solidly in favour of the measure, but the bill was defeated in spite of the proponent's lucid advocacy.

Gokhale's attention to Indian problems extended to the suffering of indentured Indian labourers in South Africa: his friendship with Gandhi no doubt inspired this interest. Gandhi had gone to India in 1896 and sought the support of the Indian National Congress in fighting a discriminatory tax imposed upon South African Indians. As a result of their meeting, Gokhale became Gandhi's political *guru*, and Gokhale wholeheartedly supported Gandhi's stand, particularly his campaign of passive resistance. At the Lahore Congress in 1909 Gokhale successfully moved a resolution supporting the struggle in South Africa and recommending that the government of India prohibit the recruitment of indentured Indian workers. He argued a similar measure in the Council the following year, but his proposed reforms were not effected until 1917.

In 1912 Gokhale was able to visit South Africa on his return from England, where he had attended sessions of the Indian Public Services Royal Commission. It was an honour for him to have been appointed to the Royal Commission, but his health would not permit him to attend all of its sessions, and, sensing perhaps that he had little time left, he wished to influence Gandhi to return to India, where he could be prepared to assume a responsible position in the Congress. Gokhale died on 19 February 1915, before the work of the Commission was finished. His death may be viewed as having brought an end to the dominance of the moderate element in Indian politics and its policy of logical analysis rather than vehemence as advocate or adversary in public policy debate.

In reviewing the strengths and weaknesses of Gokhale we find ample testimony to his command of both spoken and written English and to the efficacy of his use of the language. As Wolpert says, "Gifted as he was with a unique command of the spoken and written English language he could most effectively fashion his protests, petitions, and pleas, and by the end of his life the weight of Gokhale's influence upon British official opinion was unsurpassed by that of any Indian" (299).

Even Valentine Chirol, whose criticism of the Indian Nationalist Movement was at times vitriolic, had this to say of Gokhale's conduct on the Viceregal Council:

> Though often an unrelenting critic of the Administration, he struck from the first a note of studied moderation and restraint to which most of his political friends attuned their utterances. He naturally assumed the functions of the leader of His Majesty's Opposition, and he discharged them, not only with the ability which every one expected of him, but with the urbanity and self-restraint of a man conscious of his responsibilities as well as of his powers. His was, amongst the Indian members, not only the master mind, but the dominant personality. (169)

Gokhale's friends' "utterances"—their informative and persuasive public speeches, their council debates, their courtroom presentations, their interpersonal deliberations— apparently exhibited the strong ethical proof of their leader, whose quiet reasonableness, general equanimity, and unwavering fidelity were admired.

Gokhale's devotion to the cause of Indian nationalism is evident in all aspects of his work. He refused to compromise his belief in the equality of all men and clung to the belief that Indian reform should be evolutionary. His righteousness and straightforwardness sometimes forced him into situations where he faced unpleasant alternatives, as in the apology incident. In that instance the blow to his pride was considerable, but his comment later was, "The best part of our nature is manifested not in what we enjoy; but in what we endure" (qtd. in Wolpert 130).

His education and his personal contacts with political leaders in England inclined him toward a sympathetic view of Britain that was not shared by many Indians. Perhaps his views made him seem rather remote. Although he was politically "thin-skinned"—he suffered agonies over the dilemmas he found himself in—he attempted to face problems in a logical, a rational fashion rather than retreat into religious mysticism.

Gokhale's photographs generally show him in Western dress with a long scarf around his neck and a red silk-covered Maharashtrian hat. He wore a moustache, which was at the time an essential mark of virility, but he did not shave his hair, as was the Brahmin custom. His face seems placid, yet as his biographer Wolpert has pointed out, his benign appearance hid a temperament that was often contradictory: "he was a rationalist who believed in astrology, a statesman who founded a monastic society, a poet who taught mathematics" (25).

Of his speaking voice and his delivery, little seems to have been written. We read that he was soft-spoken, mild in his manner, reticent, and not particularly at ease with crowds: he is pictured as "too vulnerable to endure long the strain of political controversy and public responsibilities" (26). Despite any physical limitations, Gokhale did not spare himself, and we read of the taxing round of activities he imposed on himself. When he decided to stand for the Bombay Legislative Council he campaigned throughout Maharashtra in the sweltering heat.

Yet Gokhale addressed many large outdoor gatherings on his trip to South Africa and in connection with his efforts for the Indian National Congress; but of the physical conditions which prevailed under these circumstances there is little direct evidence. His effectiveness in interpersonal communication was widely acknowledged and his rapport with British Liberals has already been noted.

We find two interesting descriptions of the parliamentary situation in which Gokhale spoke, both of which are from English sources. The first is from accounts of the Viceroy's Legislative Council originally appearing in the *Times* [London]:

> the old Council Chamber at Government House presented a very significant spectacle.... The round table at which the members of the Viceroy's Legislative Council used to gather, with far less of formality, had disappeared, and the 59 members of the enlarged Council had their appointed seats disposed in a double hemicycle facing the Chair. They sat for the most part according to provinces, and the features as well as, in some cases, the dresses, of the Indian members showed at a glance how representative this new Council really was ... if the voice of the Indian National Congress did not predominate it had certainly not been reduced to silence.
>
> Not a few official members ... were inclined at first to rely exclusively upon their written notes, and there was indeed, from beginning to end, but little room for the rapid thrust and skilled parry of debate to which we are accustomed at Westminster. Most of the Indian members themselves had carefully prepared their speeches beforehand, and read them out from typed or even printed drafts before them. In many cases the speeches had been communicated two or three days ahead to the Press, and sometimes a speech was printed and commented upon in the favoured organ of some honourable member, though he had ultimately changed his mind and preserved silence....
>
> The florid style of eloquence cultivated by the leaders of the Indian National Congress fell distinctly flat in the calmer atmosphere of the Council-room, as indeed Mr. Gokhale warned some of his friends it was bound to do....
>
> Amongst Indian members it was the politician, and especially the more "advanced" politician, who figured most prominently in the discussions. The more conservative Indians were usually content to listen, with more or less visible signs of weariness, to the facile

and sometimes painfully long-winded eloquence of their colleagues. When they did intervene, however, their speeches were usually short and none the less effective. (qtd. in Chirol 162-66)

The second, a comment on the Indian National Congress, is provided in an editorial of the *Times*:

> We have produced an extensive class of talkers, and equipped them with a great deal of second-hand knowledge of English history and literature. Such a Congress as that which sat last year in Bombay, or is now sitting in Calcutta, is composed of delegates from all these talking clubs who focus the valuable results of their perennial activity. (qtd. in Gopal 283-84)

It should be remembered that conservative Englishmen thought that the Congress was an organization founded to preach sedition; with the passage of the Seditious Meetings Bill of 1911, Congressmen may have risked imprisonment for statement of their views.

No doubt Gokhale wrote out his speeches as did other members of the Congress, and his advice to fellow Council members shows that he had quickly learned to adapt his speeches to the audience and also to the demands of the speaking occasion. In his lifelong participation in public life as a member of the Indian National Congress and the Viceregal Legislature he had ample opportunity to develop his speaking abilities. He frequently found that he had to take a position between extremes, and this necessity apparently demanded that he prepare his speeches with great caution and care; but he was facilitated in preparing even long orations before deliberative assemblies by his excellent command of English, by his familiarity with the great British orators, by his appreciation of parliamentary exigencies, by his knowledge of the intricacies of parliamentary procedure, and by his grasp of historical contexts and the relevant precedents. He liked to argue by analogy (other colonies and dominions) where appropriate and also to proceed from easier decisions and not disturb settled matters; but he frequently expressed the view that the rulings handed down in previous judicial decisions often contravened the ordinary principles of justice as he understood them. He was, it was apparent, able to argue quickly, analytically, and incisively and phrase his thoughts in a style that was appropriate for the audience, the subject, and the occasion, not infrequently rising to the high style.

These characteristics can be seen, for example, in his speeches to the New Reform Club, London, on 14 November 1905, and on the Press Bill to the Imperial Legislative Council on 8 February 1910—both challenging audiences—the complete transcripts of which are to be found in the volume *Speeches and Writings of Gopal Krishna Gokhale*.

Despite the fact that Gokhale was speaking to the Reform Club on a subject of great personal importance, the general tone of his speech is controlled; the speech is not lengthy or effusive, but straightforward. The speaker opens with a short introduction that is simple and establishes his goodwill. Mindful of the honour of such an invitation, he views this opportunity to speak as "a sign, a most gratifying and unmistakable sign, of another awakening, the awakening of England to the claims of India." He next states the reason for his address:

> For the last twenty years the Indian people have been agitating for a greater voice in the affairs of their country, through the Indian National Congress. The bureaucracy, however, pays little attention to what we say in India, and so my countrymen thought it desirable that an appeal should now be addressed direct to the electors of this country.

The body of the speech contains his analysis of the causes and effects of India's problems. It is, he asserts, Lord Curzon "on whom the chief responsibility for the repression of the last three years mainly rests ... his main aim has been to strengthen the position of the Englishman in India, and weaken correspondingly the position of the Indians," and that "this reaction and this repression ... has driven my countrymen to a position bordering on despair." Continuing to ascribe blame to Curzon, Gokhale says:

> Lord Curzon is no believer in free institutions, or in national aspirations.... He has tried to fetter the Press.... he has transferred the control of [higher education] to the hands of the officials and to such Indians as will always agree with him.... he has abolished

competition, and made everything dependent upon the pleasure of the officials.... he has tried to take away, especially in Bengal, a portion of that self-government which had been given to the people a quarter of a century ago.

Gokhale regards Lord Curzon's repudiation of the Queen's Proclamation as particularly injurious. Although he calls the Proclamation a "legal fiction," he says it was nonetheless "a very important thing as laying down in theory the policy of a great nation towards a subject people."

Gokhale has built a causal relation between India's bitter despair and the reactionary measures of the viceroy. He then extends the source of blame to British bureaucracy, for "it is your system of administration in India that has enabled him to attempt all this repression...." An efficient administration of India had been the government's goal, but this would not fulfill Britain's public pledge of eventual Indian self-government, for "the higher efficiency, which comes of self-government ... you can never secure under a bureaucratic system."

The effects of over-zealous pursuits of bureaucratic efficiency are such that "nobody in the Government ... is permanently identified with the interests of the people," and because of the exclusion of the educated class from power, "The interests of the services are thus allowed to take precedence of the interests of the people." Such a policy produces a people "full of bitterness," whose despair is compounded by comparison of themselves with even Japan, where "the whole weight of the government has been thrown on the side of popular progress." Thus he specifies the evils of British rule.

Having left his hearers with a definite understanding of the coerciveness and short-sightedness of British policy in India, he concludes his speech with an appeal for self-government as the only feasible solution. He concedes that the task is difficult, but "after all they [the bureaucrats] are only the servants of the British people, and when you have definitely made up your minds, they will be bound to carry out your policy." The time is late, but he has faith that the audience will make the right judgment.

In this speech we see Gokhale using the available means of persuasion that are to be found in ethical, emotional, and logical proofs. He increases his credibility in the introduction by showing due regard for the importance of the occasion and by ascribing to his audience the virtues of wisdom and justice in their desire to learn of Indian problems. He condemns Curzon's policies but maintains that his "personal feeling towards Lord Curzon ... is one of respect" and adds, "I am anxious to be fair to Lord Curzon." In this attempt to separate the policies from the man, Gokhale is establishing his own good moral character, his ethical proof. He reiterates this approach later in the speech when he says, "My quarrel, therefore, is less with him [Lord Curzon] personally ... than with this system."

The speaker ascribes the viceroy's lack of insight to the "limitations imposed upon him by his temperament and his training," and he increases his own *ethos* when he shows that he knows the facts about India's economic condition: "On this point, I claim some right to speak, for I have been studying this phase of the question for nearly twenty years now." He does not use ethical proof extensively in the speech, but it does serve to make his arguments more acceptable to his audience.

Closely related to ethical proof is the concept of emotional proof, and Gokhale uses this persuasive device in moderation. (It might be observed that his judicious use of ethical proof itself produces a favourable emotional response.) Throughout the speech he seeks to arouse the audience's sense of fair play by showing Indians as undeserving victims of oppression. The appeal to justice is one of the strongest that can be made to an English audience, and Gokhale reaches the high point of his emotional proof in his description of Lord Curzon's repudiation of the Queen's Proclamation. He recalls that the viceroy said of the working of the Proclamation, "It says that you will have equality when you are qualified for it. Now, here we have certain qualifications which can only be attained by heredity or race. Therefore, as you cannot acquire race, you really cannot have equality with Englishmen in India as long as British rule lasts."

Lord Curzon's deliberate misrepresentation of the intent of the Proclamation must have incited in the audience feelings of

Gopal Krishna Gokhale: Spokesman for Indian Nationalism

shame that an Englishman would be so lacking in integrity. Gokhale underscored the point by continuing:

> Now, apart from the question of your national honour being involved in this—this explaining away of a 'Sovereign's word,' look at the unwisdom, the stupendous unwisdom, of the whole thing, telling the people of India that unless they were content to remain permanently a subject race in their own country, their interests and those of British rule were not identical. After this, how can any Englishman complain if my countrymen regarded ... your rule in India as maintained ... for a selfish purpose?

Throughout the speech the language is moderate. There are no stinging denunciations, no fiery tirades. With Gokhale's audience, this temperance was probably effective and appreciated.

The restrained emotion and judicious use of ethical proof make Gokhale's arguments readily acceptable. He uses cause-to-effect reasoning to establish a relationship between the misery of the Indians and the policies of the British government; he judiciously bases his case on the premises already held by the audience. For example, in assigning blame for India's condition, he builds on the idea, agreed upon by all, that a subject people cannot alone be held responsible for their own condition, so his logic is unassailable: since India is a subject nation and Great Britain controls her government, Great Britain must accept the blame for India's plight. Again, in urging the audience to accept self-government as the solution to India's problems, Gokhale uses the premise that there can be no stability for any country unless it has a government—whether imposed or indigenous. Since the imposed government (the British *raj*) has failed, the alternate form of government (Indian *swaraj*) must be tried. These enthymemes are supported with illustrative examples and the personal experience of the speaker; there is no doubt of the speaker's intimate acquaintance with the facts. His comparison of India's backward state with Japan's prosperity serves to support his contention that India must have self-government. In the long run his idea of self-government did take root; however, his method of attaining self-government by almost imperceptibly gradual means was rejected.

When Lord Curzon's oppressive administration ended and Lord Minto arrived in India as viceroy, Indians hailed the beginning of "an era of responsible association." However, the first measure considered by the Reformed Indian Legislature was the Press Bill, devised to curtail sedition by enabling the Government to impose a heavy tax (5,000 rupees) on anyone owning a printing press and to seize their property if, in the authorities' opinion, their publications were seditious. (An appeal could be made to a board of three judges, but there was no trial.) The effect of the measure was to force small Indian publishers out of business, thus effectively silencing some of the most outspoken Indian critics, who depended in large measure on the printed texts of their speeches to convey their ideas beyond the immediate locality.

Gokhale's position in the legislature was a difficult one, for he was a member of the select committee that reviewed the bill. The other Indian member, Satyendra Sinha, was on the Viceroy's Executive Council and was responsible for introducing the bill and steering it through the Council. The bill was morally wrong as far as both were concerned, but differences of opinion arose over what course of action to take. Sinha was unable to secure any amelioration of the harsh terms of the bill before he presented it; as an Indian he felt unable to present it, so he offered his resignation.

Gokhale felt that Sinha's resignation would be an irresponsible rejection of Lord Minto's programs before they had any test. Further, as Sir C. Y. Chintamani commented, "If the first Indian admitted into the Governor-General's executive council after a long struggle on the part of the Secretary of State threw up the office in less than a year after the appointment and did so on a political issue, it would produce a disastrous impression on public opinion in England" (qtd. in Gokhale 70). Gokhale persuaded Sinha to stay, and in return he agreed to move amendments to the bill.

These comments on the situation surrounding Gokhale's speech show that the real issue here was probably not the Press Bill itself but what role an Indian member of the government should take. Gokhale's problem was not so much to judge the contents of the Bill as it is to weigh the overall effect of his own behaviour in this instance. Karve and Ambekar write that "the general reaction within the country to Gokhale's attitude towards the Press Bill was naturally unfavourable. This was not unexpected, and, therefore, for Gokhale it was a calculated cost" (xlii).

The thesis of his speech is that there is no need for the bill: "the Penal Code is amply sufficient to punish sedition and ... the special legislation of last year can effectively put down incitements to violence." Gokhale notes the "irony of fate that the first important measure that comes before the Reformed Council is a measure to curtail a great and deeply cherished privilege which the country has enjoyed, with two brief interruptions, for three-quarters of a century," an effective argument from precedent. He questions the hasty consideration of the bill "by suspending the standing orders and without giving the country practically any opportunity to express its opinion on it."

Gokhale maintains that if the bill is put into effect, the punishment, "so far from restricting the area of sedition, actually widens it by reason of the unhealthy excitement it causes." Unfortunately, the government permitted the existing penal code "to remain practically a dead letter," but "a proposal to amend ... would have made its operation more simple and expeditious [and] would have caused less disturbance."

Subsequently, Gokhale indicates his reluctant readiness to accept the bill. Resuming his train of thought, he places responsibility for sedition on previous British repressions: "the crop of violence that has now come to the surface had its ground prepared five years ago." The provocative writings in a section of the Anglo-Indian press are also blamed "in turning so many of my countrymen against British rule. The terms of race arrogance and contempt ... of the Indians ... cut into the mind more than the lash can cut into the flesh. Many of my countrymen imagine that every Anglo-Indian pen that writes in the Press is dipped in Government ink." Powerful metaphors.

His conclusion is simply stated as an appeal for a return to reason, moderation, and justice:

> My Lord, I feel bound to say that this Bill by itself cannot achieve much. It is even possible that the immediate effect of its passing will be to fill the public mind with a certain amount of resentment ... the evil which they are intended to combat may only be driven underground. Force may afford temporary relief, but it can never prove a permanent remedy.... It is only in the co-operation of all classes and the steady pursuit of a policy of wise conciliation on the part of Government that the best hopes of thoughtful men on both sides for the future of this land must lie.

Gokhale's use of ethical proof is manifest when we understand the circumstances surrounding the speech as well as the ideas expressed in it. In supporting the bill Gokhale has deliberately chosen a difficult course, and he states his position very carefully:

> My Lord, in ordinary times I should have deemed it my duty to resist such proposals to the utmost of my power.... But in view of the situation that exists in several parts of the country today, I have reluctantly come, after a careful and anxious consideration, to the conclusion that I should not be justified in opposing the principle of this Bill. It is not merely the assassinations that have taken place, or the conspiracies that have come to light ... that fill me with anxiety. The air in many places is still thick with ideas that are undoubtedly antagonistic to the unquestioned continuance of British rule, with which our hopes of a peaceful evolution are bound up; and this is a feature of the situation quite as serious as anything else.

He gives two reasons for his reluctant support: the increasingly violent activities of Indian extremists and his desire to see the activities of "certain sections of the Press" curtailed. This ambiguous reference is not to the Indian press, but to the Anglo-Indian press; and to the extent that the Press Bill would curb the excesses of those journalists, Gokhale is willing to support it. His reasoning satisfies his own purposes, but is probably too subtle for his Indian audience, who wish to see a forthright rejection of the Bill. He realizes that his stand will be acceptable to the English; his problem is to maintain his own integrity and the confidence of his Indian supporters by not appearing to capitulate to the British demands. In my estimation he is not successful, and the Indians felt he was too conciliatory. In the subsequent application of the Bill it was obvious that official British opinion toward India had hardly changed.

The task of presenting Indian policies in an essentially hostile situation, before the viceroy himself, must have been tremendously difficult. Gokhale's whole temperament and training made him respect and even admire the ideals that the British government was supposed to represent. He wished to be worthy of his position yet expressive of the needs of his own people. The precariousness of his situation may explain the oblique rationalization he makes for supporting the bill.

He appears anxious throughout the speech to conciliate Lord Minto ("I entirely share the view which was so clearly and firmly expressed by your Lordship ... despite repressive measures to which you have been driven"), and he expresses his own dilemma when he comments that "the juncture is a most difficult and delicate one, [calling for] the utmost tact and conciliation."

In using argument Gokhale's basic approach is to apply the considerations of need, practicality, and desirability to the problem: (1) there is no need for the bill; (2) the bill would be impractical because it would not "prove a permanent remedy" and would "not overcome the evil altogether"; (3) the bill would be undesirable because it would incite new violence.

The intrinsic difficulties of his position seem to affect the "reasonableness" of his arguments. In the first place the statement of his position is abruptly thrust into the middle of his arguments, as though the necessity of clarifying his stand has preoccupied his mind to the extent that he disregards normal methods of order and arrangement. Some of his ideas are contradictory. He asks the government not to adopt the Press Bill because it will create further violence, yet he agrees to support it because of likely manifestations of violence in the community. On one hand he indicates that Indians are beginning to realize the dangers of sedition and violence and are able to impose self-control; on the other, he says, "I am prepared to let the Government apply to the situation even the drastic remedies contemplated by this Bill."

The chief emotional appeal that Gokhale makes is to the wisdom of expediency. This appeal operates in the arguments of the speech that have already been set out, but when he warns the English audience of the effects of the repressive Press Bill, he is playing on their fear and arguing from exigency; in his conclusion he is exhorting them to be wise and just.

It should be said that there are a number of factors that influenced Gokhale's development as a speaker. Chief among these are his education and later associations with British and Indian political leaders. His character and personality were shaped by these influences so that, as a speaker, he tried to be responsible to both points of view. Realizing the frequent incompatibility of such different outlooks, his answer was to propose that Indian reform should be accomplished gradually. Whether such an approach was the wisest, or the most useful, is a question that can not be answered categorically from the present vantage point. Gokhale was a Brahmin, and that fact doubtless dictated respect for the past and moderated instinctive urges for modernization; but he was not a spokesman for Hinduism. He was a scholar and a traditionalist and saw his role as a spokesman for evolutionary politics; he was fortunate to have enlisted as a follower no less than Gandhiji himself, whose great achievement was Indian nationhood.

NOTES

[1] Arthur Travers Crawford was commissioner of the Central Division of Bombay, and thus second only to the governor in power and influence in Western India, when he was tried on charges of corruption and bribery. Indian magistrates, whose testimony against Crawford was necessary for a conviction (yet who would implicate themselves by testifying) were assured of indulgence. Such leniency was not granted, however, and they were struck from the Bombay civil list on Crawford's conviction.

[2] Government measures to control the plague angered Indians: quarantines were imposed and houses were searched for victims. Resenting these actions, two Indian brothers murdered the plague commissioner, Mr. Rand, and one of his associates. See Lovett 49-51.

WORKS CITED

Andrews, C. F., and Girija Mookerjee. *The Rise and Growth of the Congress in India*. London: Allen and Unwin, 1938.

Chirol, Valentine. *Indian Unrest*. London: Macmillan, 1910.

Gandhi, Mohandas K. *Gokhale, My Political Guru*. Ahmedabad: n.p. 1955.

Gokhale, Gopal Krishna. *Speeches and Writings of Gopal Krishna Gokhale*. Ed. D. G. Karve and D. V. Ambekar. New York: Asia, 1966.

Gopal, Ram. *British Rule in India: An Assessment*. Bombay: Asia, 1963.

Lovett, Verney. *A History of the Indian Nationalist Movement*. London: John Murray, 1920.

Wolpert, Stanley. *Tilak and Gokhale: Revolution and Reform in the Making of Modern India*. Berkeley: University of California Press, 1962.

1970

2. Ethical Proof in Three Speeches of R. G. Menzies

In the Aristotelian sense ethical proof—that proof which resides in the moral character of the speaker—is an "artistic" proof, as also are emotional and logical proofs. It must be invented by the speaker according to the needs of the situation in which he finds himself and the rules or theories of rhetoric.

Aristotle's concept of ethical proof seems to constitute a distinct contribution to the theory of rhetoric, for we may examine the ideas of his predecessors without discovering much systematic description of this proof. The Sicilians seem to designate the proemium as the proper place to get the listeners' goodwill, but in their case this goodwill is being sought to secure acceptance of questionable proposals. Reference to the use of ethical proof is found again in the *Rhetorica ad Alexandrum*, where the speaker is advised to adapt arguments to his listeners and to establish his own authority with the audience.

Isocrates gives advice that is more specifically concerned with ethical proof: his ideal speaker—the orator-statesman—should seek to improve his persuasion by showing himself to be honourable: he is to be trained in ethics and should know how to control himself and show respect for others, while in invention (in choice of speech materials) he is to observe propriety and avoid excess.

The Platonic conception of rhetoric posits a speaker who is intelligent, informed of the truth, but eschews the consideration and presentation of matters of opinion: of propositions of value and policy. The Socratic speaker should be able to understand his audiences and have some skill in adapting arguments to them; he should have a high moral purpose. These qualities are summarized for us by Socrates' speech in the *Phaedrus*, in which he shows the dimensions of Plato's ideal rhetorician:

> First you must know the truth about the subject that you speak or write about: that is to say, you must be able to isolate it in definition, and having so defined it you must next understand how to divide it into kinds, until you reach the limit of division; secondly, you must have a corresponding discernment of the nature of the soul, discover the type of speech appropriate to each nature, and order and arrange your discourse accordingly, addressing a variegated soul in a variegated style that ranges over the whole gamut of tones, and a simple soul in a simple style. All this must be done if you are to become competent, within human limits, as a scientific practitioner of speech, whether you propose to expound or to persuade. (160-61)

Aristotle presents ethical proof as an important practical concern to the speaker. Since rhetoric deals with probabilities, the audience will inevitably need to place confidence in the intelligence and character of the speaker, whose ability to use ethical proof is therefore vital to his persuasion. By the speech itself he must create a favourable impression of his own character, showing that he is honest and is not misrepresenting the facts of the case; that he understands the facts and is able to form a judgment; that he is well disposed toward his audience and will recommend the best course of action. These ideas are set out in Book I of *Rhetoric*, where Aristotle presents an analysis of the virtues which the speaker should manifest to establish his character and sagacity, thus making himself worthy of the audience's belief.

In addition to these views of ethical proof as a function of the speaker's character, Aristotle also presents an idea of *ethos* as it relates to the audience—essentially, its characteristics. Thus, the speaker must study the forms of government; the different ages of the audience (youth, maturity, old age) and the different orders or groups of the audience (rich, noble, powerful) in order to adapt his speaking properly to his listeners. Further, Aristotle points out that if the speaker is to conciliate his audience, he must understand not only the general classifications by which the audience may be described, but also the distinguishing traits or characteristics of these types. For example, he reminds us that the motives of youthful and mature groups differ, and that the character of the wealthy differs from that of the poor. The speaker must adapt his speech accordingly.

There appears to be another area in which *ethos* takes on meaning: this is the area of style, which Aristotle discusses in Book III. He tells us that the speaker should be able to use a style appropriate to every character that he wishes to describe, since this will give reality and truthfulness to his speech and increase the audience's trust in the speaker. The language of the speaker should be current and informal; it should be characterized by propriety, moral purpose, and some elegance, which clothe the action with interest, and hence reveal the speaker as one committed to justice, honour, and expedience. In addition to these considerations, the choice of appropriate language would be based on certain fixed values held by the speaker: expediency, justice, honour.

An examination of the concept of ethical proof permits us to make two observations: (1) The use of ethical proof always involves choice on the part of the speaker and is made manifest in his invention, arrangement, style, and delivery, which are affected by the purpose of his speech and the nature of the audience itself. To a certain extent the speaker is revealing his character as he makes his choices; (2) The distinction between ethical proof and emotional proof is not always clear. Baldwin comments on the order in which Aristotle presents the three proofs—ethical, emotional, logical—and states "that the three are not mutually exclusive is evident and must have been deliberate" (11). On the other hand, Thonssen and Baird suggest that "*ethos* refers chiefly to what the speaker chooses to do; *pathos* to what the reaction has done to the listener" (386).

As we study the problem of *ethos* as it is used in speech, we may observe a speaker doing some of the following to create a favourable impression of his character: (1) telling what establishes his own virtues; (2) linking his opponent's cause with what will discredit him; (3) associating himself with what is virtuous; (4) counteracting a previously harmful impression of his character; and (5) showing that he is sincere in his inquiry into the problem.

The speaker may establish his intelligence by (1) demonstrating that he is well informed; (2) showing that he is interpreting and presenting the facts fairly; and (3) showing a sense of propriety and good judgment.

Finally, he may demonstrate his goodwill to the audience by (1) showing a willingness to permit public scrutiny of his motives; (2) tolerating dissent; (3) establishing an appropriate identification with his audience; and (4) demonstrating his competence to speak without going beyond the bounds of his authority.

In summary, *ethos* is found to be an artistic proof that depends on the speaker's moral character. His successful use of this proof depends upon his ability to make good choices at every step of the speech process and upon his ability to understand his audience.

These comments on ethical proof will serve as the basis for inquiry into the parliamentary speaking of Sir Robert Menzies during his first government. Those things which demonstrate his character, sagacity, and goodwill will be analyzed in relation to the speaking situation and the classical concept of rhetoric.

Menzies' puzzling inability to develop rapport with his fellow parliamentarians has often been noted. His speech of 20 April 1939, in which he defended himself against charges by the prime minister, Sir Earle Page, deserves to be examined, for it indicates the generally hostile attitude of the House toward him and the way in which he dealt with its direct expression.

Upon the death of the prime minister, Joseph Lyons, on 7 April 1939, an interim government was formed with Earle Page as prime minister. He was charged by the governor-general with the recommendation of a new government. The choice would very likely fall on Menzies as head of the newly reorganized United Australia Party, but Menzies would have to obtain the co-operation of the Country Party to obtain the majority necessary to form a government.

Explaining the nature of the responsibility placed upon him by the governor-general, Page said that he "was compelled to consider the qualifications of the new Leader of the United Australia Party." He noted that the nature of Menzies' leadership within his own party was "entirely a party domestic matter," adding, however, that "if the leader of that party was to become the leader of a united national effort, I was entitled to consider whether he possessed the qualifications necessary for his high office. I had to ask myself whether his public record was such as to inspire the people of Australia to maximum unstinted effort in time of national emergency" (274). Hansard reports that thus he prefaces an openly vicious attack on Menzies, wherein, contrary to his expressed purpose of examining Menzies' "public record," he brings charges based on matters that are, in two of three cases, of private concern to the accused. He bases his judgments of Menzies' unfitness on three incidents: (1) Menzies resigned his portfolio of attorney general 24 days previous. (Page charges that this action was a "desertion" that cost millions of pounds because valuable programs were left undirected); (2) Menzies made a speech 24 weeks ago in Sydney, which Page regards as an attack on the party leader, Prime Minister Lyons; (3) Menzies resigned his commission in the Melbourne University Regiment 24 years ago and had not gone to war. (This last charge was received with cries of "That is dirt!" from one of the members.)

Ethical proof plays a large part in Menzies' reply: he points out the inappropriate, unparliamentary nature of this "most extraordinary speech," describing it as an intemperate expression of Page's political opinions "as Leader of the Country Party" and not the statement of a responsible prime minister. The rashness of the attack extends to its delivery "at a most inappropriate time," when "difficult problems" must be "attacked successfully only by a concerted effort." Menzies casts doubt on the character and intelligence of Earle Page, who seems ready to jeopardize the tentative stability of the interim government in gratification of personal motives.

Recalling "whispers occasionally about the reasons for the refusal of the Country Party to co-operate with me in the formation of a government," Menzies declares the reasons "not only offensive and personal, but also paltry." In contrast to the pettiness of his opponents, Menzies promises to speak "with due restraint—indeed, with more restraint than I might have felt disposed to display on another occasion." In refusing to descend to the level of his opponents, Menzies enhances his own integrity.

He denies any ulterior motive in resigning as attorney general (though it was a move which effectively freed him for appointment as prime minister), saying that he had quit his post because of the government's failure to implement a national insurance scheme, concerning which "I had given a specific pledge in writing to my electors." Thus he attempts to establish his integrity. He is undeterred by an interruption at this point, remarking that "in due course, the honourable gentleman may have an opportunity to give his [views]. After all, I am the person who has been attacked—nobody else." This illustrates his use of mild sarcasm in coping with parliamentary exchanges. Nothing stops the development of his argument, and in making a witty reply he seems invincible to attack. In most instances of this nature Menzies does not turn off the attack with a mild tone, and his stinging replies force the point of the remarks back on his opponent, yet these episodes probably chagrined those who instigated them without building up much ethical proof for the speaker.

Defending his conduct in this matter, Menzies asks: "Is it a contemptible thing for a man to keep his word? Is it the mark of a coward for a man to keep his word on an issue which is far from popular? I have no apologies to offer for my resignation. On the contrary, I regard it as one of the more respectable actions of my public life." These rhetorical questions name the qualities which all his hearers would acknowledge to be essential in a public servant, and so Menzies establishes the probity of his character by identifying himself with these virtues.

Menzies calls the second charge "an amazing effort at ingenuity." Recalling the circumstances of the speech, he wonders "whether any honourable gentleman was present on that occasion and heard the speech?" In it he had made the point that the test of a successful democracy was leadership, and loyalty to that leadership, and the context of the remark "was a homily which I was addressing to myself and every other person in Australia who occupied any public position involving leadership of the people." Having stated the facts of the case, he declares, "I am not responsible for the manner in which my views may have been twisted." At a loss to know the source of such misinterpretations, he points out that "conversations which I had with my late leader and friend were completely inconsistent with any suggestion that he regarded my speech as an attack upon him." He has shown the harmlessness of his words, demonstrated their interpretation as such by the man he was said to have maligned, and turned the malicious aspersions from himself to his opponent.

Menzies says that the charge of his shirking military duty while a university student is "no novelty. It represents a stream of mud through which I have waded at every election campaign in which I have participated." The charge "You did not go to the war" may as conveniently be directed "to some members of the party led by the right honourable gentlemen" [Page]. Menzies tries to show that his opponent lacks good judgment and a sense of propriety in prying "into the private reasons for the actions of other people," and notes that his accuser "discovered some facts concerning my action at the time he mentions, but failed to discover others," thus suggesting Page's dishonesty in his use of evidence. Menzies states that the true nature of the case was that," in common with other young men ... [I] was a trainee under the then existing system of compulsory training.... When my period of university training expired, my activity in connexion with the system also expired. I did not resign anything." This is a blunt statement, and Menzies insists on his right to conduct his personal life on his own terms: "I ... had to answer the extremely important questions—Is it my duty to go to the war, or is it my duty not to go? The answers to those questions cannot be made on the public platform. Those questions relate to a man's intimate, personal, and family affairs." He shows his awareness of the situation and rebukes his opponent for artlessly rehearsing the same criticisms that have been made so often.

In concluding his speech Menzies expresses his disgust at the "very disagreeable" attack and asks his audience to appraise him by "the only judgment as to a man's capacity, a man's courage, a man's fortitude that has any relevance to his public conduct ... the judgment of the people who have known him and worked with him." Thus he attempts to counteract the deleterious impressions of his character. In his final appeal he expresses his belief that he is "capable of leading them," saying, "I am vain enough to hope that I have capacity enough to discharge that trust, and in the discharge of it I shall exhibit none of those miserable attributes ... suggested by the Prime Minister in the most remarkable attack that I have ever heard in the whole of my public career."

His conclusion is decidedly an appeal to the fair-mindedness of his hearers; however, it also reflects Menzies' use of ethical proof. He is content to submit his case to the scrutiny of others, confident that their good judgment of him will counteract the aspersions of Earle Page. In this case the limitations of such an appeal are evident in the political context of the situation: Menzies may reinforce the sympathies of his fellow party members, but the extent to which he could hope to influence the opinion of Earle Page and the Country Party is questionable, for James Jupp, writing in *Australian Party Politics*, says that "Menzies was political anathema to the Country Party leaders" (16). On the day that Menzies was elected head of the United Australia Party, the Parliamentary Country Party resolved that:

> In spite of past harmonious co-operation in government with the United Australia Party and a willingness to continue similar co-operation to maintain stable government, the Party is definitely unable to co-operate in a government with the Hon. R. G. Menzies, K. C., as its Prime Minister; nor is it willing to give any undertaking to support such a government if it be formed. (qtd. in Page 274)

John Curtin, the leader of the opposition, spoke to denounce the "personal aspects of the controversy," declaring he had "no confidence whatever in either the United Australia Party or the Country Party." Kevin Perkins writes that "the attack not only made members embarrassed, but shocked the nation" (79).

In his recent autobiography Menzies recollects the events in the House and the effects of the Page speech:

> Page, who had no friendly feelings towards me, was furious. His temper, which he could seldom control, got the better of him. On the floor of the House, speaking still as Prime Minister, he made a bitter and entirely false attack upon me; in the making of which he did himself more harm than he did me. Several of his own party members sat apart thereafter, to mark their disapproval of his performance.
>
> My wife was in the gallery when this abuse was hurled at me ... [She] never forgave him and never spoke to him again. (13)

And Sir Earle Page himself has written that his speech "gave the newspapers a field day. I at once became the object of vigorous and hostile comment ... my words were studied, dissected, and interpreted with an absorption seldom equaled in Australian journalism, their reiteration, while aimed at me, only fixed the role of Menzies in the public mind" (279).

This exchange did not mark the end of Menzies' difficulties: "the United Australia Party was itself in a state of turmoil. Menzies' leadership was accepted only grudgingly" (Jupp 17). He formed a coalition government with the Country Party, reorganizing the structure of his cabinet twice in two years to achieve harmony. His willingness to forget personal matters in the interests of governmental stability is shown by the fact that he subsequently included Earle Page in his cabinet as minister for commerce and transport.

As prime minister of Australia, Menzies declared war on Germany in his speech of 3 September 1939, within an hour of the British declaration. In this speech he gives a detailed examination of the events leading to the creation of a state of war between England and Germany, including the role of Australia in this action. Participation in World War I had made

Australia aware of the hardships of war; distance from Europe made her reluctant to participate in European quarrels. Australia, "like the peoples of the other Dominions and their governments, had backed appeasement to the hilt" (253).

Perhaps sensing his countrymen's mental unpreparedness for war, Menzies used the speech to set out the complete details of the diplomatic correspondence between England and Germany prior to the declaration of war, remarking at the same time on the role he played in representing the Australian government. He needed to establish the inevitability of Australia's commitment to the war. Another consideration which must have influenced the approach Menzies took in this speech was his awareness of the growing criticism of his conservative political regime. Conservative politicians had controlled the government since 1931, and as Australians recovered from the Depression they felt that they needed a government that would provide greater security for the average citizen and independence from too much overseas fiscal and political control. Thus, Menzies also needed to establish the good faith of his government in setting aside domestic programs in order to pursue the war.

The speech is therefore matter-of-fact; it is largely a recital of facts, not an impassioned call to arms. Its organization shows a brief introduction that conveys a tone of calm acceptance of the role Australia must take in the war and a resolution to carry out the role successfully. The body of the speech is almost tediously lengthy, as every detail of the diplomatic events leading to the state of war is reviewed. The conclusion is by far the most emotional part of the speech: it appeals to Australians' national honour, creates goodwill for the speaker, and concludes with the rhetorically commonplace and classic hope that the course of the war will be swift and its victories secure.

Ethical proof is used conservatively, yet effectively, throughout the speech. Menzies wishes to make it quite clear that he has not irresponsibly led his countrymen into war—that Australia's declaration of hostilities has been justified by a very real threat. He wishes them to conclude this for themselves on the basis of their own examination of the facts. In providing his audience with the facts he is establishing goodwill and demonstrating his reliability:

> In order that honourable members may have before them, and in order that we may have on record, some accurate statement of the affairs leading up to this tragic consequence I am today laying on the table a White Paper, which contains the relevant documents exchanged between the Governments, together with such explanatory matter as may serve to connect one document with another.

Continuing his introduction, he establishes his own credibility by refusing to promise an easy outcome to the war: "Nobody can foretell the course of events. Nobody can foretell how this war is going to be fought, what special dangers Australia may encounter, or what are the best services which we can render to Great Britain and the Empire." Menzies makes a patently candid appraisal of the situation; the appeal for service enhances his purpose by associating Australia with the cause of justice and recalling her past honours in dutiful service to the Crown. The closing phrases of the introduction underline this appeal and create a favourable impression of Menzies by identifying him with the national honour and justice: "but we do know that we are together in this struggle, and we are confident that our unity and determination, being based upon justice, are bound to succeed."

Much of the ethical proof is employed indirectly; i.e., by associating Australia with what is virtuous, Menzies implies his own virtue, since he is the national leader. This method of establishing ethical proof is evident in the body of the speech also, when he recalls the series of broken German promises, assigning blame to her and indirectly giving praise to Australia. He seeks to create a favourable impression of his own intentions and abilities when he recalls his role in the negotiations:

> I can say for myself that I took the opportunity on that Sunday to convey to the British Government what I thought were the views not only of the Government of Australia but also of the great majority of the people of Australia. What I said to Mr Chamberlain I repeated in substance on subsequent occasions in relation to the circumstances as they developed.

Menzies stresses that he neither seeks reckless entry into war not condones German aggression: "I went further and suggested that it should be emphasized that there was amongst all the British peoples a genuine desire for good relations with Germany, but this desire was not inconsistent with the determination to fight Germany in what seemed a just cause...."

In his reiteration of faith in a negotiated solution, Menzies demonstrates his sincere desire for peace:

> It would be a tragedy if we should fight, each believing his cause to be just when unprejudiced discussion and desire to understand each other's point of view might have avoided it.... I would not dismiss proposals made by Herr Hitler simply because they were vague or occasionally meaningless ... our approach to the problem should be liberal and generous so long as generosity was at our own expense....

He also creates a favourable impression of his character when he insists that Poland should receive fair treatment: "we must not connive at a Polish settlement which would leave Poland at such a disadvantage in the negotiations as would render it probable that its future history would resemble that of Czechoslovakia." This "liberal and generous approach to the problem" was contained in the note sent to Germany by England—"a document which exhibited a really earnest desire to arrive at a settlement."

Closing his documentation of events, Menzies ascribes blame fully to Germany, saying, "had Germany not desired war, there would not be a war today in Europe," and calling for "a clear-cut condemnation of Germany." Even here he is reluctant to indict the whole German population: "I cannot believe that what we may term Hitlerism, as exhibited in these negotiations, can possibly represent the free will and free decision of any civilized community." He thus captures a nice balance between too little blame of the enemy and too much. Wholesale, unrestrained accusation would have made him seem a ranting demagogue, as unethical and irresponsible in his speaking as any dictator. This is essentially a reasoned speech and Menzies clearly does not wish to incite inflammatory reactions in his audience.

The conclusion to the speech opens with an avowal by Menzies to permit free expression of opinion in parliament: "However long this conflict may last, I do not seek a muzzled Opposition. Our institutions of free speech and free criticism must go on." He hesitates to invoke any restrictive measures, however the wartime situation might permit their institution, which in the long run would weaken the vigour of Australia's parliamentary system:

> It would be a tragedy if we found that we had fought for freedom and fair play and the value of the human soul and won the war only to lose the things we were fighting for. Consequently, I shall welcome criticism; but I do want to emphasize that our great task, however long this struggle may endure, is in common. If we remember that, all criticism will find its right place and its true perspective.

Menzies' clear statement on this topic surely makes untenable the charge, smacking of partisan cynicism, that he did his best to undermine the parliamentary function in Australia. His announced toleration of dissent and willingness to permit public scrutiny of his actions further demonstrate his goodwill to the public. His final statement is an expression of the hope that the war "may be won so quickly as to permit a just peace, a peace that will really end war, and not a peace which will sow the dragon's teeth of bitterness and hatred and distrust."

Menzies' specific purpose in this speech was to persuade parliament to approve the printing of the White Paper, and hence to ratify the government's declaration of war against Germany. An important factor that affected his speech was the current Australian view that placed highest priority on domestic reforms and regarded the Munich aftermath, in Chamberlain's words, as nothing more than "quarrels in a far-off country of which many had scarcely heard." He faced the problem of uniting Australians in an unwelcome war effort, although this problem was not as apparent at the time of the speech as it later became.

In dealing with his problems on this occasion Menzies used ethical proof in the following ways: (1) to establish his own good character by linking himself with a just, virtuous cause and showing a genuine interest in maintaining peace; (2) to establish his intelligence by demonstrating a profound knowledge of the facts and the ability to make a wise interpretation of them and their outcome; (3) to demonstrate his goodwill to the audience by candidly inviting examination of his role in the declaration of hostilities and indicating his willingness to hear criticism.

On 24 January 1941 Menzies left Australia to attend meetings of the War Cabinet in London, visiting Australian troops in the Middle East en route. He spent ten weeks in Great Britain, attending meetings and conferring with Churchill and other officials.

In these talks Menzies pointed out the growing menace of Japan, knowing that Australian reaction to such a threat would be withdrawal of support from Great Britain in order to defend her own soil. Menzies felt that the defences of Singapore were insufficient and made specific recommendations for reinforcing them—realizing that British and Commonwealth resources were already strained and that any effective war in the South Pacific would have to involve America. As he has stated, the official reaction to his proposal was reserved: "I kept coming back to this matter during the rest of my stay in England, but without material success." He then made a speech in London to the Foreign Press Association (3 March), urging formulation of a Japanese policy and expressing a desire for frank discussion on all sides. His persistence in this matter is evidence both of his political and military realism and of his sense of responsibility toward his country.

While returning home to Australia Menzies visited the United States, where he had talks with President Franklin D. Roosevelt. Menzies was convinced that American sympathies lay with the cause of Britain and her Commonwealth allies, and in the several speeches he made to Americans during his visit he reiterated that this was their struggle as well as others'; he felt that "the key of the door was in Roosevelt's hand; that, whatever he did, the people would back him," as he wrote in *Afternoon Light* (134). Of his discussions with Roosevelt, he has written, "I was left in no doubt—though there were no actual words of commitment—that America would not stand by and see Australia attacked" (135). In another instance Menzies had apparently voiced the message of the Australian people effectively.

On his return to Australia he felt what he has described as "a lively sense of the gravity of our position," (128) and set about planning for an organized war effort. Criticism of his government seemed to have abated. In England he had been troubled by the problems of securing a united war effort in Australia and felt that a national government should be established, stating that "If my leadership and characteristics stood in the way, I should clearly efface myself" (50). But when John Curtin issued a press statement on 27 April 1941, in which he declared that "there is no political disunity in Australia in regard to the prosecution of the war," (51) Menzies was pleased; he was further encouraged by a message from his colleagues in Australia, congratulating him on his efforts in England. This was the background for his speech to the House on 28 May 1941.

Ethical proof is not abundant in this speech: Menzies received no censure for his four months' stay abroad, and he felt it unnecessary to justify his absence. He writes, "I had no doubt that things had gone reasonably peacefully during my absence. My own visit to England had clearly been well received." Criticism of his visit was raised several months later, not at the time of his return.

In his introduction Menzies says that his trip has been "the most valuable experience of my life," and hopes that his impressions will "be of value to this House." In his desire to bring the facts directly to his audience he is showing goodwill. He does not have to impress his audience with the importance of his subject; he does try, however, to impart a realization of the value of his own efforts when he lists the twenty-one countries "in which I was able to have some discussion and make some investigation." Menzies describes himself as "much more than a mere sightseer," and as "astonished to realize in how many of those countries Australia has some specific interest and how important to us are their policies and actions."

Imparting a world view of affairs to Australians was probably not easy. However, Menzies' interest in establishing wider horizons for his countrymen shows his ability to analyze Australia's problems and to grasp basic issues. Pacific defence was vital to his audience, and Menzies indicates his vigilant attention to this matter in "some discussion on the spot with those responsible for the defence of Singapore, which is one of the great key strategic places of the world from the Australian point of view." He further builds goodwill for himself by describing his visits to Australian troops in the Middle East.

He proceeds to a description of his activities in London; his impressions of the English and their leaders; the general progress of the war. He does not outline any disposition for the speech, but the material is generally arranged chronologically. Throughout it he evokes admiration for the courage of the English, praises the mettle of Australian combat troops, exhorts the audience to greater sacrifice in the war effort. The fact that his statements are made from first-hand observations of the events and people he describes adds to his authority as a speaker. He does not doubt Australia's capacity for waging war, but he does fear that political factionalism will hamper its efforts. In the conclusion of his speech he describes himself as "sick at heart at having to come back to play politics"; he insists that he is "offering no criticism [of] any party," and "we must have the proper machinery for an effective attack upon this problem." The machinery to which he refers is the "machinery of state," and he fears that it will be upset by lack of co-operation.

Attempting to mollify the effect of his words, Menzies asks that members "not impute to me any desire to criticize the effectiveness of the co-operation which I have received from the leader of the Labor Party. I have always acknowledged the value of that co-operation. I have at all times paid tribute to the attitude of my opponents." He declares that consideration for the welfare of Australia has prompted his statements. His intention is to conciliate his audience by showing that he is acting in their best interests.

Menzies does not mention the formation of a national government, which he had proposed when he was in England, but this is clearly the implicit solution that he sees to Australia's parliamentary disunity and her uncoordinated war effort. That parliament could not see the need for such a government was apparently a clear proof to Menzies "that the realities of this war have not yet struck home." A national government had been formed in England, "and there no political party has abandoned its identity, though all are co-operating.... I found them all animated by a common determination to preserve the freedom of their people."

The remainder of his speech is a plea to put away "the marching and counter-marching of politics," as it "must necessarily distract the minds of the country's leaders from the duties which at this time should be paramount." He implores his hearers to "put all these things away.... forget these differences"; the end of the war will bring time to "resume the mock battle of politics."

His conclusion shows extensive use of emotional proof, which also establishes ethical proof to the extent that it shows good sense, good character, and goodwill. Throughout the speech he has attempted to establish his good character by basing his authority on his personal experience, showing that he is sincere in his inquiry and associating himself with what is good and expedient for his audience. In the conclusion he seeks to establish his intelligence by displaying a sufficient knowledge of Australia's problems and of world events.

In referring to his own political difficulties, however, I am not so sure that he is using common sense. At the time the speech was delivered there seemed to be parliamentary willingness to unite in the war effort. If such unity actually existed, Menzies' plea for establishment of a national government might have been interpreted as a stratagem for solidifying his own political career by allowing him to remain as prime minister.

The speeches selected for this paper were chosen because they permitted an examination of Menzies' use of ethical proof and because the circumstances surrounding them gave the speaker the opportunity to deliver a purposeful, substantive speech. The speech of 20 April 1939 was significant because it

Ethical Proof in Three Speeches of R. G. Menzies

forced him to defend himself in an immediate reply to a personal attack. The charges he faced in the speech were significant, in that they were used against him many times in his political career. The speech presents Menzies in what was to be a typical role during his first term as prime minister: establishing his qualifications to lead Australia. The speech of 6 September 1939 shows Menzies leading his country into an unwelcome war that he realizes will require the postponement of important domestic programs. In the speech of 28 May 1941, he speaks under conditions when his personal prestige should have been exceedingly high. The threat of political ruin and personal abuse is still there, however, and Menzies senses it.

An examination of the parliamentary record during Menzies' first government reveals a great many occasions when he found it necessary to use ethical proof, and the ways in which he used this proof show varying degrees of effectiveness. There seemed to be little confidence in his leadership; members seized the opportunity to attack him on any issue or any occasion, from awarding contracts for an addition to the General Post Office in Sydney to accusations of installing microphones in the House for monitoring their private conversations. A passage from the House debates on Menzies' speech of 28 May indicates the kind of abuse that his opponents employed. The speaker is Mr Brennan, the member for Batman; he is referring to Australians' realization of the seriousness of war: "The people of this country maintain an attitude of cheerfulness. They live out their lives believing that they serve no useful purpose by listening to jeremiads preached in boudoirs by slippered Prime Ministers who expose themselves to no greater peril than the peril of lecturing and hectoring other people."

In reviewing these three speeches of Menzies it should be noted that there are several factors that influenced his speaking: one is certainly his thorough education and early high distinction in law, which developed his talents for speaking in situations where much was at stake. No doubt that early success made him an object of certain jealousies, while it spurred his ambition. Legal training gave him readiness in debate but little patience with non-reasoned ways of solving problems. His character and personality were shaped by these factors, so that he found it difficult to be content with anything mediocre. He often seemed discontented with the modest scope of the Australian parliament but had no difficulty making his way among important world figures and royalty.

Menzies' own writing sheds some light on these considerations, as he recalls the period of his first ministry:

> It would be stupid to deny that these events did not constitute a bitter blow to my pride, and even to my self-respect. In a very great crisis in my country's history, I had been weighed in the balance and found wanting. And yet I felt that I had done a great deal. I had not spared myself; I had worked seven days a week for at least twelve hours a day. This was, perhaps, an error, for it so absorbed my mind that I soon appeared to be aloof from my supporters in Parliament and to be lacking in human relations. But when the blow fell, it was like the stroke of doom; everything was at an end....
>
> I had enjoyed a very rapid rise to the top position.... There was not much precedent for this kind of advancement, and perhaps some resentment of it. True, I worked hard, though some of the press commentators promoted the usual legend that I was a "brilliant idler."
>
> But with so much to do officially, I do not doubt that my knowledge of people, and how to get along with them and persuade them, lagged behind. I was still in that state of mind in which to be logical is to be right, and to be right is its own justification. I had yet to acquire the common touch, to learn that human beings are delightfully illogical but mostly honest, and to realize that all-black and all-white are not the only hues in the spectrum. (56-57)

These statements are invaluable in the consideration of the deliberate and extensive use made of ethical proof in his first government speeches, and of its relative lack of effect.

WORKS CITED

Baldwin, Charles S. *Ancient Rhetoric and Poetic*. New York: Macmillan, 1924.

Commonwealth of Australia. *Parliamentary Debates*. Vol. 159, 15th Parliament, 1st Session, 20 April 1939.

—. Vol. 160, 15th Parliament, 1st Session, 3 September 1939.

—. Vol. 167, 15th Parliament, 1st Session, 28 May 1941.
—. Vol. 167, 15th Parliament, 1st Session, 19 June 1941.
Jupp, James. *Australian Party Politics.* Melbourne: Melbourne UP, 1964.
Menzies, R. G. *Afternoon Light.* New York: Coward-McCann, 1968.
Page, Earle. *Truant Surgeon.* Sydney: Angus and Robertson, 1963.
Perkins, Kevin. *Menzies: Last of the Queen's Men.* San Francisco: Tri-Ocean P, 1968.
Plato. *Phaedrus.* Trans. R. Hackforth. Cambridge: Cambridge UP, 1952.
Shaw, A. G. L. *The Story of Australia.* London: Faber, 1961.
Thonssen, Lester A. and A. Craig Baird. *Speech Criticism: The Development of Standards for Rhetorical Appraisal.* New York: Ronald P, 1948.

3. Norman Manley and Eric Williams: Speaking for the West Indies

Skill in speaking and the practice of stagecraft have been closely bound together since Isocrates proclaimed the value of rhetoric as a means of giving practical effect to the ideals of society. The classical scholar R. C. Jebb tells us that under the Isocratean system "the art of speaking or writing on large political subjects [was] considered as a preparation for advising or acting in political affairs" (qtd. in Thonssen and Baird 47). Fresh vindication of the ancient link between speech and the conduct of government may be found through examination of the rhetoric of modern West Indian society during its formative years from the eve of World War II, through the events leading up to independence, and until the present. This period reveals the development of a tradition of vigorous public address, for there occurs throughout the Caribbean a remarkable concentration of native orators speaking with all the power and versatility everywhere associated with the struggle of emerging free governments.

Norman Washington Manley of Jamaica and Dr. Eric Williams of Trinidad and Tobago are among those who may readily be associated with the nation-building processes occurring in the English-speaking Antilles. Their speeches have been examined to determine not only the content and form of the ideas but also the extent to which those ideas were the product of both the speakers' own qualities and the influence of the thought and feeling of their time, including the modifying effects exerted by their particular audiences.

Perhaps the most important key to understanding the West Indian audience is the recognition that the current social and political climate of West Indian society is deeply rooted in the past history of the area. Numerous commentators have described the manifestations of the colonial legacy universally present in the islands. Prime Minister Michael Manley has singled out the "psychology of dependence" fostered by British imperialism as one of the most prevalent forms of oppression. Speaking of the manifestations of the problem in his own country, he points to the lack of confidence and self-awareness generated by the heritage of a plantation society as responsible for "the most fundamental problem in Jamaica ... that the country was not committed to any concept of where it was trying to go" (qtd. in Anderson 65). And observers of the Caribbean scene have generally noted a weak community structure in the islands and an accompanying apathy of the population towards uniting in energetic and confident pursuit of common goals.

The rigid class lines of West Indian society, another holdover from the colonial planter period, are judged by most scholars to constitute a considerable impediment to the removal of inequalities and the creation of egalitarian societies even in Jamaica, where there is more obvious cultural and ethnic homogeneity than exists in islands like Trinidad. Professor Peter J. Wilson of Yale University attributes the class stratifications of the West Indies to unequal access to respectability. In the matter of respectability he points out that West Indians "may embrace its significance, live with the need of attaining it, seek it actively; but when all is said and done, it is their socio-economic position that ultimately declares their having—or lacking—respectability" (x). Continuing, he points out that reputation, or the worthwhileness of the individual achievement measured against the performance of the peer group, is a compensation but not a replacement for respectability, which, for the bulk of the population, is obtainable only through economic mobility.

In the West Indies the colour ranking universally recognized as a concomitant to the division along class lines is not primarily or exclusively an expression of racism, as in the United States. While there is growing racial consciousness and a marked tendency by some to deal with problems by retreating to what Professor Gordon Lewis calls "the haven of race," the primary determinant of West Indian societal divisions is economic. And, in Lewis's estimation, erosion of ethnic and colour lines and even of rigid class lines will steadily take place "so long as there continues to be cross-fertilization ... between the classes corresponding to each other in the various hierarchies, bridges built out of economic interest, political affiliations, social intercourse, and to a lesser degree, family life and religious practice, even surreptitious sexual relations" (41-42).

The effort by all West Indian peoples to achieve a positive endemic identity is made difficult not only by the paternalistic orientation of the populations and their class divisions but also by the insularity of the Caribbean in general—another legacy of political imperialism whereby the area remains fragmented and the island populations alienated from one another. Even the presence of a common language seemingly has failed to overcome the geographical and political separateness of individual islands. The longstanding British practice of dealing separately with each island community appears to have contributed to the negative attitude that prevented the success of the 1958 experiment in federation. Speeches on the issues arising out of federation showed unwillingness to strengthen the centre of the federal structure and expressed much concern over how individual countries would fare. In Jamaica Premier Norman Washington Manley voiced the concern of his countrymen that under federation the development of the small Caribbean islands would be injurious to Jamaica's interests. Stating the case simply, he said, "We conceive that in the long run there are real and great advantages in federation but that those advantages cannot be accepted at the price of anything that would destroy or injure us in a fundamental respect" (172).

The leaders who have articulated now and in the past their people's strivings to come to terms with their own emerging nationhood have understood the power of the spoken word. They have shown themselves to be richly endowed—with an awareness of the heritage from the colonial past, with a high regard for the general liberal values of constitutional democracy as expressed through a distinct West Indian medium, with a store of practical experience, and with a readiness to come to terms with the realities of West Indian life.

Among the pioneers in the development of modern Jamaica, none, perhaps, surpasses the stature of Norman Washington Manley, leader of the People's National Party, and the man who successfully gave life to the Jamaican national spirit. Professor Lewis writes that the "vast volume of political consciousness" generated by Manley's party under his leadership arose from "its advocacy of full self-government, its crystallization of latent political interest into a militant political party, its organized research ... into all aspects of Jamaican problems, and its propaganda effort" (181). These words indicate the major themes and strategies of Manley's speeches. It is significant that Lewis employs a scholarly metaphor, "vast volume," to sum up the effect of Manley's efforts, for the speeches by the "Father of the Nation," as Manley was called, taken as a whole, impart above all a distinct quality of reflective rather than emotional persuasion, and their effect is due as much to the consistent, painstaking, and unrelenting flow of Manley's rhetoric over a period of more than thirty years as it is to the sheer quality and content of his arguments.

The central inspiration of Manley's career was his commitment to self-government, to be achieved through a scheme of "Jamaican socialism" built around a two-party system and nurtured by the growth of a Jamaican national consciousness. The style Manley uses to explain his view of socialism seems designed not to confront his listeners with the necessity for making difficult, immediate judgments in unmapped territory but to encourage them to move steadily toward future goals in a conservative and stable fashion; in short, to make haste slowly. His vision is cautionary, even restrictive, rather than radical, for his ideal society lies in the future and is based on applications of British socialist theory. Accordingly, his language is frequently abstract, not concrete. Socialism, in his view, is "a patient belief that decent men will one day make a decent world" (69).

On the whole, Manley's speeches contain much patient explanation of the general Fabian socialist "goods" and a great deal of temporizing over the exact form socialism is to take in Jamaica. Manley is interested in origins and processes: in his words, Jamaicans need "to gain the broader understanding that comes from realising that we are in fact in our own way and on our own level playing a part in a process world-wide in its sweep and world-shaking in its import" (83). As for the substance and form of Jamaican socialism, Manley stipulates that it should embody what he calls "the essence of British socialism, indeed of democratic socialism the world over," which, he points out, has a "Christian inspiration" and "has always been free to adapt the means to the ends...and to accept the practical necessities of changing or different circumstances and to modify methods in the light of experience." And on a subsequent occasion, he reiterated the primacy of a Jamaican viewpoint: "The doctrinaire thinkers will have to learn by experience that Jamaica is Jamaica and what is possible here in our political framework is governed by matters special to ourselves" (89). Taken as a whole, Manley's explorations of the nature of socialism and its applications to Jamaica are presented in a tutelary fashion which seems designed to inspire reflection and self-satisfied agreement—a comfortable feeling of having come to terms with the matter on an intellectual and moral level as, perhaps, the most sensible method of dealing with it.

Besides the ability in explanation and the free drawing on Fabian socialist ideology, Manley could employ the familiar image in a way that was compelling rather than trivial. The theme of his speech at the founding of the People's National Party in 1938 was a pledge to foster a Jamaican national spirit that would produce among his people "the dawn of the feeling that this island should be their home and their country." Affirming the benefits of national self-awareness, Manley said,

> For the immature and primitive, a faith and a sense of destiny are requisite. History will give intuitions of the destiny, but until faith in its reality is born, the psychic and ethical value of progress and culture cannot exist. History cannot teach them, for they arise out of an inner process and their roots require an emotional soil. (lxvi)

What Manley was doing was to seek to overcome his people's psychological alienation and lack of self-confidence—to help them "throw off the legacy of fear and inferiority and want of pride that an ugly past has left" (69). To Manley, the first step to achievement of a national spirit must be willingness to face the reality of "the poverty of the masses...to look at the plight of our young men with honest open eyes" (338). His strategy of plainly citing problems of his society and the shortcomings in the Jamaican character, then of issuing a direct challenge to his audience to overcome these deficiencies, becomes the major organizational pattern in many of his speeches. He addresses himself candidly to the dangers of Jamaicans lingering in the shadow of colonial paternalism as a "shepherded people" when they should be "facing the hard road of discipline, developing your own capacities...your own people to the stage where they are capable of administering their own affairs" (15). He is dismayed by those "who would love to see everything settle back into the old complacent jog trot" and rebukes those "who love our thatched huts and the picturesqueness of Back-o'-Wall and those who look at smiles on people's faces and believe that all is well because people will smile, nature is beautiful and one season follows another" (17). He insists that smug self-satisfaction must be overcome, for "when everybody is contented even in the midst of poverty and degradation, when the bright flashing teeth and smiling faces that are the sort of popular legend of the happy Jamaican—it is inevitable that government will do as little as it possibly can." Nor does he spare himself. He says quite candidly, "I have lived in that feeling myself, I have felt those sentiments" (103). As often, he stresses common ground with his audience.

While Manley has a vision of a better Jamaica, he displays in his speeches no inclination to take the role of prophet or charismatic leader; his distaste for the Messiah image is well documented by his biographer, Rex Nettleford. As if to secure acceptance of his ideas on their own merits rather than on his personal authority, Manley consciously plays down his own contributions. Of his ideas he remarks, "I claim no originality for them." And of his role in the party, he says,

I have the honour to be associated with [it]. I do not claim to be the founder of it. I have no desire that it should be associated with my name beyond the fact that it will be honoured to accept my services.... My own position is perfectly clear. I have never pretended to be a labour leader and I have no ambition to be a labour leader. (12)

In Manley's view, the only solution to Jamaica's problems is the rejection by all of complacency and a conscious embrace of "discipline, honesty, loyalty, hard work ... for the good of the masses of the people and not for self-interest."

Here is a mild reformer calling the attention of his audience to their weaknesses in simple terms and homely illustrations that present a gentle satire of the easy-going Jamaican. Manley speaks for reform, yet his proposals are not cataclysmic or revolutionary, but essentially conservative and evolutionary: "We are starting in our infancy, and we will have to pass through many stages before we attain the goal we seek—the assurance and confidence and power that belong to manhood." The salvation Manley promises, paradoxically enough, comes through the work ethic of the Anglo-Saxon: the torpor of dependence created by the plantation system will be removed by an application of the former oppressor's values. In Manley's words, realization of Jamaica's goals will require "courage.... It will want a new discipline in what is today the most undisciplined country on God's earth" (21). Thus Manley enhances the thematic qualities of his message by proposing to substitute the metaphor of the Protestant ethic for that of the incipient Arcadianism.

While Jamaica embarked on overwhelming political changes in 1938, in Trinidad and Tobago it remained for the arrival in 1956 of Dr. Eric Williams and his party, the People's National Movement, to initiate a comparable transformation. As chief minister and later premier, Dr. Williams promised with the PNM to build up a democratic regime not based on race or class, which aimed to economic, political, and social reform and appealed to "the intelligence rather than the emotions of the electorate whose political education it places in the forefront of its activities" (*Perspectives 8*). An examination of Williams's speeches since he assumed office reveals his conscious effort to translate his societal vision into practical terms: the themes he develops in his speeches stress the necessity of long-range planning, industrialization, education, separation of race and politics, and self-conscious development of nationalism.

These familiar aims are so commonly found in the contemporary political rhetoric of developing countries as to be almost cliches. Nonetheless, when Williams lays out these simple elements in his speeches, in the process exhorting his audience to secure these goals by seeking a new morality which supplants selfish individualism with collective ideals, his speeches rise above the pedestrian level of political harangue. His ability to instil vitality into such inherently dull subjects as economic planning is the result of his skillful composition, which is clear, powerful, and direct yet sufficiently discursive to permit him frequent sallies into historical analysis and argument from example whereby he conducts the political education of his listeners.

Williams was a brilliant Oxford scholar, researcher, and faculty member at Howard University before he entered West Indian politics, and his remarkable insight and depth of learning are evident in his speeches. Professor Gordon Lewis notes the Burkian cast of Williams's role as politician and speaker, describing Williams as

> the philosopher in action, bred out of the radical intellectual's conviction that the cloistered virtue of academic life becomes sterile save as it seeks to translate its knowledge into social purpose, bred, too, out of his professional historian's conviction that ... the historian must be judge as well as witness. (213)

In many ways, Williams could be compared to Fidel Castro as a speaker, for both excel in the lengthy harangue to a large outdoors audience that is minimally educated, deficient in knowledge of international politics, history, and economics and eager to be directed by an acknowledged leader and didactic teacher whose primary aim is to create national cohesiveness, island pride, and social progress. While Castro most famously delivers his hours-long speeches in the Plaza of the Revolution,

Williams has made his "University of Woodford Square" his principal rostrum, but he is as likely to speak in the Town Hall at San Fernando (where the audience tends to be predominantly East Indian), brought vividly to mind in Michael Anthony's intriguing *Bildungsroman*, or on the Port of Spain savannah.

Williams's style reflects his Burkian outlook: it combines appeal to intellection with appeal to deep-set emotion. His speeches do more than convey his reasoned view of political and social problems; they seek a harmony with the audience based on mutual respect and kinship.

One of the basic strategies consistently used by Williams to unify his audience and to promote his own identity with them is the invocation of the archetypal metaphor of the master-slave relationship. He sees his listeners sharing a common oppression in which he also partakes. He says that "in Trinidad the Negro, the Indian, French and Spaniard, English and Portuguese, Syrian and Lebanese, Chinese and Jew, all have messed out of the same pot, all are victims of the same subordination, all have been tarred with the same brush of political inferiority" (*History* 278).

On other occasions Williams portrays the horrors of colonialism in a style more graphic and vigorous, as in the following passage from his speech "The National Community," delivered at night at the Old Arima Race Stand on 28 October 1965 and running to about 12,000 words:

> You know one of the famous pastimes of the old planters in Trinidad—the West Indies generally? They would take a slave girl, sleep with the girl and then they would take the daughter, their own daughter, sleep with the daughter, and then they would go through the different generations. It was a regular pastime. They had a name for it. They called it 'washing their blackamoors white.' Lightening the generations. It was consciously done. (*Reorganisation* 116)

One of Williams's frequent variations on the master-slave metaphor is his portrayal of the slave as the sacrificial victim of English and American mercantilist greed. Here is his assessment of the effect on the West Indies of the long association with these countries:

> Thus, one century after British emancipation in 1833, the entire West Indies were again ablaze—revolt against the American-supported dictatorship in Cuba, hopeless poverty in Puerto Rico and the Virgin Islands, an absentee plantocracy crucifying West Indian humanity upon a cross of sugar cane everywhere, Haiti under American occupation, a pervading apathy and sickness in the smaller islands broken only in periods of disorder, as the Disturbances Commission stated in respect of Trinidad. ("Perspectives" 12)

The evils that Williams portrays were deliberate, and Williams warns his listeners not to "be tempted to regard them as either blunders or stupidity or perverseness on the part of those who enunciated them. They are neither blunders nor stupidity nor perverseness." It is important to the speaker that he assign blame; he sees colonialist policies, of whatever origin, as the root cause of his people's present plight, and he finds no difficulty in identifying the colonialist scapegoats. He tells his audience, for example, that should his proposals for a solution to the Chaguaramas issue not be accepted by the Americans, then "the only possible explanation we can find [is] the continued domination of the habits and thinking of colonialism to us as non-whites."

Time and again in dramatic language Williams forces his audience to face the ugly realities of their colonialist heritage. But the lesson is also instructive of the means of their redemption. Having depicted the pernicious effects of colonialism, he asks his listeners a rhetorical question and then proffers his intended answer:

> What is the exact significance of all this for us today? Among other things it is this: all the difficulties from which we suffer and the problems we have to overcome, all these are not native to our country as a Territory or to us as a people. The unbalanced state of our economy, our insularity, even the timidity with which some of us approach the privileges and responsibilities of independence, all these are due to the course of economy, politics and history which were imposed on us for 300 years.
>
> We are now getting out of it, and the more we understand what was done to us, the more easily we shall throw off the evil heritage that it has left behind. (16)

Thus Williams assures his audience that awareness of their demeaning historical experience will be their salvation; certainly his dramatic presentations of that experience help to make their redemption psychologically inevitable.

And from time to time, balanced against the picture of the depraved oppressors, Williams evokes the romantic myth of Rousseau's noble savage, as when he refers to "the superior magnanimity of the African slave over the sordid soul of his master." Or when he declares that "slavery is not by nature ... the humblest antecedents are not inconsistent with greatness of soul" (*History* 282).

But on the whole, when Williams depicts his audience, it is in terms that call them to account for their laziness and self-indulgence, their selfish careerism that seeks mere personal aggrandizement. Declaring that the national character of the people of Trinidad and Tobago, "as developed and encouraged by generations of slavery and colonialism," is an "overwhelming advantage" to the achievement of nationhood, he says:

> Some of those who protest against colonial exploitation seek in the same breath to demand the perquisites enjoyed by the expatriates, seeking thereby not only to foist upon the people of Trinidad and Tobago a perpetuation of colonial standards and colonial privileges, but also to maintain the same distributive injustice which precipitated the nationalist movement; as if a parasite ceases to be offensive because it is indigenous. (283)

He speaks with asperity of those "who see in nationalism and self-government nothing but an opportunity for establishing their own little clique and having around them a mass of clients and proteges whom they push forward at the expense of others."

In Williams's view Trinidadians suffer not only from the notion that government exists merely to provide special privileges but also from "the confusion of anti-intellectualism" that is inevitable "with a mentality conceived in slavery, cradled in indenture, and nurtured in colonialism" (qtd. in Lewis 394). If Williams appears to risk historical distortion by an overdrawn picture of colonialist evils and a too-consistent condemnation of all that Britain did, does he not restore some balance to his analysis through his straightforward acknowledgment of imperfections on the other side? Williams's understanding of his listeners' shortcomings is important: since his listeners lack the tradition of enlightened community participation, appeals for unity based on reason would probably fail. Invocation of the dramatic master-slave metaphor is a more effective means of inspiring sentiment for national rather than selfish aims.

The power, directness, and vividness of Williams's style is conveyed not only by his skill in invoking the master-slave metaphor, but also in his use of strategies of analysis, arrangement, and argument that project strong contrast and comparison and are designed to force a choice upon his listeners. In all of his speeches he customarily traces the historical development of present problems. His purpose is not merely to inform: any pedagogical quality that might attach to a straightforward recital of facts is dissipated by his treatment of points so as to build a case in favour of his own view.

In a speech that Williams delivered, entitled "Race Relations in Caribbean Society," he justifies his claims that West Indian governments were traditionally "the organs of the plantocracy and the enemy of the people" when he examines the findings of the 1736 Commission of Enquiry in Antigua and declares that behind the Commission findings lay "the philosophy ... very clearly stated in French law—that nothing would ever make the slave equal to his master." Continuing his analysis he examines emancipation in Jamaica and declares that when "equality threatened, ... the British government in 1865, under pressure from the planters, formally suspended the constitution and instituted direct government by the Crown." Pursuing his theme, he discourses on the history of the theory of race, branding Thomas Carlyle a "neo-fascist" and repudiating "Gobineau's inequality of races, which is associated with the intolerance of fascism, the vapourings of Nietzsche, and the indecency of South Africa. Froude would have no respectability today ... Macaulay would be stoned to death." By such accumulation of evidence through historical review, Williams seeks to substantiate his claim of the "bankruptcy of the slave-plantation economy." He shows his ability to exploit a basic image through a series of specific examples; the effect of his analysis relies upon contrast and accumulation.

Williams augments the force and clarity of his strategy of cumulation by using short, dramatically worded internal summaries that reiterate the point he has just made and invite a comparison favourable to Trinidad. In a speech entitled "The National Community" Williams announces his intention to clarify "the progress that the P.N.M. has made towards ... national community ... and see what happens in other nations, the majority of them independent." Summing up his remarks on the United States, Williams says, "Then one will recognise that the United States is not a national community in the sense that the P.N.M. has sought to establish a national community in Trinidad and Tobago." Continuing, he says of Canada's sense of national identity: "They thought they had one for 98 years in Canada and suddenly they woke up to find that they don't have one"; and of Belgium: "If they still have one they don't know what the devil it is." In this manner he goes on to consider a total of twelve different countries, in each case either implying or specifying the superiority of the Trinidad and Tobago national community. His style throughout the passage conveys both force and control, the goal clearly persuasion.

One of Williams's most effective rhetorical techniques that enhances the clarity and directness of his message and effectively forces his audience to choose is his constant posing of either-or propositions, often in conjunction with argument on principle. The following passage illustrates these qualities in combination and reveals the energetic quality of his style: it moves forward with sudden shifts in direction, parenthetic elements, and rhetorical questions. Williams tells his audience that

> the greater the solidarity at village levels, the more established and stronger is the community at national level. This does not happen in these other places, where, whilst we are getting together ... in Quebec they are pulling apart; in Brussels they are dividing; in Ceylon after

a hundred years of, if not partnership, co-existence, you suddenly destroy what you thought had been put together. We in Trinidad are moving together, other places are moving apart.

    I emphasise that, friends, because I want to impress upon you that you must not take the moving together for granted. Canada did it and look at it after 98 years. You don't want suddenly to find that after eight or 98 years you suddenly have now to make desperate efforts to patch it up again, it has come apart. We understood this from the start and went out for inter-racial solidarity. We used to say, you either get together or you cut each other's throats. Which do you prefer? And look at what is happening all over the place. And if you get at each other's throats, will you tell me in the name of all that is holy what is going to happen to your children being mixed up in these schools? Do you want the fights to start in the schools? ("Perspectives" 14)

Thus we see Williams, in the passages quoted, struggling to inculcate a positive national consciousness by hammering home the lesson of the colonialist metaphor, trying to rouse his people politically, and affirming the individualism and integrity of Trinidad and Tobago. Williams's ideas are conveyed in a style that is rich in imagery, clear, powerful, and direct, displaying effective use of language to convey the vivid physical perception of suffering and shame. He is so much at ease in discoursing on the evils of colonial oppression and his style seems so calculated to offend that the question must be asked whether he achieves the appeal to "the intelligence rather than ... the emotions" that he promised in 1958. Does his relentless pursuit of the colonialist metaphor and his resolute ascription of blame produce in his audience what Lewis calls the acceptance of symbols "as substitutes for, instead of merely being aids to the solid feelings of national community arising out of common social experience?" (395). I think not. Williams's faults are the defects of his virtues. There is, perhaps, too much stimulation of the imagination, but his evocative richness provides his audience with something perceptible and immediately useful.

When one compares Manley and Williams one discovers that they have certain aims in common (self-government, the development of national consciousness) and share some themes (repudiation of the colonialist legacy of dependency, self-doubt), but there are differences as well.

Although the comprehensive treatment both men give to speech materials shows a clear debt to history, Williams emerges as the impetuous judge of history, mercilessly condemnatory, while Manley appears as the self-conscious ponderer of past events, searching for applications. Manley is more conventional in his use of history than Williams and does not consistently use language to heighten the implication of his statements as Williams does. Manley's well-developed explanations, his logical progression of those ideas are an illustration of style matching sentiment. Williams's forceful style is both didactic and evocative; the distortion it evinces is the price he pays for directness.

Both Manley and Williams appear to be well within the mainstream of modern West Indian oratory, wherein they must come to terms with the force of the past while dealing with present conditions and shaping future policy. Their speeches reveal men of superior capability seeking solutions to the basic problem which faces the West Indies today, as it did nearly forty years ago—the development of genuine national interest and identity. The answers given by Manley and Williams demonstrate the variety of achievement to be found in West Indian public discourse.

WORKS CITED

Anderson, Jervis. "A Reporter at Large: Home to Jamaica." *New Yorker* 19 Jan. 1976: 63-85.

Lewis, Gordon K. *The Growth of the Modern West Indies*. New York: Monthly Review P, 1968.

Manley, Norman. *Norman Washington Manley and the New Jamaica: Selected Speeches and Writings 1938-68*. Ed. Rex Nettleford. London: Longman Caribbean, 1971.

Thonssen, Lester, and A. Craig Baird. *Speech Criticism: The Development of Standards for Rhetorical Appraisal*. New York: Ronald P, 1948.

Williams, Eric. *History of the People of Trinidad and Tobago.* New York: Praeger, 1962.

—. *Perspectives for Our Party.* Port of Spain: People's National Movement, 1958.

—. "Race Relations in Caribbean Society." in *Caribbean Studies: A Symposium.* Ed. Vera Rubin. Seattle: University of Washington Press, 1960.

—. *Reorganisation of the Public Service: Three Speeches.* Port of Spain: People's National Movement, 1965 (?).

Wilson, Peter J. *Crab Antics: The Social Anthropology of English-Speaking Negro Societies of the Caribbean.* New Haven: Yale UP, 1973.

1976

4. R. G. Menzies as Parliamentary Speaker

In the history of Australian politics two men stand out as the major speakers of a vast assemblage of generally undistinguished politicians, many of whom must be properly judged as either verbose or else taciturn, though capable, members. Though some partisans might wish to advance the claims of George Higinbotham or W. A. Holman, it is relatively easy to support the thesis that the only two Australian parliamentary speakers worthy of being thought in the tradition of Burke, Fox, Pitt, Gladstone, and Churchill are Alfred Deakin and Robert G. Menzies, the former the cynosure of an earlier, more fundamental age, the latter the leader of his country in its transition from post-colonial dependency on Britain to contemporary hegemony in the Pacific.

From the numerous comments that he made on public speaking, it is clear that Menzies regarded speech communication as one of the politician's most effective instruments in influencing both small group and national behaviour and in maintaining a leadership role.

For Menzies, the ideal speaker, like Cicero's or Quintilian's, was the good man engaged in political life, which he believed to be "the most responsible civil activity," an art demanding "exposition, persuasion, and inspiration," but requiring certain conditions to be met for it to flourish. These he sets out in an essay entitled "Politics as an Art":

> The essence of a speech is that it should reach the hearts and minds of our immediate audience. It must therefore be made to them and not merely in their presence.

> The speaker should have something to say which he is resolved to convey to his listeners in the simplest, most intelligible, and most persuasive language.... The search for elaboration rather than simplicity is a mark of the second-rate. Lucidity has always seemed to me to be one of the cardinal virtues.
>
> Two modern devices are ... acting adversely to good public speech. One is amplification by the microphone.... It is impairing our faculties of speech by making the proper pitching and modulation of our voices irrelevant.... It is destroying the faculty of listening because people who are accustomed to the deafening blare of an amplifier find the unassisted voice thin and (so they think) inaudible....
>
> The other dangerous modern device is ... that important speeches are ... prepared and distributed before they are spoken.
>
> This has made fashionable and perhaps inevitable the reading of speeches.... The speech ceases to be the obvious expression of the speaker's personality and ideas, since anybody may have written it.... His speech loses flexibility. It all too frequently ceases to persuade because persuasion depends upon the creation in the mind of the listener of a feeling that the speaker is addressing him, man to man, and is dealing with the point that is troubling his mind. (*Speech* 185-89)

It is clear from these words that Menzies had firm ideas on what constituted good speaking and that he valued speech as an "obvious expression of the speaker's personality and ideas." With these comments of his in mind, it should prove useful to preface the examination of his parliamentary speaking by noting his methods of speech preparation and the general characteristics of his delivery.

Menzies personally carried the principal responsibility for the preparation of his speeches. Commenting on his methods, Edgar Holt writes that "Menzies was so fastidious about words, that he rarely permitted anyone to write a line for him. His professional opinion was that a politician should be competent to express himself in his own idiom" (123). His effort to improve upon his own use of language led him to frequent reading of the major poets as a means of sharpening his appreciation of the effect of words: "their weight, meaning, and sound endlessly fascinated him.... He would sometimes take up a book of verse and read for a while when he was about to prepare an important speech" (126).

These continuing efforts to achieve precision in language enabled him to achieve both grace and individuality in his speeches; he selected the language to express his special point of view in phrases of particular force or nuance, so that his speeches became an accurate expression of both his personal experience and his considered judgment.

Three factors aided Menzies in the preparation and presentation of his speeches: his ability to discover the essentials of a problem; his skill in making simple, lucid summaries; and his excellent memory. (It may be noted that Menzies spoke extemporaneously in the House of Representatives, since the standing orders forbid members to read their speeches.)

In preparing policy speeches or formal statements to parliament, Menzies customarily wrote out his speeches with a lead pencil in longhand, although he preferred the methods that he used for public political speeches and after-dinner speeches, when his practice was to assemble facts and ideas and then to prepare a rough outline containing summarized notes and headings; he did not prepare the actual words, for he felt that "the language of the speech was best dictated by the mood of the audience" (124).

At no time did Menzies use speech writers; he handled the complete preparation himself, except for the collection of data, which his ministers undertook. As he pointed out in *The Measure of the Years*, he felt that the pressure on politicians to give many speeches—in his case "perhaps a hundred a year"—tended to "debase their own currency by introducing a routine element into what they say" (9). And he had firm views on the use of speech writers to satisfy the demand for excessive communication:

> I had an obstinate objection to having other people's words put into my mouth, and ... except for formal lectures and statements on foreign affairs made by me to Parliament, my practice has been to speak from brief notes, allowing the language to come spontaneously as the actual speech developed. (9)

The impression of him as a man of intellectual integrity and candour was undoubtedly enhanced by the originality of his speeches, for they gave his audience an immediate insight into his thinking and allowed them to judge his ideas without the confusion of trying to distinguish his personal point of view from that of a speechwriter or public relations man. No doubt his speeches derive much of their quality of originality and directness from his habits of preparation; certainly his methods were appropriate to his view that speech should be the obvious expression of the speaker's personality. Australians are said to admire bluntness and honesty in speech, which suggests that insofar as Menzies' speeches conveyed the sense that he spoke openly and directly to his listeners—"man to man" as he has expressed it—they made a positive contribution to his ethos.

Menzies' technique of speech preparation was sufficiently refined to enable him to broadcast or televise his speeches without rehearsal; Edgar Holt tells us that in preparing for such an appearance, Menzies marked the time on every page of his script and made his own adjustments as he delivered it (126). As a result, his attention to detail gave him complete mastery over the speech. In undertaking conscious refinements of language and arrangement, he would have been able to command the elements of unity, coherence, and continuity so as to achieve the simplicity, clear sense of purpose, and individuality that he admired in a speaker. Not the least advantage of such thorough preparation would be the flexibility and confidence he could gain in delivery.

Menzies not only paid careful attention to the preparation of his speeches; he possessed considerable skill in delivery as well. The visual impact of his large figure clad in his customary double-breasted suit or the green robe of the Order of the Thistle was considerable; in fact, his habitual appearance in a dark double-breasted suit gave him an air of timelessness and contributed to the impression of him in his later years as an institution. In keeping with his imposing build, Menzies' movements were deliberate rather than quick; in speaking, he stood firmly and employed gestures sparingly, occasionally using an unhurried lifting movement of his hands to accompany his words. By contrast, his face was remarkably expressive of his moods and reactions; he could silence an offending backbencher with a glance or, just as readily, give encouragement with a wink or a nod. The dominant feature of his face was his heavy black eyebrows, which contrasted strikingly with his silver hair:

> A cultivated growth, they appeared to be stuck on. They gave the face a mephistophelian look. He manipulated them to register surprise, incredulity, appreciation.... His eyes were used with dramatic effect. Whenever he dispensed charm he directed a quite brilliant glitter upon his subject. Laughter was rarely employed, certainly not belly laughter. But there was ample room on the face to display mood, although it was all done as if by command from some secret source. Face and head were constructed on monumental lines—a combination ruling out mercurial changes of expression. The technique was slow motion. (Holt 103, 124)

Holt continues this description, adding: "The clue to his style was timing.... He used the pause in speaking like a man who had spent his life in the theatre." This allusion to a "theatrical" quality in Menzies' delivery is corroborated by the testimony of another observer, Leon Gullett, who writes that Menzies was "master of every debating tactic and has histrionic or dramatic ability of a high order" (167). Conceivably, Menzies' delivery could be described as theatrical or dramatic, but since his style was neither bombastic nor fustian, his delivery could never be flamboyant or ranting; nonetheless, he could be impressively deliberate, magisterial, avuncular, and at times urbane or debonair, particularly when engaged in repartee or banter.

Perhaps Menzies' success in achieving effective delivery came from his self-possession and control, qualities which are important to speaker and actor alike. Even under the most difficult circumstances he never failed to give an impression of authority; his use of the variables of pitch, rate, and intensity assisted in the creation of this impression.

His speaking rate, determined by timing randomly selected passages of some of his taped addresses, is at the lower end of the average range—a moderate 120 words per minute; he avoids extreme fluctuations, using a slower rate to emphasize difficult or important ideas and a faster rate to set out illustrative or background material or to summarize arguments. Speaking at an even, moderate rate, he could remorselessly pour sarcasm, denunciation, and logic on his opponents, pausing occasionally for emphasis before pronouncing a particular word or before inserting a repetition or short summary of a point he had just made.

Menzies' voice has been described as "fairly light but penetrating and flexible." Those who have heard him address open-air meetings attest to his vocal resources: in replying to interjectors one writer reports that his voice "becomes almost stentorian in its volume, yet it retains its quality and clarity." These descriptions concur with the writer's judgment, insofar as it is possible to draw conclusions on the basis of parliamentary broadcasts and taped speeches. Within a rather restricted range, Menzies achieves variety in all three vocal elements, although his most characteristic modifications are those of intensity. Frequently, when he comes to a point that he wishes to stress, his voice becomes louder and his tones are orotund in the best sense of the word. Thus, although his replies are immediate and sharp and an entire speech conveys the impression of authority, incisiveness, and efficiency, he achieves such results with an air of ease and satisfaction. His accent is identifiably Australian, but could not be described as "broad," or "uneducated"—the accent which, Sidney Baker says, the English associate with near-illiteracy and which is spoken by every Hollywood version of an Australian (129).

One of the most accurate impressions of his speaking is contained in the following short paragraph by a London writer who heard him deliver a speech in 1941 to the National Defense Public Interest Committee at a luncheon meeting in the Dorchester Hotel:

> To begin with, there was nothing impersonal about him. There was the different voice, distinctly Australian. His comparatively easy-going manner, the suggestion of delight he could take in pouring phials of acid on stuffed-shirts and mandarins. At the same time his intelligence was as plain as a pikestaff, and you watched him with a certain amount of caution, treated him with respect since you knew instinctively that he could bite pretty sharply. He was aggressively independent, a master of sarcasm and subtle insinuation. (Hole 455)

Lord Birkenhead's daughter, Lady Eleanor Smith, commented that Menzies, "in the speed and pointedness of his speeches," was reminiscent of her father, a former Lord Chancellor, who was noted for his brilliant wit and sarcasm (qtd. in Hole 455).

Turning to a consideration of the characteristics of Menzies' parliamentary speaking *per se*, it is obvious that his speeches in the House exhibit those qualities—lucidity, directness, simplicity, and mastery of facts—set out in his essay "Politics as an Art." The basis for this judgment is a reading of all his speeches of his First Government and those during his years in opposition as well as his speeches on foreign affairs and selected domestic issues during his subsequent prime ministerships (1949-66).

Much of the lucidity of his speeches derives from his concern for precise use of words and correct definition of terms. For example, in a 5 September 1957 debate on the Japanese trade agreements, Menzies challenged his opponents' allegations that importation of Japanese goods would produce "serious injury" in Australian industry, pointing out that the word "serious" has

> a dictionary meaning of 'important or not slight.' An illness may be serious or slight. Yet no medical man would seek to set out in advance a category of illnesses which would inevitably be 'serious.' He would properly reply that the gravity of an illness can be judged only at the time and in the light of existing circumstances.... This consideration is relevant to the present argument. How could anybody in advance say of an immense variety of industries, great and small, that importation of some specified quantity of successfully competitive goods was to be regarded as threatening or causing serious injury? A comparatively small importation might in one case be significant and even deadly; in another case, of a great industry with large productivity it might be negligible. (405)

Because Menzies could command the precise word to express his ideas, he was a formidable opponent. He also had the ability, as this passage illustrates, to discredit his opponents by citing ambiguities in their language. By implying that his opponents' irresponsible assertions demonstrate their inability to grasp the complexities of the issue at hand, he impugns their intelligence. Passages from Menzies' speech on the Conciliation and Arbitration Bill provide a further example of his ability to turn his opponents' deficiencies of language against them.

His precision in the use of language is an ability that is related to advocacy, and no doubt this was derived from his legal training. His preparation and experience in law provided him with invaluable insights into constitutional law, and it gave him training in the skills of analysis, organization, use of argument and evidence, and methods of attack and defence. The rather unorthodox instruction in case presentation which he received from Sir Owen Dixon taught him to go straight to the important points in an argument and develop them in a persuasive fashion. Menzies appreciated the various aspects of forensic speaking, for he wrote, in *Afternoon Light*,

> The truth is that a barrister with years of experience and considerable skill gets to know far more of human psychology and human behaviour than most men. He really gets to know a great deal about truth and falsehood, and what makes people 'tick.' He is not deceived by plausible stories. And above all, he is trained to distinguish between the relevant and the irrelevant. (327)

Menzies' own speeches in the House of Representatives demonstrate his remarkable grasp of essentials, his appreciation of tactical requirements, and his ability to make a clear statement of his arguments; to a considerable extent, he seems to have applied the skills of advocacy to his own speaking. His precision in the use of language, noted earlier, was another of his abilities directly related to advocacy; much of the intelligibility of his arguments in refutation and constructive speaking was based on his ability to choose words that would convey his ideas in the clearest and simplest fashion. There is nothing obscure or vague in his speeches: they are incisive and coherent. In the give-and-take of debate, he surpassed his colleagues to such an extent that all his critics, regardless of their opinions of him as a politician, acknowledged his superiority.

Systematic argument and lucid expression of assumptions based on constitutional or legal points of view characterize

Menzies' speeches in debate. Dr. J. F. Cairns, a Labor member of parliament and long-time opponent of Menzies, describes a technique which he claims Menzies used in attempting to present his ideas clearly: "He was a great builder of straw cases, a great searcher for simplification and simplifier of people's positions and of issues. This enabled the ordinary man to grasp them" (qtd. in Perkins 243).

In examining Cairns's claim that Menzies used the "straw man" technique, the present writer could find no examples of his use of that method *per se*. In many speeches he uses what might be considered a modification of the technique when he builds a case on a matter which his opponents, through muddled thinking or failure to delineate their own case properly, have inadvertently admitted into the argument. Citing his opponents' ambiguities, he launches an attack on grounds which, he points out, they have implied in their case. An example of this technique may be drawn from his speech of 24 March 1960 on the activities of wool pies (the term "pies" refers to improper price agreements):

> But, Sir, the motion put forward ... went beyond wool pies. It extended into the area of restrictive practices.... Restrictive practices are, I imagine, attacked in the case of wool because it is said that they tend to reduce prices. In every other respect that I can think of, however, they are attacked because it is said that they increase prices and thus increase profits, and therefore produce what the distinguished Leader of the Opposition (Mr. Calwell) was good enough to describe, a few times at least, as a "profit inflation."
>
> [*Mr. Calwell*: That is right.]
>
> That is right! I am very glad he is here, because I regard his words with great interest. Several times he has made it clear that this is a profit inflation. Therefore, I imagine that my distinguished friend will agree that this is just one phase of the attack, which the Opposition is going through the motions of making, on the subject of alleged excess profits and how to deal with them. Pies, coupled with the honourable name of General Motors-Holden's Limited, represent the two ends of the scale. (605-08)

Having ridiculed his opponents' analysis of the issues, Menzies then exploits the argumentative grounds they unwittingly provided as he presents a defense of his government's policies on the related matters of restrictive practices, monopolies, and overseas investments in Australia. There is much evidence to support Cairns's testimony that Menzies was a "great searcher of simplification." Menzies' 1940 budget speech contains an excellent example of his ability to describe in simple terms the inflationary effects that would be produced by Labor's proposals. In many of his speeches Menzies uses exposition when he argues, as he frequently does, from legal or constitutional authority, from precedent, or from the record of previous parliamentary debate or action. In arguing from such authority, he explains its nature and intent and its application to his case.

His arguments *ad verecundiam* (from constitutional authority or parliamentary precedent) seem always to have been particularly well-received, perhaps because the provision for judicial review of parliament by the High Court made it important for members to know in advance of recommending any measure what its constitutional validity was and whether there was a possibility of successful challenge in the court.

When Menzies spoke on matters of constitutional or parliamentary law, he frequently appeared as a judicious advocate rather than as a partisan spokesman, for he eschewed party considerations and treated his opponents in a straightforward, courteous fashion. Under ordinary circumstances, however, the topics under discussion in the House did not permit a non-partisan approach; on these occasions Menzies spoke as a political leader who was quite conscious of differences—one whose maxim was to go straight at his opponent and at the point.

Menzies excelled in refutation, frequently drawing the support for his own case from the statements of his opponents. During the 15 October 1947 debates on Labor's proposed bank nationalization, Menzies quoted from a book written by his opponent, Labor leader Dr. H. V. Evatt, in which he contradicted the notion of nationalization. Menzies prefaced his citation with customary sarcasm: "Oh, that mine enemy should write a book!

I shall read an extract from page 199 of the first edition of this valuable book; I do not know whether there has been a second edition" (688). Thus Menzies adroitly arranged to have Evatt destroy himself. Menzies casts his opponent as a weak reed, vacillating from theory to theory, his notions without acclaim from any quarter.

Using a variation on this type of refutation in his speech of 24 March 1960 on wool pies, Menzies discredited his opponents' case by showing that their ideas had already been discarded by their own more prestigious colleagues. On this occasion, he argued against Labor's demands for an excess profits tax and used the experience of two former Labor prime ministers to show the impossibilities of devising what he called

> an equitable and just system of excess profits tax on companies which would not grievously handicap the new company established by some enterprising Australian starting from scratch. The late John Curtin had to abandon it. The late Mr. Chifley had to abandon it and, indeed, he was very frank, he said—"In ordinary peace-time circumstances this tax operates inequitably." This is the excess profits tax—"It penalizes new industries by preventing the building up of reserves and consequently favours old established industries which have had the opportunity of building reserves in the past." (605-06)

Using refutation of this sort, Menzies made his opponents look foolish, for he showed that he not only knew more than they of the history of the issue in the Labor Party, but had, moreover, the insight to recognize that the question of a tax on excess profits touched on a basic economic problem that went beyond mere partisan solutions. Closing his case, he stated:

> Now, Sir, I will just put that in summary. Of the total company profits—and this is all behind this motion, the object of the exercise—this is the case that the Australian Labor Party under new and garnished leadership thinks it has—of the total company profits earned in Australia, one-third comes to the Government as income tax ... 35 per cent goes back into enterprises ... and near enough to 31 per cent is paid out in terms of dividends. Now, Sir, those, I think, are very interesting figures, and I refer to them because I believe that the Opposition has put this sorry little motion forward today as part and parcel of its general campaign on profits.

Menzies valued logic and coherence in his own arguments. He frequently attacked the arguments of his opponents by citing their inconsistencies, as he did on 5 September 1957:

> The arguments of the opponents are inconsistent when they say that on one hand, Japan will act in bad faith, and on the other hand, they say the treaty is all in Japan's favour.... There is a certain logical indecency about having arguments that contradict each other, and in this case they do. (404)

Menzies' arguments from legal authority have already been noted; phrases such as "If he had mastered his brief" and "No amount of cross examination could reveal" occur frequently throughout his speeches and reveal the legalistic cast of his mind. Occasionally he rounded off the point he was making with a quotation in Latin—a rhetorical inflation that may have done more to provoke resentment, however, than it did to reinforce his argument.

Hansard abounds, also, in illustrations of Menzies' handling of heckling exchanges: during one debate he referred to Queensland as a fertile state, and when a member from that state interjected with "Hear, Hear," Menzies replied, "Except in ideas, as I am reminded by looking at the honourable member for Griffith." A debate on the Broadcasting Bill contains an exchange in a similar vein:

> Mr. Pollard: Why did not the Government prohibit the importation of all books and make a good job of it?
>
> Mr. Menzies: If the Government did that it would cause no hardship to the honourable member.

His skill in handling interjections, questions, and personal abuse was so well known that opposition members were once warned not to interject when he was speaking. Menzies was subdued or silent only in the face of the most insolent personal attack, such as one made upon him by Earle Page. Menzies thrived on the polemics of debate: he seemed to require conflict in order to do his best; if opposition was not forthcoming, he provoked it. The ease and obvious pleasure with which he employed witty ripostes and clever repartee to despatch his adversaries gives an impression of him as an extraordinarily skillful player who valued the game and appreciated the challenge that a skilled opponent could provide.

Australians enjoy a contest, they love a battler, and Menzies never disappointed them in that respect. No doubt his ready response to personal attack helped to create an impression of courage. There were times, however, when his propensity for sharp riposte and his disdain for his opponents' unfavourable estimates of him had regrettable consequences in that the sarcasm he unleashed in vitriolic diatribes spoiled the inherent force of his argument and distorted or temporarily destroyed the image he otherwise presented of a judicially calm politician and statesman.

Insofar as we may assume from Menzies' frequent argument from the authority of the law that he wished his audience to view him as "a person whose object is the discovery of the truth rather than as someone against whose propositions they should be on their guard," he could be said to have carried the considerations of good advocacy into the House. Thus he must have realized that excessive sarcasm can erode the impression of the user's sincerity and reliability and create undue sympathy for its recipient. In the latter case, Menzies' ability to let his opponent destroy himself by his own testimony helped to break down whatever sympathy the sarcasm may have engendered; but the impression remains that Menzies frequently scored too easy a victory against outclassed opponents who in debate rarely seemed his equal either in knowledge of the subject or in argumentative techniques and competence.

The most obvious exception to this comment on the calibre of his opponents was Dr. H. V. Evatt, who was elected leader of the parliamentary Labor Party in succession to J. B. Chifley in 1951. In him alone, perhaps, Menzies found a worthy opponent—a man who was a closer match for him than any other Labor politician. Evatt entered parliament during Menzies' wartime prime ministry and soon made it clear that, unlike John Curtin, he opposed any cooperation with Menzies and preferred to work for Labor's return to office. One observer wrote at the time that Evatt had "a pugnacity which does not do justice to his great powers." Evatt and Menzies seemed destined to oppose each other: graduates of rival universities, each had been a brilliant debater as a student and had subsequently made his mark in the legal profession before entering parliament—Menzies as a leader of the bar and member of the Privy Council, Evatt as a judge on the High Court and as first chairman of the United Nations General Assembly.

Their long feud in the House reached its climax in the debates of 19 October 1955 on the report of the Royal Commission on Espionage, which had concluded that there was evidence of Communist activity in Canberra. Evatt spoke for two hours in a discursive speech that accused Menzies of instigating the investigation for political purposes; further, Evatt pronounced the evidence examined by the Commission to be false: the Soviet government, he said, had replied to his request for authentication of the documents by stating that they were "falsifications fabricated on the instructions of persons interested in the deterioration of the Soviet-Australian relations and in discrediting their political opponents" (1695). The realization of the true import of the Molotov letter sent the House into such an uproar that order could hardly be maintained.

When Menzies spoke later in the debate he implacably examined "what I might loosely describe as the substance of the right honourable gentleman's main charges" and made full use of Evatt's blunder: "He made a monumental exhibition of himself last week. I am not adding to the monumental exhibition; I am merely sealing the tombstone on top of it." Speaking to the accompaniment of numerous interjections and Evatt's steady intonation of the word "smear," Menzies excoriated Evatt's aspersions on the Royal Commission, reminding the House that the only appropriate question was "whether dangers to the country had been revealed and ... what steps ought to be taken to prevent repetition of those dangers."

Although Evatt had made a personal attack on him, Menzies merely reminded the House that his record of service "for over a quarter of a century ... in the heat of political controversy" had made him "not entirely unknown, either in character or act, to the Australian people." This use of litotes, a form of understatement in which a proposition is affirmed by asserting the negative of its opposite, is a stylistic device by which Menzies frequently injects irony into his speeches; he also utilized the more commonplace trope, meiosis (simple understatement), for humorous, satiric, or emphatic purpose.

Throughout the speech Menzies concentrated his efforts on defending the Royal Commission, thereby indirectly clearing his own reputation and casting doubts on the probity and motives of Evatt. Saving his direct attack on Evatt until the close, Menzies declared that "honourable public opinion" would acquit the members of the Commission, but not Evatt, who, he said,

> has, ... for his purposes, ... and with the enthusiastic support of every Communist in Australia, sought to discredit the judiciary, to subvert the authority of the security organization, to cry down decent and patriotic Australians and to build up the Communist fifth column. I am, therefore, compelled to say that, in the name of all these good and honourable men, in the name of public decency, in the name of the safety of Australia, the man on trial in this debate is the right honourable gentleman himself. (1858-65)

This speech amply illustrates Menzies' mastery of debate. Reporting on the debate, the *Sydney Morning Herald* declared on 30 October 1955:

> This was R. G. Menzies at the peak of his debating form, his unrivalled powers in that line evoked by the historic occasion, but even more by the consciousness that he had a detested opponent at his mercy.
>
> The bitter raillery, the contempt, the venom, came sizzling over the wireless. Menzies was not only defending the Judges and Security, but paying off old scores. (15)

The debate on the Royal Commission demanded Menzies' best efforts, and he rose to the occasion.

Indeed, he seemed to speak better in circumstances where something was at stake, or where the outcome was uncertain and his words might affect the resolution of a problem. Since the deliberative setting demanded the settlement of urgent problems and there was a likelihood that Menzies would be contradicted, his speeches in that setting are generally superior to those given on epideictic occasions. His occasional speeches have been called "extremely disappointing and pedestrian," perhaps owing to the fact that in most cases the situations which called them forth had no more significance for him than the opening of the Wagga Wagga flower show.

Certainly the atmosphere of the Australian parliament did not encourage extensive debate on important issues. Not only was the average member ill-equipped to speak on such subjects; the parliamentary procedures and the operation of the Liberal Party tended to curtail debate by its members, whose apparent satisfaction with Menzies as their leader and spokesman increased their disinclination to participate in debate in which their own shortcomings would be made apparent to their constituents and the national audience. In such circumstances Menzies' skills as a parliamentarian and speaker helped him both to achieve and to sustain a position of great authority; in fact, so outstanding were his abilities that it would not be inaccurate to conclude that his very brilliance contributed to the paucity of debate.

While Menzies' parliamentary speeches contain abundant evidence of his mastery of facts and his capacity for clear expression and skillful argument, they also indicate occasional self-satisfaction and an impatience with ideas which differed from his own. The continuous party strife, apparently indigenous in the Australian parliament and often carried to the point where the focus of debate was distorted by discursive statements and a barrage of personal abuse, seemed not to perturb Menzies, who handled abusive attacks masterfully.

In many respects, the opposition which Menzies found in the House provided no real challenge to him; he easily turned his opponents' weaknesses to his own advantage. His speeches in the House reveal the adjustment he made to the parliamentary circumstances: those who disagreed with him he appeared to regard as odd or misguided; his excellent exposition and argument were occasionally marred by sarcasm.

His emphatic support for Britain and his search for a role as a statesman-speaker in the larger arena of international affairs may be viewed as another adjustment which he made to the parliamentary situation and a natural aspiration for a man of his ability. It may also have been a reaction to Australian culture in general.

R. M. Crawford points out that until well into the period following World War II Australian society was generally unable to provide sufficient opportunity for its talented citizens: it "could nourish the beginnings of some great talents, but could not bring them to fruition"; the "immaturity" of the society gave its bright young people "a choice between achievement in exile and frustration at home" (53). This has been profoundly true in the case of writers, musicians, and artists; perhaps it is not unreasonable to assume that similar forces were at work to an extent in Menzies' case. Australia's courts furnished him his initial opportunities, and her parliaments enabled him to perfect his techniques of leadership and oratory; but they gave insufficient scope for his talents.

The Suez Canal crisis of 1956 was an occasion when Menzies was called upon to function as a world statesman; it was an opportunity for him to rise above everyday politics, to seek the "long view," without which "democracy becomes a mere squabble for bread and circuses; statesmanship disappears, and the adroit manoeuvres of evanescent politics prevail," as he wrote in *Speech is of Time* (198).

In his speeches on this occasion he generally used the problem-solving arrangement, creatively modified by digressions; he developed his own ethical proof (and that of his client, Britain) while proposing Egyptian untrustworthiness; sought to build emotional proof by arousing feelings of national pride, moral indignation, and concern for economic well-being; used the strategies of analysis and exposition, argument from authority, and refutation of contrary arguments; and couched his speeches in a style that was clear, forceful, direct, varied with wit and sarcasm, and phrased in language embellished by antitheses, parallelisms, rhetorical questions, and restatement—but not extravagantly. That is, in these, his last great speeches on the international scene, he applied, once more, the basic principles of speech communication that he had learned, mastered, and practised in Canberra.

WORKS CITED

Baker, Sidney. "Language," in *The Pattern of Australian Culture.* Ed. A. L. McLeod. Melbourne: OUP, 1963.

Commonwealth of Australia. *Parliamentary Debates.* Vol. 193, 18th Parliament, 1st Session, 15 October 1947.

—. N.S. No. 8. 21st Parliament, 1st Session, 19 October 1955.

—. N.S. No. 16. 22nd Parliament, 2nd Session, 5 September 1957.

—. N.S. No. 26. 23rd Parliament, 2nd Session, 24 March 1960.

Crawford, R. M. *An Australian Perspective.* Madison, WI: U of Wisconsin P, 1960.

Gullett, L. "Robert Gordon Menzies." *Observer* 3 May 1958: 167.

Hole, Tahu. *Anzacs into Battle.* London: Hodder, 1942.

Holt, Edgar. *Politics Is People: The Men of the Menzies Era.* Sydney: Angus, 1969.

Menzies, Robert G. *Afternoon Light.* London: Cassell, 1960.

—. *The Measure of the Years.* London: Cassell, 1970.

—. *Speech Is of Time.* London: Cassell, 1958.

Perkins, Kevin. *Menzies: Last of the Queen's Men.* San Francisco: Tri-Ocean P, 1968.

5. Speeches as an Artifact of Historiography

In a monograph entitled *The Whig Interpretation of History* Herbert Butterfield makes the point that the historian's task is to recover the richness of the past, to understand the entire context of events so as to achieve "the elucidation of the unlikenesses between past and present" (10). If the historian fails to learn what was important at a given period, substituting instead the standards, values, and judgments of his own present experience, he will have drawn a fallacious view of the past. While the historian must be concerned with significance, he must not assume that past events will necessarily bear a likeness to present events; nor should he allow himself to overdramatize events, indulge in moralizing, or assume the posture of arbitrator. In short, he ought to confine himself, as far as possible, to an examination of a single point in history, mastering the details as a means of finally grasping the complexity of whole processes.

The necessity of bringing past events into present focus is a concern which the historian shares with the rhetorical critic, for whom the central task is to understand the influence of thought and feeling of his day, of the modifying effects of individual audiences, and of the role of the public speaker as a communicator in a particular society. John Donne described the singular ability of oral communication to reflect and reveal the times when he wrote that "rhetorique will make absent and remote things present to your understanding" (615). Through an examination of speeches, more particularly than other literary artifacts, the historian may not only trace national and political events but also understand more fully the growth and development of ideas and assess the place of those ideas in society.

For example, the speeches in the British Parliament on the revolt of the American colonies give an exact picture of Great Britain's position as no creative or imaginative literature does. In his *Straws and Prayer-Books,* James Branch Cabell, the prolific Virginia novelist, wrote, in elaboration of his theory of fiction, that

> it is the privilege of the novelist ... so to delude mankind that nobody from birth to death need ever really bother upon his, upon the whole, uncompromising situation in the flesh.... The endeavour of the novelist, even by the lowest and most altruistic motives, is to tell untruths that will be diverting. (232)

The "Great Commoner," William Pitt, Lord Chatham, while rejecting the notion of separation from the mother country, yet emerges as a champion of the American colonies when he states, in his speech of 11 December 1777 in the House of Lords, "I rejoice that America has resisted," and warns his countrymen that "we have not, nor can procure any force sufficient to subdue America." And he substantiates his claim of the insufficiency of British forces in America by this description, at once graphic and vivid:

> They told you, in the beginning, that 15,000 men would traverse all America, without scarcely an appearance of interruption. Two campaigns have passed since they gave us this assurance. Treble that number have been employed; and one of your armies, which composed two thirds of the force by which America was to be subdued, has been totally destroyed, and is now led captive through those provinces you call rebellious. Those men whom you called cowards, poltroons, runaways, and knaves, are become victorious over your veteran troops; and, in the midst of victory, and the flush of conquest, have set ministers an example of moderation and magnanimity well worthy of imitation. (qtd. in Goodrich 141)

These facts and illustrations would be completely alien to poetry, as well as to drama and the novel.

The shortcomings of the novel and drama as aids to the historical record are apparent, for they follow the event at some distance: the Spanish Civil War took place from 1936-39, yet *For Whom the Bell Tolls* did not appear until 1940; Sean O'Casey's *The Plough and the Stars*, set in the period of the 1916 Easter Rising, came out in 1926. There is substantial question whether the novel, even when designed to depict life as it is, does so effectively. Harrison Steeves argues that no single novel, on its own, "has any probative value in social evidence"; we may make presumptions as to its value only in terms of the whole weight of the fiction of a period, but "that value will depend upon the ethical consensus of the writers as well as upon their ability to sift facts and make judgments.... At this remove from the scene, it is probably impossible to measure the truth of the fiction to the life depicted" (101-02).

It is easier to assume truthful depiction in a novel than it is for poetry. Desmond Pacey, commenting on Oliver Goldsmith's poem "The Rising Village" as historical record, voices a reservation that applies to poetry in general when he writes: "The poem has been hailed as a valuable document in the history of pioneer settlement, but this claim cannot be sustained: the uniformly favorable picture which Goldsmith paints is not in keeping with the facts of the Nova Scotian economy at this time as we know them from other sources" (14).

But what of the reliability of oral rhetoric and its relation to history? Max Lerner posits a view of the interrelation of rhetoric and history when he describes what he calls "a naturalistic approach" to the history of ideas which emphasizes the shifting, unpredictable struggle for survival of ideas, and calls for recognition

> not only [of] the conditions of the creation of ideas but also the conditions of their reception, not only the impulsions behind the ideas, but also the uses to which they are put, not only the thinkers but also the popularizers, the propagandists, the opinion skill-groups, the final audience that believes or disbelieves and acts accordingly. (6)

While Lerner's view may give emphasis to the role of the articulate members of society, it reveals an awareness of the essential Aristotelian concept of the audience which underlies spoken discourse and makes it a useful tool for the historian.

Speeches as an Artifact of Historiography

Because the speaker must prepare for an audience to whom he will deliver the speech directly, he must understand that audience and adjust his message to it. In turn, the critic who examines the speech will need to recognize the impact of complex forces at work in the entire social setting and in the speech: the unfolding and development of ideas and structure, the resolution of contrary ideas or their uneasy accommodation and juxtaposition. It is precisely in the notion of adjusting ideas to the audience that we discover what is one of the chief distinctions of oral communication, as opposed to other forms of communication. Professor Carroll C. Arnold writes of "'adjusting' as an active process ... [which] cannot *fully* describe the character and purposes of most imaginative, fictive works. They have 'informative and suasory' purposes, but they almost invariably have aesthetic purposes too" (5).

The persuasive speaker is engaged in shaping the ideas of his listeners, a task which in the Aristotelian view presumes the conditions and methods of dialectic, a situation which seldom obtains in poetry. Adopting the Aristotelian perspective, the critic may thus expect to find in important speeches given in times of controversy the bases of the settlement of differences. Hence, practicality and utility are the hallmarks of true persuasive rhetoric: the persuasive speaker aims not primarily for eloquence, but, as Goodrich says, his "true aim is to address just and pertinent remarks on the subject under contemplation" (viii). The conditions of dialectic also imply an element of uncertainty of outcome. The speaker must exercise his judgment in choosing strategies and arguments; but he is inevitably forced to deal with probabilities, since in many matters policies must be decided even though all the facts may not be available or the audience reaction may be impossible to gauge. It is the resultant uncertain struggle to bring ideas to life for the audience and to win acceptance of those ideas that gives force and vitality to history and makes spoken discourse, or public address, an undeniable aid to the historian in search of the past.

In respect of urgency, directness, immediate impact upon the audience, and the testing of ideas in an adversary situation, oral communication has no equal among literary forms, which differ in purpose and method. The writer may express himself in isolation, for he faces no real audience and, unlike the speaker who is not free to remain silent but must make a reply, the writer may choose not to comment or to comment when events are past, in words that are reflective and interpretive. The ancients recognized differences between rhetoric, on the one hand, as having for its purpose practicality and effect and dealing with logical determinations, and poetic, on the other hand, as seeking permanence and beauty, and employing imaginative and emotional depictions. Charles Sears Baldwin writes that to ancient critics "the distinction may have been familiar enough to be tacitly assumed," and he points out that Aristotle separated rhetoric and poetic, treating them as distinct processes of conceiving, ordering, and uttering (3-4).

More recently, Walter Ong has differentiated between the writer's and the speaker's task in terms of audience. He comments that "the writer's audience is always a fiction," playing a "made-up role" assigned by the writer (17). Continuing the theatrical metaphor, Ong admits that both the writer and the speaker may attempt to conceal themselves from their audiences by putting on masks, which are an inevitable part of all human communication; but he points out that the directness and urgency of the oral communication situation contains "a momentum that works for the removal of masks.... No matter what pitch of frankness, directness, or authenticity he may strive for, the writer's mask and the reader's are less removable than those of the oral communicator and his hearer" (17). Thus, spoken discourse, which places the speaker in direct contact with his audience, revealing his motives and exposing his arguments, may be more useful than other genres of literature in the understanding of past events and historical contexts, and hence to the attainment of authenticity in historiography, whether of lives, events, or movements.

Although the historian must take note of oral rhetoric as it influenced men and events, the relationship between historian and rhetorician is not always harmonious. The historian fears that an examination of speeches may lure him away from his duty to give a strict presentation of facts; his search for picturesque and interesting elements to enliven his account may take him from what the historian James T. Shotwell, in *The History of History* (1939), admits as an understandable—perhaps inevitable—slight warping of the facts to "the sphere of conscious distortion" (qtd. in Thonssen and Baird 316).

Yet the practice of incorporating speeches to animate historical presentation has been customary since the ancient historians. Livy and Herodotus included speeches in their accounts, and Ephorus is considered to have gone so far as to make up many of the speeches which he wove into the fabric of his historical narratives. The fifth-century historian Thucydides even served the speaker on occasion by writing out introductions to the speeches he included in his accounts. The classical scholar Rex Warner, in his *Men of Athens*, tells us that Thucydides was a careful reporter who combined concern for accuracy with an understanding of the processes of history in order to produce "an aid to right action" (200). Thucydides set aside gossip and romantic embellishment and stated his aim to be "judged useful by those who want to understand clearly the events which happened in the past.... My work is not a piece of writing designed to meet the taste of an immediate public, but was done to last for ever" (qtd. in Warner 201). Thucydides did not eschew dramatic methods, including irony, but Warner points out that he did not thereby insert his own style into the speeches that he reported. Warner supports this claim by his own study of Thucydides' reporting of the speeches of Pericles, which study leads him to believe that the frequent poetical phrases of the speeches are rightly attributed to Pericles, for they do not match the presentational style of Thucydides.

The usefulness of speeches which are incompletely or inaccurately reported is of serious concern to rhetorical critic and historian alike, who must be alert to the degree of authenticity of a given text and the consequent limitations on its utility. But the problem is not adequately addressed by the critic who, like Hugh Blair, dismisses reported speeches out of hand as "a mixture which is unnatural in history, of fiction with truth" (491). Blair prefers that the historian deliver, "in his own person, the sentiments and reasoning of opposite parties, or the substance of what was understood to be spoken in some public assembly; which he may do without the liberty of fiction."

That there is, in fact, a place for the reported (or even re-created) speech is the thesis argued by Professor Judy Hample in her article, "The Textual and Cultural Authenticity of Patrick Henry's 'Liberty or Death' Speech." Acknowledging that the available text is unauthentic, having been put together by Henry's first biographer with the use of eyewitness accounts and testimonial recollections, Hample claims that the general substance of the speech is unimpaired; its survival attests to the fact that our society, like that of Patrick Henry, "promotes an emphasis on moral virtue, tradition, heroism, and eloquence" (303). Here, then, is a picture—perhaps extreme—of rhetoric as tradition, wherein the speaker's words are not more important than their reinforcing value in terms of the societal myths they reveal. A speech such as Patrick Henry's "Liberty or Death" speech, for which no authenticated text may be found and which has passed into the realm of oratorical masterpieces, is probably more fictive than historical and its consideration as pure rhetoric is inappropriate.

Nevertheless, Professor Hample's discovery that spoken discourse provides an index of the social and economic values of the times is a truism. Rufus Choate noted this characteristic of speeches when he said,

> It is the peculiarity of some schools of eloquence that they embody and utter not merely the individual genius and character of the speaker, but a national consciousness—a national era, a mood, a hope, a dread, a despair—in which you listen to the spoken history of the time (qtd. in Peterson xxviii).

And Hugh Blair, in his lectures at the University of Edinburgh, elaborated on the view of public address as a reliable index of national attributes. Contrasting the oratory of France and that of Great Britain, he noted "characteristical differences" in style. Pointing out that "in France, the style of their orators is ornamented with bolder figures; and their discourse carried on with more amplification, more warmth and elaboration," Blair attributed the distinctive qualities of French oratory in part to the genius of the people, which leads them to attend fully as much to ornament as to substance; and, in part, to the nature of their government, which, by excluding public speaking from having much influence on the conduct of public affairs, deprives eloquence of its best opportunity for acquiring nerves and strength. (339).

Other, more recent writers have concurred in Blair's ascription of authenticity to public address and have expressed dismay that so little attention is paid to its place in society. Herbert A. Wichelns suggested that the neglect of public speech seems related to its ephemeral nature and to the ease with which speeches may be transmuted into other forms of literature:

> We have not much serious criticism of oratory. The reasons are patent. Oratory is intimately associated with statecraft; it is bound up with the things of the moment; its occasion, its terms, its background can often be understood only by the careful student of history. Again, the publication of orations as pamphlets leaves us free to regard any speech merely as an essay, as a literary effort deposited at the shrine of the muses in hope of being blessed with immortality. (182)

It is evident that many critics and historians continue to feel more comfortable with the notion of speech as specialized literature rather than as spoken rhetoric. In a recent review of Irving H. Bartlett's book *Daniel Webster*, the reviewer, Mark Harris, applauds Bartlett's conclusion that Webster's chief accomplishment lay in the fact that he "helped take American oratory out of the political forum and establish it as a literary form in its own right ... emerging as a Homeric figure who, more than any other leader of this generation, could create a heroic past for his countrymen" (19). Apparently, Webster's position as the chief orator of his day is something that the reviewer and even the author feel unable to come to terms with, for they fail to grasp what Arnold calls the distinctive characteristics of "oral communication as *action* rather than as 'literary effort deposited at the shrine of the muses in hope of being blessed with immortality'" (7).

One may expect that, until the true characteristics of oral rhetoric are understood by the historian, public address will continue either to be overlooked or to be treated as a piece of ephemeral literature to be weighed when the speaker is safely dead. The historian, who needs to understand social environments, should realize that he cannot completely comprehend those environments until he takes into account the public address that took place in them. He must recognize that he can make the proper use of oral rhetoric if he understands that its central principle is indeed the idea of adaptation of ideas to a specific audience; that this process of adaptation necessitates the treatment of probabilities; that it implies that oral rhetoric has intense practical, suasory qualities; that it is carried out in situations surrounded by controversy. Perhaps, then, the historian will even echo the sentiments of Albert C. Baugh, who has written, "In passing from Gibbon to Burke, we pass from history to actuality" (1089).

WORKS CITED

Arnold, Carroll C. *Criticism of Oral Rhetoric.* Columbus, OH: Merrill, 1974.

Baldwin, Charles S. *Ancient Rhetoric and Poetic.* Gloucester, MA: Peter Smith, 1959.

Baugh, Albert A. *A Literary History of England.* New York: Appleton-Century, 1948.

Blair, Hugh. *Lectures on Rhetoric and Belles Lettres.* Halifax: Milner, 1847.

Butterfield, Herbert. *The Whig Interpretation of History.* New York: Norton, 1965.

Cabell, James Branch. *Straws and Prayer-Books.* New York: McBride, 1924.

Donne, John. "Sermon XXVI." *Complete Poetry and Selected Prose.* Ed. John Hayward. London: Nonesuch, 1929.

Goodrich, Chauncey A. *Select British Eloquence.* New York: Bobbs-Merrill, 1963.

Hample, Judy. "The Textual and Cultural Authenticity of Patrick Henry's 'Liberty or Death' Speech." *Quarterly Journal of Speech* 63.3 (1977): 298-310.

Harris, Mark. "A Legend Instead of President." *New York Times Book Review* 23 July 1978: 6.

Lerner, Max. *Ideas Are Weapons.* New York: Viking, 1939.

Ong, Walter J. "The Writer's Audience Is Always a Fiction." *PMLA* 90.1 (1975): 10-20.

Pacey, Desmond. *Canadian Literature in English.* Mysore: CCLR, 1979.

Peterson, Houston, ed. *A Treasury of the World's Great Speeches.* New York: Simon, 1954.

Steeves, Harrison. *The Shaping of the English Novel in the Eighteenth Century.* New York: Holt, 1965.

Thonssen, Lester, and A. Craig Baird. *Speech Criticism: The Development of Standards for Rhetorical Appraisal.* New York: Ronald, 1948.

Warner, Rex. *Men of Athens: The Story of Fifth-Century Athens.* New York: Viking, 1972.

6. | B. G. Tilak and G. K. Gokhale: Advocates and Adversaries

In the history of India's long struggle for equality and representative government, two men, Gopal Krishna Gokhale and Bal Gangadhar Tilak, stand out as champions of Indian rights. These two great predecessors of Gandhi and Nehru who, as contemporaries, prepared the ground for the modern Indian state, were quite opposite in temperament, motivation, and methods of expression, yet the early Indian Nationalist Movement readily encompassed, and emphasized from time to time, the views of both. Each worked persistently for Indian nationalism, employing rhetoric that may be characterized as polemical and agitational, comprising, as it does, what Charles W. Lomas calls a "persistent and uncompromising statement and restatement of grievances through all available communication channels, with the aim of creating public opinion favourable to a change in conditions" (2).

While each sought change and fearlessly confronted British control, a comparative analysis of the style of the two speakers suggests many differences: Gokhale dissents, claiming Indian rights within the existing system; Tilak defies, claiming Indian rights apart from the existing system. A quite comprehensive insight into their essential differences has been provided by B. P. Sitaramayya, the historian of the Indian National Congress, who has written,

> Gokhale's plan was to improve the existing constitution; Tilak's was to reconstruct it. Gokhale had necessarily to work with the

bureaucracy; Tilak had necessarily to fight it. Gokhale stood for cooperation wherever possible and opposition wherever necessary; Tilak inclined towards a policy of obstruction. Gokhale's ideal was love and sacrifice; Tilak's was service and suffering. Gokhale's methods sought to win the foreigner, Tilak's to replace him. Gokhale depended upon others' help, Tilak upon self-help. Gokhale looked to the masses and the millions. Gokhale's arena was the Council Chamber; Tilak's forum was the village *mandap*. Gokhale's medium of expression was English; Tilak's was Marathi. Gokhale's objective was Self-Government for which people had to fit themselves by answering the tests prescribed by the English; Tilak's objective was Swaraj which is the birthright of every Indian and which he shall have without let or hindrance from the foreigner. Gokhale was on a level with his age. Tilak was in advance of his times. (qtd. in Shay 110)

Both Gokhale and Tilak were Maharashtrians, born into the Chitpavan Brahmin clan, which traditionally took the role of leading social reformation. Both men were well educated, Gokhale having won government scholarships in English and mathematics, Tilak having specialized in Sanskrit, mathematics, and astronomy. While Gokhale set for himself the goal of mastering every nuance of the English language as the most appropriate vehicle for his thoughts, Tilak (whose command of English was also exemplary) took pains to inform his audiences that he was most at home in his native Mahratta and apologized that he had no ability to address them in Hindi, which language, he contended, ought to replace English in common usage. Certainly, the high level reached by both Gokhale and Tilak in their use of English argues against either of them deserving the scornful appellation "métèque," which F. W. Bateson applies to "the writer with a non-English linguistic, racial or political background" who, as a cultural interloper, fails to grasp "the finer rules of English idiom and grammar" (qtd. in Burgess 7).

Both were spokesmen for the Brahmin community, and both were able to reach educated audiences; however, Tilak is credited with having reached far larger audiences. During his lifetime he was given the title *Lokamanya*, revered leader, and is consistently credited by all his biographers with unusual charisma, having succeeded in enlisting the support of the masses of India in the cause of nationalism. He was, in the words of Richard Cashman, "a politician whose career and achievements have been mythicized" (3).

In any culture myths provide a ready means of appeal to the audience. Their invocation lends authenticity to the speaker and his message, provides a unifying context for the speaker's demands, and serves as a vehicle for expressing powerful symbolic violence, which for the Indian masses was a wholesome cathartic that assisted them in achieving a sense of equality with their British masters.

Tilak's speeches and journalism reveal him as a mythmaker and as the object of myth. Drawing on the powerful unifying force of religion, Tilak reshaped and enlarged the Hindu festivals of Ganapati and Shivaji, to make them more effective political vehicles. These two popular regional figures were well chosen as symbols of Tilak's protest movement: Ganapati, the elephant-headed deity, was known as the "Overcomer of Obstacles"; Shivaji epitomized the warrior tradition of Maharashtra, for he killed his Muslim enemy by striking the first blow. It was not difficult for Tilak to connect both of these personages with *swaraj*, the movement for Indian Home Rule, and, in reinterpreting the Shivaji tradition, he made the point that violent action in defence of freedom was above customary moral considerations. His 24 October 1905 editorial in *Kesari* declared that the question of Shivaji

> should not be viewed from the standpoint of the Penal Code or even of the *Smritis* or Manu.... Great men are above the common principles of morality. These principles do not reach the place on which great men stand. Did Shivaji commit a sin in killing Afzal Khan?.... Shrimat Krishna preached in the *Gita* that we have even to kill our own *guru* and our kinsmen. No blame attaches to any person if he is doing deeds without being actuated by a desire to reap the fruit of his deeds.... If thieves enter our house and we have not strength enough in our fists to drive them out, we should without hesitation lock them up and burn them alive.... Do not circumscribe your vision like a frog in a well; get out of the Penal Code, enter into the lofty atmosphere of the *Shrimat Bhagavad Gita* and then consider the actions of great men. (4)

Thus, Tilak redefines and reshapes the meaning of Shivaji to his own ends, forcing his audience to listen through his employment of a style that is typically direct, outspoken, and simple. Exclaiming his conclusion at the outset, Tilak leads his listeners on by means of rhetorical questions, answering them with reaffirmations of his basic principle expressed as aphorisms, and developing the reaffirmations with homely analogies. Tilak's style is simple and vigorous and capable of rallying his listeners to demand *swaraj*: they become Shivaji, and their fight for *swaraj* becomes a crusade to be carried out by whatever means are available. Thus Tilak redefined the essence of Shivaji for his own purposes, enlisting religion in support of his politics and reinforcing his position as a Maharashtrian Brahmin leader.

When extremism followed in the wake of Tilak's provocative interpretations of Shivaji, he was seized by the British and tried on charges of sedition. His incarceration helped to confer mythical status on him: he thus became a living symbol of the Shivaji tradition. And Tilak consciously presented himself in his speeches as a simple man of the people and the epitome of Maharashtrian traditions. "I speak to you as I am a poor man myself," he said to his audience in Chikodi (269); and, on another occasion he emphasized his own humility when he described his relationship to the Indian patriot Ghose: "I have learnt many lessons sitting at his feet. I revered him as my father and I venture again to say that he, in return, loved me as his son" (323). The familiar image of the *guru* and his disciple would not be lost on Tilak's hearers.

As Tilak's political stature increased, he continued to enlist the militant Hindu nationalism of Shivaji in support of his fight for *swaraj*, expressing himself in a style that never failed to make his ideas accessible to his audiences and that created a context in which he presented himself as the epitomization of cultural traditions. His simple definitions, for example, are presented in terms of the experienced realities of his listeners, as in his customary definition of *swaraj*, which he repeated with slight rephrasing on numerous occasions. As he said at Allahabad in 1917, "Every one knows what home rule meant. Home rule was nothing but to have the management of their home in their own hands. That was the simplest definition that could be given of the word.... It was their birthright" (281).

Tilak frequently also used figurative analogies and homely illustrations to restructure events in terms that are meaningful to his audience, because they show the practical realities of everyday life. *Swaraj*, his most frequent theme, is often presented in terms of home ownership, as in "The National Demand," his speech at the Calcutta Session of the National Congress:

> We are entitled to the possession of the whole house, and if we allow you to share our power with you in that house, it is a concession made for you in the hope that you will soon clear out of it. You have managed the house so long; you have been living in the house; we will allow you to live in the house for a longer time, but eventually you must acknowledge that from today we are masters of the house. (315-16)

Describing the impact of the British *raj* on India, Tilak says, on another occasion, at Lucknow (30 December 1916), "They have tried to clear India of the jungle that was there. But further on, after clearing the jungle, there is one thing they do. They do not want to sow in the ground thus cleared." And, on another occasion he likens India to "an emasculated man" whose health must be restored by administering "tonic to the brain and that is Simla or Delhi" (312-13).

Tilak's presentation helps to direct his audience's attention to his theme. While his language is not dramatic, it has marked propagandistic overtones, for it clearly and consistently depicts the British as the oppressors and allows his Indian audience to feel a sense of justification in their struggle. Tilak tells his listeners in Calcutta (2 January 1907) that under the present scheme of things they are the underdogs held down by the superior cunning of abusive British administrators, an "alien Government ... ruling over us not by its innate strength but by keeping us in ignorance and blindness" (49); his audience could readily respond to the stark power of this familiar archetypal metaphor of the oppressed and the oppressor.

Tilak's simple directness is further manifested in his ready use of aphorisms and epigrams, serving both as effective summaries of his arguments and as compelling goads to action: "Three P's—pray, please and protest—will not do unless backed by solid force" (21); "Great things cannot easily be gained and things easily gained are not great" (236); "Your fault lies not in the want of capacity or want of means but your fault lies in the want of the will" (247). *Swaraj* was the theme nearest him, and he referred to it with epigrammatic force in the statement which is most often associated with him: "Swaraj is my birthright, and I will have it" (qtd. in Wolpert 191).

Direct and outspoken, Tilak was sometimes carried away by his subject, haranguing his audiences in a garrulous fashion, as in his speech "The Rights of the Poor Raiyat":

> One who suffers might groan, but we cannot help it. You must, therefore, work in earnest.... This is the time for work.... Let us stop quarrelling among ourselves, let us not listen to those who talk against Home Rule, make up your minds and have a firm resolve, do not stop working, be perfectly loyal, work in such a way that the people in England will come to your side, and then God will surely fulfil all your desires. God helps those to succeed who work earnestly. (269)

The torrent of exhortation in Tilak's speeches never seems to subside. He is very close to his audience, and while he understands their feelings, he does not excuse them but urges them to act on their own behalf. Rather than suffer in silence, he chides them: "Do not be afraid of speaking out things, which are plain in themselves. There might be some trouble, but nothing can be had without any trouble. Home Rule is not going to be dropped into your hands from the sky" (268-69).

Tilak's contemporary, Gokhale, certainly exhorted his audiences just as earnestly, but his premises were drawn from a different perception of the British *raj* and its impact on Indian society. Gokhale was certainly a Hindu, but he was not a spokesman for Hinduism; nor did he advocate a return to the Hindu past as a solution to problems as did his famous pupil Gandhi. Gokhale cast his lot with the West, specifically with the British representation of Western culture as he had experienced it through his education and his personal contacts with the English. Perhaps his Hindu background shaped his view of reform as an evolutionary process and gave him the patience to endure such slow progress.

Unlike Tilak, who sought a unifying concept in the revitalization of traditional Hindu myths, Gokhale urged education of the masses for their advance into Western government and technology. Gokhale's revolt against the English rule of his day was primarily a moral one, for he felt that Indians should be treated with equality: to do otherwise was contrary to Britain's own announced principles, hence irrational and incomprehensible. Gokhale was unwilling to believe that an inherent hatred could exist between Indians and Britons; ill-feeling on both sides could only be increased if violence, rather than reason, were permitted to dictate policy. An example of Gokhale's typical appeal to reason may be found in his speech at Poona (1 September 1889) on the Crawford case, in which he protested the dismissal of Indian magistrates implicated in the scandal:

> In the interest of India and England alike, the Government of this country ought to be carried on with absolute impartiality.... If our English friends will kindly disabuse their minds of all bias against us, if they will take a calm and dispassionate view of everything, if sentiment will give way to reason, then they will find that in treating the natives of this country with courtesy, consideration, and equality, consists the best safe-guard of the British Rule. (142)

Gokhale's style is straightforward; his expression plain, unaffected, and wholly suited to the expression of his profound personal conviction in the ultimate rightness of his protest. What Gokhale required of a responsible Indian public servant included what his biographer Stanley A. Wolpert calls the courage "to place before the bar of British public and official judgment those arbitrary and inequitable practices of the government of India which he considered patently 'un-British' in the highest sense, and therefore in need of rectification" (299).

Gokhale's belief in his ideal of equality was so strong that he was harsh on the slowness of British officialdom to implement the Queen's Proclamation of racial equality. Speaking on the problem at the 1894 Madras Congress, Gokhale gives vent to his exasperation in a remarkably Burkean passage that clearly reveals his forensic and deliberative capacities:

> We have had this question in every shape. We have examined it from every point of view. Our invention has been exhausted. Reason is fatigued. Experience has given judgment. But Anglo-Indian obstinacy is not yet conquered. (*Cheers*.) And remember, Gentlemen, this that we have to conquer is perhaps the worst kind of obstinacy, for it is not based so much on wrong judgment; it is not based even so much on prejudice; it is obstinacy based on the strong foundations of self-interest and love of domination. (10)

The passage is a good example of Gokhale's style, for it shows cogent analysis expressed in short sentences; the use of key words or phrases; and simple, cumulative repetition, all combining to give lucidity and directness to his speech.

These qualities were important, since Gokhale often gave speeches to audiences who needed to learn something about Indian affairs and who were frequently in a position to alter the course of events in India. The conversion of his listeners to the justice of his claims was of paramount importance, and it is understandable that his speeches should strike a note of evangelicalism through their sense of command and injunction. Skillful use of question, exclamation, statement, and appeal are evident in Gokhale's style on such occasions, as in the following passage from his speech urging government initiative in economic development:

> Is it not the duty of Government to see that the subject population is properly fed and clothed and housed? ... Does not the security of the country lie in the real prosperity of its teeming millions? ... But 'Let alone' is the policy of Government. Free-trade, or rather political economy, is working out her laws, say they. Well! We think the laws of political economy are largely amenable to human control. The Government must take the initiative here. They should support the falling industries of the land, if they want India to be prosperous. (qtd. in Wolpert 104-105)

While Gokhale uses a method of direct challenge through exclamation and question, he is nonetheless restrained in his criticism of his opponents and modest in his appraisal of himself. Speaking to the Reform Club in London on 14 November 1905, he condemns Lord Curzon's policies but maintains that his "personal feeling toward Lord Curzon ... is one of respect." He ascribes the viceroy's lack of insight to "the limitations imposed upon him by his temperament and his training," while of himself he simply says, "On this point, I claim some right to speak, for I have been studying this phase of the question for nearly twenty years now."

Gokhale's remarkable restraint is also apparent in his judicious use of emotional appeals. He did not seek, as did customarily Tilak, to stir up the emotions; but he did permit himself to lay out fairly and openly to his English listeners the opinions of Indian society. Recalling on the same occasion that Lord Curzon had misrepresented the Queen's Proclamation as implying "certain qualifications which can only be attained by heredity or race," Gokhale must have incited feelings of shame that an Englishman would be so lacking in integrity. But, rather than indulge in a stinging denunciation of the viceroy, Gokhale merely underscored the emotion:

> Now, apart from the question of your national honour being involved in this—this explaining away of a 'Sovereign's word,' look at the unwisdom, the stupendous unwisdom, of the whole thing, telling the people of India that unless they were content to remain permanently a subject race in their own country, their interests and those of British rule were not identical. After this, how can any Englishman complain if my countrymen regarded ... your rule in India as maintained ... for a selfish purpose? (336)

The appeal is to reason and justice; Gokhale is calm and clear. Even the design of his speeches is simple and unpretentious. After a brief introduction he sets out the causes and present state of India's problems, poses his solution and answers objections, then follows to his conclusion where he impresses his listeners with the virtues of his solution. His movement through the speech is steady; his language is clear; he is unobtrusive, yet authoritative. It is the manner and method of an efficient teacher.

Tilak and Gokhale were contemporaries, and both were accomplished spokesmen who achieved impressive records of public service, yet the two men were considerably different.

Gokhale at all times was a speaker who was careful in his approach to his material and careful in his statement of it. Restrained, thorough, and predictable, he favourably impressed both his Indian and English audiences with his devoted labours for Indian equality. Tilak, in contrast, was essentially a popular speaker who successfully propagated for his Indian audiences the notion of Hindu chauvinism. A successful agitator and organizer, he was a brilliant innovator who was sufficiently practical not to seek martyrdom in a rash collision with authorities. In their different ways, both Tilak and Gokhale were models of service and self-sacrifice whose speeches represent the rich variety to be found in the Indian political heritage. Each was an admirable advocate, each was a formidable adversary, but both were devoted partisans for Indian self-determination and progress.

WORKS CITED

Burgess, Anthony, Introduction. *All About H. Hatterr*. By G. V. Desani. Harmondsworth: Penguin, 1972.

Cashman, Richard I. *The Myth of the Lokamanya: Tilak and Mass Politics in Maharashtra*. Berkeley: University of California P, 1975.

Gokhale, Gopal Krishna. *Speeches and Writings of Gopal Krishna Gokhale*. Ed. D. G. Karve and D. V. Ambekar. New York: Asia, 1966.

Lomas, Charles W. *The Agitator in American Society*. Englewood Cliffs, NJ: Prentice, 1968.

Patwardham, R. P. *The Select Gokhale*. New Delhi: Maharashtra Information Centre, 1968.

Shay, Theodore L. *The Legacy of the Lokamanya: The Political Philosophy of Bal Gangadhar Tilak*. New York: OUP, 1965.

Tilak, Bal Gangadhar. *Bal Gangadhar Tilak: His Writings and Speeches*. Ed. Aurobindo Ghose. Madras: Ganesh, n.d.

Wolpert, Stanley A. *Tilak and Gokhale: Revolution and Reform in the Making of Modern India*. Berkeley: University of California P, 1962.

7. Public Address and Caribbean Studies

In *The Whig Interpretation of History* Herbert Butterfield asserts that the tasks of the social historian are to recover the richness of the past and to understand the entire context of events and phenomena so as to achieve "the elucidation of the unlikenesses between past and present" (10). And he provides a caveat: failure to appreciate a society's value system by substituting the standards and judgments of his own experience will jeopardize the utility of the investigation and invalidate its conclusions.

The necessity of bringing past events and movements into meaningful present focus is a concern which the social scientist shares with the rhetorical critic, for whom the central task is to understand the influence of thought and feeling of specific audiences; that is, of the public speaker as communicator in a particular society. John Donne, in his Sermon XXVI, described the singular effectiveness of oral communication in reflecting and revealing political and social phenomena when he said, "rhetorique will make absent and remote things present to your understanding." And it is through the study of speeches, more than any other literary artifacts, that the social scientist may not only trace national and political events but also understand more adequately the development or growth of ideas and then assess the significance of those ideas in the formation of societal patterns.

In large measure public address has been neglected or misused as an aid in the understanding of social and political matters because its true nature as oral rhetoric has been overlooked; it has too often been regarded as a minor literary genre. Unlike poetry, fiction, and the drama, public address is prepared for delivery to an immediate, present audience and has a primary goal of persuasion. The speaker, unlike the writer, is required to adapt his message to his audience, meeting objections in the process and coping with an uncertain outcome. It is because the essential characteristic of speeches is—as Aristotle noted in the *Rhetoric*—adaptation and adjustment, that they provide us with the surest intimations of the feelings, values, ideas, and expectations of an audience.

The shortcomings of the novel and drama as artifacts for the social scientist are apparent: first, they commonly follow events at a considerable distance, and hence most are subject to the effects of post-facto rationalization on the one hand or inadequate understanding of the social milieu. (James Jones's *From Here to Eternity*, set in 1941, appeared in 1950; Sean O'Casey's *The Plough and the Stars*, set in the 1916 Easter Rising, was published in 1926.) And there is substantial question among literary critics whether the novel, even when avowedly realistic or naturalistic, can claim to be objective. Harrison Steeves argues that no novel, on its own, "has any probative value in social evidence"; we may make presumptions as to its value only in terms of the whole weight of the fiction of a period, but "that value will depend upon the ethical consensus of the writers as well as upon their ability to sift facts and make judgments.... At this remove from the scene, it is probably impossible to measure the truth of the fiction to the life depicted" (101-102).

It is easier to assume truthful depiction in a novel than it is for poetry. Desmond Pacey, commenting on the Canadian Oliver Goldsmith's poem "The Rising Village" as historical record, voices a reservation that applies to poetry in general when he writes: "The poem has been hailed as a valuable document in the history of pioneer settlement, but this claim cannot be sustained: the uniformly favourable picture which Goldsmith paints is not in keeping with the facts of the Nova Scotian economy at this time as we know them from other sources" (48).

But what of the reliability of oral rhetoric and its relation to social history? Max Lerner describes what he calls "a naturalistic approach" to the history of ideas which emphasizes the shifting, unpredictable struggle for survival of ideas, and calls for recognition

> not only [of] the conditions of the creation of ideas but also the conditions of their reception, not only the impulsions behind the ideas, but also the uses to which they are put, not only the thinkers but also the popularizers, the propagandists, the opinion skill-groups, the final audience that believes or disbelieves and acts accordingly. (6)

While Lerner's view may give emphasis to the role of the articulate members of society, it reveals an awareness of the essential Aristotelian concept of the audience which underlies spoken discourse and makes it a useful tool for the historian. Because the speaker must prepare for an audience to whom he will deliver the speech directly, he must understand that audience and adjust his message to them. In turn, the critic who examines the speech will need to recognize the cultural imperatives at work on the audience as well as to consider the sociolinguistic aspects of expression, or style. Therefore, speeches, which reveal the interaction of speaker and audience, may be of greater value than other forms of literary evidence to the social scientist in searching for authenticity in political or social phenomena.

Skill in speaking and the practice of statecraft have been closely associated since Isocrates proclaimed the value of rhetoric as a means of giving practical effect to the ideals of a society. Fresh vindication of this longstanding link may be found through an examination of the Anglophone Caribbean societies, which give evidence of a tradition of public speaking that has been undaunted by even the most severe proscriptions and can claim a remarkable number of indigenous orators (often from the most humble origins, and many from the ranks of slaves) who deserve the same recognition that is belatedly being accorded to such early black Americans as Frederick Douglass and Henry Garnet. Their speeches, where we have full, reliable texts, often reveal great eloquence; and it is not difficult to understand why they wielded such power, persuasion, and ultimately effect on the political and social issues of their time and helped in the inexorable development of imperial enclaves into independent sovereign states. And while my frame of reference is especially the Anglophone Caribbean, I have no doubt that what I have to say applies also to the former French and Spanish possessions.

Perhaps the most difficult problem is the availability of speech texts, and from this derive two major issues: first, How can texts of the speeches on matters of social significance by the leading political figures of the Caribbean be retrieved before they are wholly lost to posterity?; and second, Are severely edited or paraphrased speech texts of sufficient value to be reliable evidence for social researchers?

Now, there are several volumes of speeches available, especially from Trinidad, such as *His Best Orations* (being those of Captain the Honourable A. A. Cipriani); the sermons of the Reverend Clive Abdulah, Episcopal bishop; *A Collection of Addresses* by Sir Hugh Wooding; and a large number of texts of individual speeches by A. N. R. Robinson, former minister for external affairs, and Dr. Eric Williams, the prime minister. In a way, the almost Victorian enthusiasm of the Government Printing Office in Trinidad is a guarantee that future historians will be better equipped to write about the island's social and political development during the past twenty-five years than about any other Caribbean society. One can speculate that Dr. Williams's own research emphasized the need for adequate primary materials.

Elsewhere, printed speech texts or manuscript notes are more rare, one exception being sermons—in Jamaica, the Reverend K. D. Carnegie has reversed a twentieth-century tendency and has committed over one hundred of his sermons to print. Perhaps they merit this temporary reprieve, but the politically (and perhaps socially) more effective speeches of Sir Alexander Bustamante have not been recorded for posterity; hence we do not know exactly what he said during the tumultuous days of the thirties and outside of parliament. As Lady Bustamante has explained, "In those days speeches were never recorded, neither were they prepared speeches—one just spoke as one felt."[1] Ironically, it is exactly those impromptu speeches that would provide us with the most useful documentation of contemporary political and social events.

Fortunately, an almost verbatim account of Albert Gomes's moving speech on "The Black Man," delivered in Port-of-Spain in 1931, has been preserved in the pages of *The Beacon*; but there seems to be no record of Uriah Butler's speech to oilfield workers in 1937, as a result of which he was arrested and the outbreak of violence was precipitated.

Even today the situation is fraught with apparently insurmountable difficulties. Repeated requests for copies of speech texts from public officials throughout the Caribbean have been unsuccessful, so that I have been unable to obtain anything from the following, for example: Prime Minister Robert Bradshaw of St. Kitts-Nevis; Prime Minister William Bramble of Montserrat; Peter D'Aguir of Guyana; and Premier George Price of Belize. Likewise, though Sir Grantley Adams became the first prime minister of Barbados and later first prime minister of the short-lived West Indian Federation after an early career in which he became influential as spokesman for the impoverished sugar-plantation workers, it has proved impossible to obtain texts of speeches that do not appear in *Hansard*. Yet perhaps his major statements are those made outside parliamentary halls or the United Nations—where, as member of the United Kingdom delegation in 1948 he defended in language of some force and elegance British colonial policies against Soviet-bloc attacks.

Some politicians and social activists have, however, aided the cause of objective social and political history by preserving texts or notes for at least their principal speeches: they include Eric Gairy of Grenada, Sir Philip Sherlock of Jamaica, and Janet Jagan of Guyana.

There is, therefore, an immediate need for the retrieval of such speech transcripts, manuscripts, and outlines as may yet be located in private libraries and papers; for the accurate transcription of recorded and sound-filmed speeches; and for the preservation of those most ephemeral of literary artifacts, the texts of individual speeches issued by candidates of minor political parties and produced by job printers. In view of the rarity of these materials, it would seem advantageous to establish two central depositories: one in Jamaica, for that country, Bermuda, the Bahamas, and Belize; the other in Trinidad for the remainder of the West Indian islands and Guyana. Any duplication would, of course, prove advantageous.

Hardly less important than the recovery of such printed or manuscript speech texts is the authentication of their accuracy; and in this we could be guided by the highly sophisticated principles of textual criticism established by the celebrated Fredson Bowers. There is, of course, need to be certain that there were no significant emendations to prepared texts, no additions, no excisions, and that the transcript is in fact a *bona fide* record of the delivered statement, for though (for example) Calvin Coolidge is remembered for his observation that "The business of America is business," his actual words were "The business of the American people is business." The verbatim record shows that he did not have the skill at constructing a pithy, balanced aphorism after all, and allows a somewhat different interpretation from the customary one.

The value of speeches which are incompletely or inaccurately reported is of serious concern to rhetorical and social critics alike, for their degree of authenticity determines in large measure the limitations of their utility.

The problem is not adequately addressed by the critic who, like Hugh Blair, dismisses reported speeches out of hand as "a mixture which is unnatural in history, of fiction with truth." Blair prefers that the historian deliver, "in his own person, the sentiments and reasoning of opposite parties, or the substance of what was understood to be spoken in some public assembly; which he may do without the liberty of fiction" (491).

That there is, in fact, a place for the reported (or even re-created) speech is the thesis argued by Professor Judy Hample in her article, "The Textual and Cultural Authenticity of Patrick Henry's 'Liberty or Death' Speech." Acknowledging that the available text is unauthentic, having been put together by Henry's first biographer with the use of eyewitness accounts and testimonial recollections, Hample claims that the general substance of the speech is unimpaired; its survival attests to the fact that our society, like that of Patrick Henry, "promotes an emphasis on moral virtue, tradition, heroism, and eloquence" (299). Here, then, is a picture, perhaps extreme, of rhetoric as tradition, wherein the speaker's words are not more important than their reinforcing value in terms of the societal myths they reveal. A speech such as Patrick Henry's "Liberty or Death" speech, for which no authenticated text may be found and which has passed into the realm of oratorical masterpieces, is probably more fictive than rhetorical and its consideration as pure rhetoric is inappropriate.

Nevertheless, Professor Hample's discovery that spoken discourse provides an index of the social and economic values of the times is a truism. Rufus Choate noted this characteristic of speeches when he said, "It is the peculiarity of some schools of eloquence that they embody and utter not merely the individual genius and character of the speaker, but a national consciousness—a national era, a mood, a hope, a dread, a despair—in which you listen to the spoken history of the time" (qtd. in Peterson xxvii).

Accordingly, though Professor Nettleford's *Manley and the New Jamaica: Selected Speeches and Writings, 1938-1968* (1971) is a most valuable aid to our understanding of that nation's social and political structure and history, it is not without its deficiencies, which result in the main from his need to truncate or paraphrase. Likewise, *A Destiny to Mould: Selected Discourses by the Prime Minister of Guyana* (1970) could be subjected to the same criticism were it not that it, too, helps fill a need of some major significance. Nonetheless, the goal of compilers of speeches should always be for textual authenticity even at the expense of long and apparently uninteresting or graceless passages of the most pedestrian prose, such as are to be encountered in the speeches of Fidel Castro and Eric Williams, who seem to feel that an endless speech is the same as a timeless one. The greater the social significance of the speaker, the greater the need for textual accuracy. To require social scientists to base their conclusions on texts of public addresses that are not complete or authentic is akin to making statements on the Bard's style and characterizations from a reading of Lamb's *Tales* or asking F. R. Leavis to base his assessment of Jane Austen on *Masterplots*.

And when we have eventually recovered and examined major Caribbean speeches, are they of any significant value to the social scientist? The celebrated Hugh Blair, professor of rhetoric and belles lettres in the University of Edinburgh, noted over a century ago that French speeches, *vis à vis* British, are "ornamented with bolder figures; and their discourse is carried on with more amplification, more warmth and elaboration." This, he concluded, was the result of "the nature of their government, which, by excluding public speaking from having much influence on the conduct of public affairs, deprives eloquence of its best opportunity for acquiring nerves and strength" (339). That is, he saw speech style as an index of national traits and attitudes—a view that has since been widely endorsed.

Whether Caribbean speeches in French have the same characteristics as those identified by Blair, I am unaware; but it does appear that the flourishes and embellishments common to much British oratory both at home and abroad is absent from Anglophone oratory of Caribbean indigenes, being replaced by a noticeable directness, succinctness, and forcefulness that may have influenced many to conclude that it lacks the characteristics of true oratorical literature.

Perhaps the earliest Caribbean speech delivered in English of which we have record is a sermon "Preached before the Governour, Council, and Assembly, at their first meeting at Saint Jago de la Vega, in Jamaica, Feb. 1, 1671." And it was apparently thought so salutary that the Council and Assembly directed that it be printed in the public interest. It was accordingly issued in London "at the Sign of Three Daggers, in Fleet-Street" as a nineteen-page pamphlet two years later. The title of the sermon, which was delivered by Henry Houser, "Minister of Gods Word in St. Katherines Parish," is "An Exact

Model or Platform of Good Magistracy," and it is an exegesis of Exodus 18:21, "Thou shalt provide out of all the people able men, such as fear God; men of truth, hating covetousness."

After the usual explication of the text, the preacher provides the traditional application to the lives of his congregation and concludes in these words, which in all probability could have been applied to every Midlands town and any colonial outpost:

> How doth every street ring with cursing and swearing and profaneness? How little conscience do men make of this day to live in open filthiness and lasciviousness of the flesh? ... Sin is grown to such a height, as if the Work of God were but a scarecrow, and all Religion but a Fable.... Truly, wickedness reigns in every state, in every condition, in every place: and now even at this time, as if we would defie God to his Face ... every one strives (as it were) who shall outdare him most in our Atheism, Libertinism, and Profaneness, in all Riot and Excess, in Impenitency.
>
> Yea, let this whole island say it is His mercy that Fire, and Sword, and Pestilence, and other Miseries and Calamities did not prey upon me, as upon others. Oh, Lord, ... had not thy Mercies exceeded all Limits, our sins ere this had sunk us all, our Island had been made a second Sodom and Gomorrah.

Of course, life in the tropics had always had its attractions, but Jamaica must have been quite some place in the 1670's.

In 1825 the Reverend William Shrewsbury published his *Sermons Preached on Several Occasions in the Island of Barbadoes* (in the chapel in Bridgetown) so that, as he wrote in his prefatory note, "the world may judge of the character and tendency of those doctrines which the Wesleyan Missionaries preach in the West Indies; and that the members of the Methodist Society in Barbadoes may ... be encouraged to persevere in their Christian profession."

Two of Shrewsbury's sermons were delivered before slave congregations: they are the shortest, the most simplistic, and stylistically the least sophisticated of the collection, but their theme is readily conveyed by a brief excerpt:

> You will sometimes say, when we charge you to repent, that you are not as bad as many other people, and that you have never committed any great sin. No! But you have; you have every one been

guilty of the foulest crime that was ever committed on the earth ... verily, you have all been concerned in the death of the Son of God. *Your sins* caused him to die.... You would not repent in your own country. God has, therefore, by bringing you to this land, punished you for worshipping devils, and trusting gree-grees [charms and amulets] and a great many wicked things that you and your fathers have done. But mercy is mixed with the punishment, for he has brought you hither for good, that you may repent and be saved. (408-09)

Now, this is not atypical of evangelical preaching of its era, but it does seem ill-adapted to its particular audience, and it provides additional material for the study of the sociology of religion in the Caribbean. (One wonders whether the preacher thought that British military and civil personnel were also assigned to Barbados for their own good and as "punishment for the great many wicked things" that they and their fathers had done.)

An interesting short speech, which exists in only a putative text, is Sir Henry Morgan's famous call to unity and action: originally published in Esquemeling's *Buccaneers of America, 1684-1685*, it was reprinted by Clinton Black in his *Story of Jamaica*. Its brevity, antitheses, and noteworthy common sense recommend it as a model for the speech to actuate, and though it is in all probability merely the peroration of a much longer harangue or hortatory address, it would be an excellent model for contemporary speakers who are much given to verbosity and prolixity. The received text *in its entirety* is this: "If our number is small, our hearts are great; and the fewer persons we are, the more union and better shares we shall have in the spoil."

Samuel Sharpe, described by a Wesleyan missionary, the Reverend Henry Bleby, as "the most remarkable and intelligent slave that I have ever met," was a leader of the 1832 Jamaican revolt. In *Jamaica's Heroes*, an anonymous pamphlet published in 1963, we are told that at Retrieve plantation, "with gifted eloquence he held the group spellbound with a speech on the injustices of slavery, the equality of man, and the movement in England for freeing the slaves," and that

After hearing Sharpe making powerful, fluent speeches to his fellow prisoners several times, Bleby understood how he had such an effect upon his audiences and had been able to command so much influence among the slaves. He possessed the gift of delivering in words, feelings that came from the heart. Bleby wrote, 'He appeared to have the feelings and passions of his hearers completely at his command. Having heard him speak just once, Bleby ceased to be surprised at what Gardner, another condemned prisoner had told him, that 'when Sharpe spoke to him and others on the subject of slavery,' he, Gardner, was 'wrought up almost to a state of madness.' (15-16)

This makes it quite clear that at least some of the great national oratory of the Caribbean is to be sought not so much in the formal environments of pulpit, parliament, or courtroom, but in the meeting places of the folk: the small rural chapels and meeting-houses, the street-corners, the assemblies, and the markets.

When Sharpe was executed at Montego Bay on 23 May 1832, he walked with equanimity to the gallows and delivered a brief speech that ought, by rights, to be included in the anthologies, for it is every bit as eloquent as the final statements of more celebrated infamous persons, such as John Brown and Ned Kelly, the Australian bushranger. (A version of Sharpe's speech was printed in the *Jamaica Watchman* on 3 June, where it is described as having been delivered "in nearly the following words.")

Hardly less able as a mass orator was Paul Bogle, the central figure of the 1865 rebellion at Morant Bay, but unfortunately his Stony Gut Baptist Church lay sermons and public speeches are all, apparently, now lost to us, though we do have Governor Eyre's speech on the same topic. Here is an excerpt from his bombastic speech to the Colonial Parliament after the apprehension of Bogle. He loses his structure among the polysyllables, triads, and fustian:

> The misapprehensions and misrepresentations of pseudo-philanthropists in England and this country, the inflammatory harangues or seditious writings of political demagogues, of evil-minded men of higher position and of better education, and of worthless persons without either character or property to lose.

Public Address and Caribbean Studies   111

> The personal, scurrilous, vindictive, and disloyal writings of a licentious and unscrupulous press, and the misdirected efforts and misguided counsel of certain Ministers of Religion, sadly so miscalled, if the Saviour's example and teaching is to be the standard, have led to their natural, their necessary, their inevitable result amongst an ignorant, excitable, and uncivilized population—rebellion, arson, murder.
>
> These are hard and harsh words, gentlemen, but they are true; and this is no time to indulge in selected sentences or polished phraseology.

One can only wonder what Eyre's more elaborate passages and "polished phraseology" would be like.

Clearly, the collection and study of public addresses can aid us in almost any area of Caribbean studies, for they are a record and measure of a society's interests and thinking. Some years ago Herbert A. Wichelns suggested that the neglect of public address by social scientists, especially, seemed related to its ephemeral nature and to the ease with which speeches may be transmuted into other forms of literature:

> Oratory is intimately associated with statecraft; it is bound up with the things of the moment; its occasion, its terms, its background can often be understood only by the careful student of history. Again, the publication of orations as pamphlets leaves us free to regard any speech merely as an essay, as a literary effort deposited at the shrine of the muses in hope of being blessed with immortality. (182)

But the researcher who wishes to understand social environments should realize that he cannot accurately comprehend them until he takes into account the multifarious speeches that were delivered and that were adapted in an endeavour to influence both social behaviour and political or historical events.

Accordingly, for a better and more complete understanding of Caribbean affairs, we need to encourage the discovery and accumulation of authentic speech texts as primary materials of social history. We should encourage the cooperation of folklorists and others in gathering rural sermons and parish political speeches; we can collect the speeches of the expatriates, such as Claude McKay, Marcus Garvey, and W. A. Domingo;

we can supplement the present holdings of speeches of such political figures as Lord Constantine, Captain Cipriani, the Jagans, Hugh Shearer, and George Gordon. Many of these speeches will prove inconsiderable, and not of any greater consequence than much state and local oratory; but unless the grain is garnered, the quality of the crop cannot be properly assessed.

In his keynote address to the 1972 Carifesta, in Guyana, Denis Williams made the pronouncement that "In countries passing from colonial status to Independence, the immediate post-colonial period is characterised by a surge of creativity in the arts," but that "immediately preceding and just following the break-up of colonialism, it was the politicians and not the artists who seized the creative initiative and maintained it here in the New World" (102). The principal artifact of politicians, of course, is the speech, and hence through their retrieval and analysis we will be better able to assist in the advancement of Caribbean studies.

NOTES

[1] Professor John J. Figueroa, then professor of English and dean of the School of Education at the University of the West Indies in Mona, Jamaica, wrote on 21 July of that year concerning the proposed compilation of an anthology of important Caribbean speeches, "You have chosen a difficult job, because Jamaicans are great extemporary speakers, and I am not aware that many of their speeches have been properly recorded. You are right that Philip Sherlock has been an outstanding speaker; so, incidentally, has been his brother, the Reverend Hugh Sherlock."

WORKS CITED

Blair, Hugh. *Lectures on Rhetoric and Belles Lettres*. Halifax: Milner, 1847.

Bustamante, Lady. Letter to the author, 23 August 1971.

Butterfield, Herbert. *The Whig Interpretation of History*. New York: Norton, 1965.

Hample, Judy. "The Textual and Cultural Authenticity of Patrick Henry's 'Liberty or Death' Speech." *Quarterly Journal of Speech* 63.3 (1977): 298-310.

Houser, Henry. *An Exact Model or Platform of Good Magistracy; or a Sermon*. London: Francis Tyson, 1673.

Jamaica's Heroes. Kingston: United Printers, 1963.

Lerner, Max. *Ideas Are Weapons*. New York: Viking, 1939.

Pacey, Desmond. *Canadian Literature in English*. Mysore: CCLR, 1979.

Peterson, Houston, ed. *A Treasury of the World's Great Speeches*. New York: Simon, 1954.

Shrewsbury, William J. *Sermons Preached on Several Occasions in the Island of Barbadoes*. London: Butterfield, 1825.

Steeves, Harrison R. *The Shaping of the English Novel in the Eighteenth Century*. New York: Holt, 1965.

Wichelns, Herbert A. "The Literary Criticism of Oratory." *Studies in Rhetoric and Public Speaking in Honor of James Albert Winans*. New York: Century, 1925. 181-216.

Williams, Denis. "Art and Society." *Kaie: The Literary Vision of Carifesta 72*. Ed. Celeste Dolphin. Georgetown: National History and Arts Council of Guyana, 1973. 100-110.

1981

8. African Speeches in English

References to the oral tradition in Africa have frequently conveyed the impression that the storyteller was the principal, if not the sole, member of a tribe or community to practice in any consistent and skilled fashion the arts of spoken communication and that his main function was restricted to the unadorned transmission of traditional literature: histories, biographies, myths, legends, and similar factual or expository genres. But the oral tradition properly encompasses what nowadays is denoted by the terms rhetoric, public speaking, public address, interpersonal communication, or—in the older literary or philological tradition—oratory.

Nurtured, as they were, on the community respect for the storyteller, the leaders of modern African social and political development have, for the most part, been remarkably competent at public speaking; and their speeches, in many cases, have risen from the pedestrian level of practical, prosaic political artifacts to that of the rhetorical genre the epideictic address, which is marked by its essay-like examination of a subject—sometimes fanciful, sometimes philosophical—and characterized by its concern for style: a concern that is exhibited in the very poetic feel for language that distinguishes the oration per se from the everyday political speech or the occasional remarks of a public figure.

Not surprisingly, the number of speeches that can properly be considered part of any country's oratorical literature are few; and the number of epideictic speeches consequently even more rare. Each year in the United States, for example, over five thousand commencement speeches are delivered: but studies have shown that even the themes of most are wholly forgotten within a week, and it is a rarity that survives a decade or a generation: something like Churchill's Westminster College (MO.) "Iron Curtain" speech. A few years ago, Arthur Pollard remarked in his *English Sermons*: "The secular trends of our day have all but destroyed the sermon as literature, and yet in the Church of England alone some twenty thousand sermons are preached every Sunday. It is well, therefore, for this reason that we should still treasure the great sermons of the past as a standard by which to measure the present performance" (53). But the desideratum is: What determines whether a sermon—or any other genre of speech—is "great"? Essentially, whether it has survived the occasion of its initial delivery; whether it was merely functional, utilitarian, or had substance and style that superseded the immediate occasion and audience and impinged on the general, lasting concerns of people everywhere, and at all times. It is this occasional, extraordinary, and exemplary speech that can be considered a part of oratorical literature, just as it is the rare essay, the rare play or poem that can be considered literature in its purest sense.

But the arduous duty of reading and evaluating speeches *as literature* has not been observed as rigorously as it should: we are alternately inundated with meretricious, ephemeral ones or else unable to find copies of speeches that should have been preserved.

Since about 1950, African politicians and statesmen—no less than their counterparts in Trinidad and Tobago, India, and Guyana—have been careful to preserve their speeches—though it should be acknowledged that this is more characteristic of those in power than those out of power, who must be content with pamphlets or duplicated hand-outs, by and large. Accordingly, we can agree with Socrates in the *Phaedrus*, that "There is nothing of which our great politicians are so fond of as delivering speeches and bequeathing them to posterity." As a result of this propensity to publish and thus perpetuate, we have volumes of speeches by Jomo Kenyatta, Julius Nyerere, Kwame Nkrumah, Sir Abubakar Tafewa Balewa, Kenneth

Kaunda, and Nnamdi Azikiwe. But they have, in general, been regarded properly only as aids to a proper appreciation of history and political science and not as legitimate components of the literature in English of the countries that the speakers represent. Only occasionally do we discover individual orations or small collections of speeches by the more erudite and literary spokesmen, such as Albert Luthuli, Desmond Tutu, and Nelson Mandela, and all to often even major statements of their condign, eloquent and effective predecessors are overlooked or disregarded in a reprehensible enthusiasm for the more contemporary and not always effective or relevant.

The place of deliberative and forensic speaking in many African societies was very similar to that in Ciceronian Rome, when individuals could participate personally in the exercises of the council or court. Margaret Laurence is one of the many writers who have written on this subject. In *Long Drums and Cannons* she says:

> every significant or controversial issue was discussed in council, either a council of kings and elders, or (as in the case of the Ibo), a general council of elders and people. All points of view were heard. It was the right of anyone to speak his mind freely and to be listened to, however lengthy or irrelevant his oration might be.... The advantage of this council system was its fairness to all points of view; its disadvantage was its crippling slowness. (202)

But in these last characteristics it was not significantly different from our Western legislative and judicial procedures.

Increasingly, the function of the African storyteller "assumed more importance in his dual role as educator and entertainer" and "moved in the direction of exaggeration and innovation, from educational historian to poet and entertaining orator," to the end that, as R. A. Freeman suggests (perhaps a little extravagantly) in *Pageant of Ghana*:

> The art of oratory is in West Africa carried to a remarkable pitch of perfection. At the public palavers, each linguist stands up in turn and pours forth a flood of speech, the readiness and exuberance of which strikes the stranger with amazement, and accompanies his words with gestures so various, graceful and appropriate that it is a pleasure to look on.... These oratorical displays appear to afford great

excitement for every African native is a born orator and connoisseur of oratory. (3)

Yet, with the high standing accorded to ritual and ceremony in African communities, it is not astonishing that ceremonial, or epideictic, speaking seems to have been held in highest regard as a form of public communication and display.

When European languages were introduced as commercial and then colonial languages, those who mastered the intricacies of the new grammars and syntaxes were the recipients of enhanced community status as intermediaries with access to power and decision-making. Casely Hayford himself is the authority for believing that in the Gold Coast, at least, "From the earliest times of barter, when the Europeans wanted to speak with the black man, it was through the black man who could speak English with some intelligence ... and we have educated men who have been chosen by the government to assist them in their deliberations" (62).

Quite obviously, the colonial environment militated against the achievement by Africans of mastery of English at anything approaching the literary level, even though some inexplicably managed it; yet they were truly exceptions. In his introduction to *Voices of Ghana* (1958), Henry Swanzy commented:

> What then, of expression in English? It is here that one wonders whether the spirit of the people inclines against creative literature and in favour of polemical and pragmatic writing. A communal society does not have the neuroses and tensions of individualism, the diseased oyster that produces the pearl. At any rate, until the revolutionary 1940's, almost all the expression of Gold Coast writing was political journalism or law, from the pen of men like the politician E. Casely Hayford. (14)

This is certainly correct, though it tends to minimize the role of oral discourse in an environment in which the written word has a circumscribed influence. The testimony of Sir Magnus Sampson's editorial efforts would seem to indicate that Casely Hayford's principal contribution to Gold Coast high culture was effected through his public addresses, occasional speeches, and epideictic orations.

Lalage Brown, in his brief yet instructive assessment, "The Development of African Prose Writing in English: A Perspective," devotes part of his study to the eminent public speakers. As he writes, oratory is an art

> which has been, and still is, highly praised in Africa. Because of the place of oratory in the African tradition, when Africans started writing in English, it is arguable that some of the more interesting things that they put on paper were those designed to be presented verbally—such things as sermons and political speeches. (40)

Unfortunately, it is just these initial literary documents (sermons and political speeches)—the very things that establish a literary tradition—that are most fugitive and ephemeral. They are customarily financed by the speakers themselves (or their sympathetic sponsors and supporters); issued in inexpensive leaflet or pamphlet format by job printers who keep no inventory for subsequent researchers; either not sent to libraries and similar depositories, or (once sent) disregarded as subliterary and unworthy of accession. Few of the species survive, and they are generally political policy statements, strident harangues, or inconsequential homilies by undistinguished clerics, preserved in the pages of diocesan magazines.

Ironically, most of even the major sermons and speeches from the pre-World War II period are now irretrievably lost to us and leave a serious lacuna in the African heritage. As Lalage Brown notes, "Nowadays, sermons may seem a drug on the market; and very unfortunately, the words of the man who has the widest fame [in Africa] as a maker of sermons, Dr. Aggrey, have only come down to us second-hand." Likewise, Dr. D. D. T. Jabavu, whose *The Black Problem* (1920) contains many of his addresses to educationists, enjoyed a more vast audience in his time than his book and a number of paraphrases and synopses would indicate. All of his speeches, which are interesting examples of the conflation of biblical and tribal wisdoms, "have a moral point and are in a format which involves starting with a text and including proverbs and a homely story to illustrate them." That is, they appear to combine in an idiosyncratic manner the rhetorical principles of the traditional African storyteller and of European oratory, yet for the present this possibility must remain conjecture, since (as Ruth Finnegan points out in her *Oral Literature in Africa*, "For all the passing references to the significance of oratory [in African cultures], there seems to be little documentation on the actual practice of public speaking as a skill in its own right" (445).

A somewhat analagous situation in New Zealand, however, might provide some encouragement: there the Maoris have maintained a strong oral tradition in the absence of a written one, and they have developed both a distinctive, systematic rhetoric and a terminology that is in remarkable harmony with that of classical Greco-Roman rhetoric, so that *whakatu* means to make a speech, *whatataki* is the exordium of the speech, and *whakarongo* means to inform, as distinct from to persuade. This, naturally, was what the classical rhetoricians firmly believed: that the principles they expounded had, in fact, a universal validity.

Pursuing this subject somewhat further, Anne Gere notes that

> Despite the differences in culture, the Greek definition of oratory as consisting of deliberative, forensic, and ceremonial discourse seems to work well in the African context. There appears to be no form of African oratory which falls outside this definition, and there are many examples of each. Deliberative oratory appears frequently in communal decision-making; the judicial situations whether in courts or the more ritualised *egwugwu* (secret cults which often perform judicial functions), provide forensic oratory; and ceremonial oratory appears in situations as diverse as funerals and gatherings to honor the accomplishments or good fortune of an individual. (14-15)

But many Africans (such as Sir Abubakar Tafewa Balewa, former prime minister of Nigeria and a Hausa; Edward Blyden; and millions of others from the north-west to the south-east of the continent) have been influenced in their speeches by another oratorical tradition—that of Arab and Muslim rhetorical theory and practice. Accordingly, when one reads the prime minister's speech to the United States Congress (26 July 1961), for example, one must bear in mind that its composition has been influenced, at least indirectly, by two at-times divergent rhetorical canons. In the Muslim rhetoric, according to H. Samuel Hamod,

> He who speaks well is well educated; he who is well educated is more qualified to render judgments and it is his advice that he should follow. Eloquence and effectiveness were equated. This higher form of communication was entitled *balagha*, but was not recorded systematically in any textbook.... Mohammed stressed that truth was the most important quality, and truth should be the first criterion of judgment: however, he did not underestimate the importance of style. Thus the Koran is logical and practical and also a work which is stylistically beautiful.
>
> Mohammed's ideas became the basis for all future Islamic preaching; the goal of speaking became persuasion instead of entertainment: truth served by beauty. (98-99)

Therefore, when we attempt to evaluate African speeches in English, we must not be oblivious to the oral traditions of the tribe or community, we must not overlook the potential influence of Arab-Muslim rhetoric, and we should try to take into consideration the particular role assigned to speakers who have developed eloquence in an alien language. In sum, we must be alert to the shortcomings of applying a strictly European rhetoric to the evaluation of African speeches, even those delivered in English before audiences whose first language is also English. Yet until we have a better understanding of the dynamics of African interpersonal communication under the influence of Eurocentric cultural forces, we must, by default, resort to the application of the Greco-Roman rhetorical imperatives.

At the same time, however, we must recognize the danger of evaluating most African speeches—like any others—by applying the criteria of literary criticism rather than rhetorical criticism. As Herbert A. Wichelns asks,

> What is the relation of rhetorical criticism, so understood, to literary criticism? The latter is at once broader and more limited than rhetorical criticism. It is broader because of its concern with permanent values: because it takes no account of special purpose nor of immediate effect; because it views a literary work as the voice of a human spirit addressing itself to men of all ages and times. But this universalizing of attitude brings its own limitations with it: the influence of the period is necessarily relegated to the background ... and the speaker who directed his words to a definite and limited group of hearers may be made to address a universal audience. The

result can be confusion. In short, the point of view of literary criticism is proper only to its own objects, the permanent works. (213)

Because of the circumstances of their delivery, then, it would seem that most African speeches up to the present, even, should be evaluated from the rhetorical rather than the literary viewpoint, as only this will take into account the exigencies that occasioned them.

The vast number of speeches in any culture are—like the majority of novels, poems, essays, or plays—not of great consequence either in local or universal terms. They tend to be shortlived because deficient in invention, substance, or style; alternatively, their ephemeral existence can be laid to a strictly utilitarian or propagandistic purpose which, once served, removed any justification for their composition. But as we reexamine the oratorical literature of colonial Africa, it would seem that three speakers, at least, stand out as of uncommon skill and grace, and hence worthy of greater recognition and exposure: Edward Blyden of Liberia, Iska Seme of South Africa, and Casely Hayford of Ghana.

The selected published works of Edward Blyden were recently issued under the appropriate title *Black Spokesman*. Perhaps no Anglophone African of the nineteenth century became so renowned as Blyden as a public speaker, though others before him had written or spoken on essentially the same themes and had expressed the same general sentiments. But, as Lalage Brown observes:

> The great series of spoken political texts comes, of course, from Edward Wilmot Blyden, a consummately artistic propagandist who devoted serious effort to his political and semipolitical addresses. He was writing before he had a speech published in the 1850's, and he didn't retire until 1906; so for half a century he was going up and down West Africa making his neat and polished speeches (and also preaching and lecturing in Britain and the United States on such texts as: "Ethiopia shall soon stretch out her hand to God"). (41)

(Blyden's first published speech, the 1857 annual address before the Monrovia Common Council, was entitled *Liberia as She Is and the Present Duty of Her Citizens*.)

Throughout his speeches and derivative tracts, essays, and articles, Blyden develops a small number of themes, nearly always stated in some mnemonic form, such as parallel grammatical structure: for example, Emancipation (social, intellectual, and religious), Immigration (of wholly committed, identifiably African "exiles" from the diaspora), Illumination (through enlightened government by and for Africans), and Harmonization (the development of a sense of solidarity transcending tribal, regional, and national allegiances). He favoured a West African church and the truthful chronicling of African history and culture and opposed both inordinate dependence on technology and urbanization, which he feared would diminish "the softer aspects of human nature" characteristic of the African personality. Further, throughout his life, but especially in his later years, when he was director of Muslim education in Sierra Leone, he espoused the culture of Islam and initiated the rapprochement between that religion and Christianity in West and Central Africa. His interests were truly wide-ranging, while his views were equally farsighted.

Blyden's speeches often have a homiletic quality, and the techniques of the sermon—particularly in the use of illustrative devices, such as analogies and extended metaphors, application of a principle to everyday-life situations, and recapitulation— are readily noted. In his speech on "The Return of the Exiles and the West African Church," delivered initially in St. Paul's School, Lagos, on 2 January 1891, he compares a European-supported Christian church to a railway ticket stamped "Not Transferable," and so argues for the United Native African Church that was his special interest. And in the same address he develops an interesting figurative analogy between African-initiated enterprises and experiential learning at sea:

> We shall never learn to swim unless we venture into the water. Let us launch out into the deep and try the vast ocean of life, with its sweeping gales and dashing waves. If our tiny bark should be shattered by storms and we return to the port with broken spars and tattered sails, we should be learning by experience. We should learn to be careful not to spread the sail too wide before we are sure of the strength of the gale. And what if we should founder? Many a gallant

ship, with able commander, has suffered this fate; but we shall not founder if we are careful to take Him into the ship with us, whose power can calm the boisterous sea and say to the raging waves, "Peace, be still."

Now, this short excerpt illustrates certain common traits of Blyden's rhetorical method: he develops common ground by using the "we/us" rather than the "I/you" approach; he uses a maritime illustration well-suited to his audience; he incorporates a rhetorical question which is then answered so as to develop his point; he dispels the fear of failure and so enhances his ethical proof with his listeners; he makes use of parallelisms and balance; he imbues his analogy with a dramatic quality in the pitting of the "tiny bark" against the indomitable seas; and finally, he implies victory through the intercession of reliable and supreme support.

In a longer and more philosophical disquisition, "Training the Mind," which was delivered to the Young Men's Literary Association of Sierra Leone on 19 May 1893, Blyden expounds some of his personal philosophy: he exhorts his audience to read widely in the classical literatures and in the Arabic and modern, but especially those authors who treat of subjects "in some way connected with your race, with Africa, or with some work in which humanity generally is interested"—and he recommends (after Shakespeare, Milton, and Tennyson) Wordsworth because, he says, "I think he suits the African mind on account of his love of Nature, his simple and cordial manliness and sympathy with every interest of actual life and with every effort for freedom." (He advises against Swinburne on the ground that "No one can fully grasp the beauty and force of [his poetry] without more than an ordinary knowledge of Latin and Greek"; and he likewise proscribes Byron because, "brilliant as he sometimes is, he is a man of false and distempered mind.") In essence, this speech clearly reveals the considerable extent of the speaker's knowledge and interests and spells out his humanistic philosophy of education for modern Africans.

But the speech also reveals in great clarity the components of his oral style: compound elements and triads abound;

aphorisms and maxims are prolix ("So long as you have good books to read, you need not complain of the disadvantage in having few"; "The cross precedes the crown"; "No man ever lost anything by fairness and justice") and result in the ascription of considerable ethical proof to the speaker, as Aristotle observed in the *Rhetoric*; there are powerful similes ("a mind properly drilled is like a blacksmith whose muscles have been exercised"); there are quotations, paraphrases, and allusions of biblical origin; and there are examples and anecdotes to enrich the conversational texture.

This speech, then, perhaps more clearly than most of his others, presents Blyden as a consummate occasional speaker and as an accomplished stylist; and it is not to be wondered that—as many chroniclers have attested—several of the leading African speakers of the present century deliberately modelled their methods and styles on his.

Pixley Ka Isaka Seme, a Zulu born in Inanda, Natal, was one of a group of talented young South Africans who shared a vision of leading the native peoples of the continent towards political enfranchisement, tribal cooperation, and full and equal participation in a multi-racial society in which the benign influence of religion would reduce factional animosities and ensure the progressive attainment of material well-being.

In 1902 Seme was admitted to Columbia University, having been sponsored by the Reverend Joseph Pixley, a member of the Board of Missions of the African Methodist Episcopal Church. After his graduation, he was admitted to Jesus College, Oxford, and subsequently read law in London and was admitted to the Middle Temple. He returned to Durban, where he established his practice. But his return to South Africa provided something of a culture shock: he was appalled at the treatment afforded to Blacks and at the bickering among their purported leaders. "We are one people," he declared; "These divisions, these jealousies are the cause of our woes." This analysis, of course, was somewhat simplistic, but it motivated him to call a meeting in Bloemfontein on 8 January 1912 (at which he delivered the principal address) that resulted in the founding of the South African Native National Congress, later simply the African National Congress.

Seme became vice-president of the A.N.C., editor of its journal, *Abantu-Batho*, and one of its principal spokesmen, advocating for almost forty years a centrist, responsible policy of racial cooperation that was almost indistinguishable from that of Dr. Booker T. Washington, president of Tuskeegee Institute, who rose to national fame following his 1895 speech to the Cotton States Exposition in Atlanta, Georgia. That speech was largely replicated in Seme's 1932 speech to the A.N.C. But just as Washington's philosophy of gradualism and vocationalism had its opponents, led in the main by Dr. W. E. B. DuBois, so did Seme's; and as the economic and social ills of the 1930's increased, Seme's policies became increasingly irrelevant in the eyes of his leftist adversaries. After three years of his presidency, the A.N.C. was moribund: the disaffected had left, and his supporters were reduced to about thirty.

Though he was indefatigable as a speaker during his long public life, perhaps no speech surpassed in rhetorical excellence the Curtis Medals Oration that Seme delivered at Columbia University on 5 April 1906. It states with brevity, clarity, and force the quintessence of his lifelong philosophy, so that it can justifiably be considered his most representative public statement. (In the tradition of the time, it was published by the university as a booklet; but the university library no longer owns a copy. Fortunately, the speech was printed in *The Colored American Magazine* and in J. M. Webb's *The Black Man: The Father of Civilization, Proven by Biblical History*.

Seme's oration, entitled "The Regeneration of Africa," has many of the stylistic characteristics of Blyden's speeches, and insofar as these are in general common to most eighteenth- and nineteenth-century speeches in the "high" style, this is not especially remarkable. But he does make greater use of comparison and contrast, of exemplification, and of literary tropes than his predecessor. As a result, his style at times has a decidedly poetic quality and enjoys the hue and heft of inspired, inspirational eloquence. The several passages that utilize parallelisms and antithesis would be easily committed to memory, and so it is understandable that "The oration seems to have become known to other Africans studying in America in later years; and more than half a century later, it could be quoted in its entirety by Dr. Kwame Nkrumah" (Brown 41).

"The Regeneration of Africa" presents material that is today commonplace: that an adequate and honest history of Africa will demonstrate the full achievements of the black race; that unity is a prerequisite to strength; and—differing from Blyden— that science and technology must be harnessed for the common advancement. Like Blyden, Seme himself sought to establish a united black African church, but failed; it, too, was an ingredient in his recipe for regeneration.

Yet Seme's evident pride in Africa is apparent, and his erudition is clear. He reveals an advanced understanding of cultural anthropology, noting the integrity of all cultures and denying the validity of any hierarchy based solely on Eurocentric criteria; he stresses the accomplishments of African art and architecture, going beyond the then normal limitations to utensils and personal adornments to include the great Ethiopian pyramids and their elaborate decoration; he emphasises the need for racial pride and self-consciousness, anticipating Alain Locke's clarion call for these in *The New Negro* exactly twenty years later; and he recognises the inevitability of martyrdom before the achievement of individual liberty and racial respect. To him, industry and education, science and religion, churches and colleges, commerce and business, peace and war, were all necessary for the achievement of pan-African solidarity and racial self-fulfillment. In observance of the principles of Ciceronian rhetoric, he provides a succinct recapitulation of the substance of his oration in his peroration:

> Agencies of a social, economic, and religious advance tell of a new spirit which, acting as a leavening ferment, shall raise the anxious and aspiring mass to the level of their former glory. The ancestral greatness, the unimpaired genius, and the recuperative power of the race, its irrepressibility, which assures its permanence, constitute the African's greatest source of inspiration. He has refused to camp forever on the borders of the industrial world....

> The regeneration of Africa means that a new and unique civilization is soon to be added to the world.

Admittedly, Seme's remarkably clear vision was somewhat premature; but that, of course, is in the nature of inspirational leadership and without which progress is slow and uncertain. More commendable, surely, is the fact that this vision was that of a twenty-year-old undergraduate, that it has proved so accurate in particulars, and that it was so impressively stated.

It is to be regretted that Seme's leadership potential was never fully realised. The cause was probably his firm belief—held with religious conviction, it would appear—in the legitimacy of only his own vision of African development and his disparagement of other, less-reactionary views. When he died in 1951 he was duly honoured for his efforts, but hardly lamented. Nonetheless, his 1906 oration, "The Regeneration of Africa," fully deserves to be retained in any collection of major or representative speeches by Africans.

The last of the three pre-World War II public speakers that I have selected for comment is Casely Hayford, of whom it has been written:

> He was ... a good after-dinner speaker.... He was clever, too, at using such informal occasions to make an important political point. He made, for example, a very polite and flowery speech of welcome to a new governor, praising his wife for the novels she wrote, but in the middle of it, hinting that what they wanted from the governor was a solution to the land problem. Such sly digs, as well as Casely Hayford's generally sinewy style, ensured that his speeches were quite widely read by politicians and intellectuals. (42)

Actually, few of Hayford's speeches that are included in the collection *West African Leadership*, edited by his fellow-Ghanaian, Sir Magnus Sampson, read well. This is perhaps an indication that they were extemporaneous or impromptu in their delivery, though the fact that with only a few exceptions they were given before organizations as presidential or inaugural addresses would seem to have warranted their careful prior preparation and composition.

Though there is little doubt that Hayford was a popular and effective public speaker, Sampson's evaluation appears to be excessively generous:

> His appeals not only touched the imagination, but moved the hearts of people. A born orator whose cultured voice and simple and delicious phrases charmed the ears of all who listened to him. There was the stamp of originality with a touch of genius in all his utterances. His resources were inexhaustible, and he was equally skillful in the setting forth of his own case and in answering his opponent's case. He was one of the finest speakers that West Africa has known.... It may be stated without contradiction that among the fine band of orators of the Gold Coast ... no one has eclipsed Casely Hayford's power of succinct expression and his gift of lucidity. (26)

On the evidence of the eleven speeches that Sampson has collected, it seems possible to conclude that he did make use of the method of indirection, of interposing a major point in an unlikely context, and that his method of elucidation was primarily dependent upon the inclusion of anecdotes, proverbs, Biblical allusions, and the accumulation of specific examples. That is, his methodology and style conform to the accepted norms of political and occasional speaking of the 1920's. There is none of the lush prose of Blyden or Seme, but there is a genuineness, a conciliatory tone that becomes apparent. These speeches seem predicated on the belief that compromise and conciliation are always possible, profitable, and preferable to confrontation; they suggest that the largesse of the colonial government can be depended upon for the capital necessary for development and should not, therefore, be deprecated; that colonial unity is essential to progress; and that progress (as he told the National Congress of British West Africa in 1923), should be achieved "in a right and constitutional manner," and "by relying upon that Divine assistance which has hitherto, as a congress, guided our feet."

One reaction to a reading of Hayford's speeches is that he seems at this remove to have been unnecessarily pusilanimous; but in his situation and time his was in all probability the counsel and course of defensible pragmatism.

African Speeches in English 129

In an address to the Cape Coast Literary and Social Club on "Patriotism," Hayford provides, in the conclusion of his speech, a typical example of his elevated style and of his handling of his basic themes, both of which suggest the influence of the Chautauqua lecturers and of Robert Ingersoll:

> Once more I bring West Africa a message of hope, a message of triumph. The last message that I had the privilege and the honour of delivering has, under God, borne fruit. Today entire West Africa has clasped hands over a common need, a common constitutional demand. She is asking for an effective voice in her affairs. She is asking for self-determination; and we believe she will not ask in vain. It will be uphill work, we know. There will be slackers; there will be obstructionists; there will be traducers. But the Eternal Power, whose fiat set our sphere going, will sustain us until our little world attains unto that degree of free and democratic life which will enable us to develop according to the genius of our race within a free, united British Empire.

It does seem an example of hyperbole to claim that an agreement among a half-dozen colonial people's assemblies "asking for an effective voice" in their own affairs is "a triumph," but this must be understood in its immediate context.

While it is generally acknowledged that creative writing in English in the former British African colonies did not reach a fully literary level until the post-war years, it is clear that the speeches of at least three African orators on occasion did so much earlier—in what some writers have described as the closing days of the era of great public speaking. That they came from Liberia, Ghana, and South Africa suggests that their aptitude and skills were generally distributed among Africans and not the result of particular tribal or community circumstances. The regard in which they were—and still are—held indicates that they became the exemplars for succeeding generations in their own territories and beyond, so that today (even though oratory has declined from its former pre-eminence as a literary art) we can still find signs of their influence in the speeches of the new leaders of African affairs.

Sadly, these new leaders have not shared a common vision of postcolonial Africa. The first, Kwame Nkrumah of Ghana, though guided at times by his mentor, Dr. W. E. B. DuBois, the celebrated American black writer, educator, and sociologist, became increasingly narcissistic and authoritarian until his eccentricities and unpredictability aroused general disaffection and he was removed by a coup d'etat; then the idiocies of Idi Amin in Uganda made him and that nation a laughing-stock of the continent; and the pretensions of "Emperor" Bokassa of the Central African Republic strengthened the international view that the former colonial peoples were incompetent to govern themselves. This view was, unfortunately, strengthened by incessant and widespread civil wars that gave evidence that public speaking and discussion and debate had ceased to have any relevance to the determination of public policy and national (or regional) goals.

Even in South Africa, where peace and progress seemed assured after the Boer War at the turn of the century, turmoil surfaced after the crucial election in 1948 that ushered in the policy of apartheid and Afrikaner supremacy that survived for almost half a century. This "new" policy has hardly novel, in fact, for it was Cecil Rhodes who said, in his famous speech "The Basis of South African Government" (1887), "We must adopt a system of despotism, such as works so well in India, in our relations with the barbarian of South Africa." It was the adoption of this system that motivated Olive Schreiner to deliver her famous address "The England of My Love Is Dead" (1900) and that gradually transformed the thinking of Jan Christiaan Smuts, so that in 1934 he could say, in his inaugural address as the chancellor of the University of St. Andrews:

> I am not against experiments in human government. The extraordinary difficulties and complications of modern government call for revised methods and new experiments. What I am here concerned with is the serious threat to freedom and self-government which is involved in the new experiments now being tried out in the Continent. They are all based on a denial of liberty—not as a temporary expedient but on principle....
>
> Remembering the great appeal of Pericles, which rings through the ages, let us seek our happiness in freedom and bravely do our part in hastening the coming of the great day or freedom.

However, apartheid was enshrined as the policy of the National Party, and speeches to explain it as separate development of the races or as a form of Christian Nationalism were frequent, strident, and patently defensive. Among the most vehement of its advocates were Dr. Malan, Dr. Verwoerd, and Prime Minister Pieter Botha; and their adversaries included Alan Paton, author of *Cry, the Beloved Country* and of a moving speech, "Why We Must Go on Dreaming"; Ambrose Reeves, Episcopal bishop of Cape Town, who was exiled for having defied apartheid and opened his cathedral "to men and women of all races to all services at all times," whose sermon "Separation and Segregation are Impossible" was printed in Johannesburg's *The Watchman* in November 1955; Helen Suzman, longtime liberal member of the South African parliament who has been outspoken against Nationalists, whom she has characterized as "right-wing zombies," and argued for new thinking, as in her speech "Equal Opportunity for All," which was delivered in the House of Assembly on 4 February 1970 as part of the no confidence debate on the government of Prime Minister John Vorster.

In spite of having admirable public speakers, advocates for change and progress, Africa seems to have become mired in internecine strife, and it is apparent that Pixley Seme saw the root causes quite clearly when he declared in his A.N.C. speech in 1912: "The demon of racialism ... must be buried and forgotten. We are one people. These divisions, these jealousies, are the cause of all out woes and of all our backwardness and ignorance today." Improvements in literacy and communication may well contribute to the diffusion of the thoughts of Africa's best advocates and their adversaries and reduce the attractiveness of military action, thus increasing freedom and liberty and improving the standard of living of people throughout sub-Saharan Africa.

WORKS CITED

Brown, Lalage. "The Development of African Prose Writing in English: A Perspective," *Perspectives on African Literature.* Ed. Christopher Heywood. New York: Africana, 1971. 40-45.

Finnegan, Ruth. *Oral Literature in Africa.* Oxford: Clarendon P, 1970.

Freeman, R. A. *Pageant of Ghana.* London: Heinemann, 1958.

Gere, Anne Ruggles. "West African Oratory and the Fiction of Chinua Achebe and T. M. Aluko." Diss. U of Michigan, 1974.

Hamod, Samuel H. "Arab and Moslem Rhetorical Theory and Practice." *Central States Speech Journal* 14.2 (May 1963): 98-99.

Laurence, Margaret. *Long Drums and Cannons.* London: Macmillan, 1968.

Pollard, Arthur. *English Sermons.* London: Longmans, Green for the British Council, 1963.

Sampson, Magnus J., ed. *West African Leadership: Public Speeches Delivered by J. E. Casely Hayford.* London: Cass, 1969.

Swanzy, Henry, ed. *Voices of Ghana: Literary Contributions to the Ghana Broadcasting System, 1955-57.* Accra: Ministry of Information and Broadcasting, 1958.

Wichelns, Herbert A. "The Literary Criticism of Oratory." *Studies in Rhetoric and Public Speaking in Honor of James A. Winans.* New York: Century, 1925. 181-216.

9. The Rhetoric of Cheddi Jagan and Forbes Burnham

In his keynote address to the 1972 Carifesta in Guyana, Denis Williams observed that

> In countries passing from colonial status to Independence, the immediate post-colonial period is characterised by a surge of creativity in the arts.... Immediately preceding and just following on the break-up of colonialism it was politicians, not artists, who seized the creative initiative and maintained it, here in the New World as well as elsewhere. (102)

It has long been recognized that the literary artifact of the politician is the speech, and it is through the study of the speech, more perhaps than any other literary genre, that the social historian may trace most adequately the development of ideas and assess their significance.

During the 1920's and 1930's the growing social and political awareness in the Caribbean gave rise to a number of speakers whose skill moved crowds, persuaded governments, effected change, and developed a tradition of oratorical eloquence. Alexander Bustamante and Norman Manley in Jamaica, Arthur Cipriani and Albert Gomes in Trinidad—and their counterparts in the other islands and territories—maintained a long oral tradition by speaking almost always spontaneously and in what often approached literary language on a wide range of subjects and themes. By enunciating the thoughts, ambitions, and sentiments of the common man and woman, they prepared a later generation to face the post-war problems that were associated with anti-colonialism and rising nationalism. Gradually "the people of the West Indies became not so much ... the thing spoken of, but rather the subject being addressed and the person spoken to," according to A. J. Seymore (53).

Thus the reasoned or affecting speeches of Eric Williams, Grantley Adams, and Eric Gairy—together with a number of less memorable politicians—determined in large part the history of the region by influencing national decisions.

Gordon Rohlehr writes of this time:

> While Guyana started on its fragmentation in mid-fifties, Trinidad was applauding the emergence of Dr. Eric Williams, party politics, and a new sense of both history and destiny, which the prime minister seemed to be offering.... The oral tradition was flowering and gaining a new polish of sophistication ... on the political platform, and the dream of Federation, alive since the 1920's seemed to be nearing centre. (57)

This fragmentation, this "great erosion of the spirit" as Rohlehr called it, resulted in Martin Carter's "movement from rhetoric to reticence" and moved Derek Walcott, looking at the poverty and futility of the average person's life in the Caribbean, to comment that the poet's art could be of little use: "Politics and prose," he thought, could do as much or more.

It was in this context that Cheddi Jagan and Forbes Burnham became the leading spokesmen in the politics of Guyana. Both are able speakers, if not orators of the highest rank, and have influenced the thought and actions of their audiences and those who have read the texts of their speeches. Jagan's "charm, his personality, his ability to speak to the people as one of themselves, overcame every Indian party that was set against him," while Burnham (who had won the Best Speaker's trophy at the University of London Law School) "had an ability to think on his feet, and to think more trenchantly and more wittily than anyone who opposed him. As a result, ... even his enemies would enjoy his speeches, his humour, and his quick ripostes" (Simms 186).

Unfortunately, many Guyanese speeches—like those delivered elsewhere in the West Indies—have been transient and ephemeral, neither committed to manuscript nor reported, except in paraphrase or precis. As Lady Bustamante has explained: "In those days speeches were never recorded; neither were they prepared speeches. One just spoke as one felt." And this practice has continued: C. A. Nascimento and R. A. Borrowes, the editors of Forbes Burnham's *A Destiny to Mould* (1970), a collection of articles and speeches, note that he "very seldom writes out his speeches, and as a result, a great many ... have had to be culled from tape recordings" (xxxv).[1] Consequently, most of the non-parliamentary public address has been lost, even though both Jagan and Burnham (like Eric Williams) have issued many of their speeches in leaflet and booklet form. However, the disdain for prepared texts has helped to perpetuate the stylistic characteristics of extemporaneous delivery that are increasingly rare elsewhere.

Jagan delivered his maiden speech in the Legislative Council on 6 January 1948. Years later, he observed rather deferentially, "I associated law with excellent public speaking and oratory, but at that time I had not been initiated into this art" (47). Yet, as Peter Simms says, "he showed from the beginning an understanding of parliamentary life. He also showed considerable moral courage as he consistently put forward views that he knew would not be popular with his colleagues" (86). Ostensibly responding to the Governor's Address, Jagan provided an explication of the policies of the Guyana Labour Party, of which he was then neither member nor supporter, and "within a month he had obtained such moral ascendancy, that he had made himself their spokesman. It was no mean achievement" (87).

Then he proceeded, gadfly-fashion, to identify those budget items that discomforted the compilers and delighted the critics. Quite undeterred by the constraints of the place and occasion, he eschewed platitudes and ceremonial commonplaces of speech. He demonstrated that fiscal legerdemain was being employed; that corporations were juggling accounts with administrative collusion; and—with a nice balance of irony and forcefulness—that while $600 was allocated to the S.P.C.A., there was no provision "for the prevention of cruelty to the working-class people of British Guiana." That is, he revealed a critical acumen, an appreciation for principles and priorities, and a speedy perception of consequences and implications that sometimes eluded him in later years. In structure, the speech is haphazard, and in style it is undistinguished, yet it is fair to conclude with one critic, that this speech "was certainly one of a man who was not afraid to express his opinions in correct parliamentary form" (88).

After the People's Progressive Party won the 1953 election, Jagan delivered his first speech as prime minister on 17 June. Though the attorney general proposed that protocol required a Loyal Address to the Queen as the initial business, Jagan chose to respond to the governor's address at the opening of the legislative session: symbolic gesture bested propriety.

He first expressed "grateful appreciation" for the Royal message and then immediately proceeded to a statement of his government's principal policies:

> We will strive to the utmost for the happiness and well-being of the people of British Guiana, and will remove every obstacle which may be placed on the road to peace, progress, and prosperity....
>
> We, however, harbour no illusions ... we shall continue to struggle for a democratic Constitution for British Guiana. The House ... is fully conscious of the legacy of privation, malnutrition, unemployment and disease which is bequeathed to us by the old order. We are aware of the pressing needs of the people.... We will initiate schemes for the reorganization of the material resources of the country and for raising capital ... the government will honour and fulfill all its obligations and undertakings.

In many ways this resembles the counterpart speeches of other leaders in the anti-colonialist movement; like them, it has a high degree of predictable, stylized content and phraseology. In fact, much of the lexicon of the movement and of Third World politics is observable. There are the concepts of service to oppressed and abused people, the confrontation with realities rather than illusions, the honouring of treaties and obligations, and the provision of a more equitable life based on self-identified goals and priorities. This, according to Paul Corcoran, a political scientist interested in language and rhetoric, amounts to

> a display of style with no meaningful content ... little more than a survival of the formulaic tropes and scheme of classical rhetoric. Rhetorical devices such as slogans ... strongly reinforce the formulaic, ritual-like stylization of political language. Hence, speeches become embarrassingly trite, and ... produce a language reduced to slogans and unpredicated incantations. (197)

But this is not so severe a criticism as it at first might appear: almost all ceremonies, whether introductions, awards, or inaugurations, have culturally mandated commonplaces and prescribed length, structure, and tone. Jagan's policy speech comports well with the requirements of epideictic oratory; in fact, it has the added characteristic of some specificity, which is a change from the normal vacuousness of its genre, and a well-controlled truculence that replaces a more frequently used pusillanimous tone. Pride becomes more apparent than complaisance, and surely this is apposite for a speech celebrating political victory.

Later in the year, Winston Churchill suspended the colony's constitution and expelled the government. Subsequently, the P. P. P. split into Jagan and Burnham factions, and many observers identify this series of events as the beginning of the racial and ideological divisions that have since bedevilled the nation. In this situation, the Annual Congress of the P. P. P. was held on 22 December 1956. Jagan's speech reviews the international situation, emphasizing the progress of decolonization, Third World power, and socialist governments. Then it gives a dispassionate analysis of shortcomings that amount to "leftist deviationism": overrating the capacity of the party to effect immediate change; failure to observe the Stalinist injunction to be flexible in attacking enemies and finding allies; and disregard for the Maoist caution against unenlightened dogmatism, or "all struggle and no unity." This self-searching results in a series of recommendations, including the development of a common front with the "revolutionary bourgeoisie" against imperialism and a clear differentiation of goals: "We are primarily interested in struggle ... Burnham and John Carter are primarily interested in 'office'."

After alluding to the cause of the rift in the P. P. P., Jagan slips into the "formulaic, ritual-like stylization" of language that Corcoran alludes to and which is fraught with the emotionalism of anathematizing a doctrinal miscreant:

> All the time Burnham was with us, we had to control his right deviationist tendencies, and at the same time not expose him for fear of disrupting our party.... The Burnham clique were prepared to deviate to [the right] to sacrifice our proletarian working-class, internationalist outlook for narrow nationalism.

Now, while this may sound like an immoderate *ad hominem* attack, it must be remembered that Burnham's family, educational, and occupational background would naturally incline him more toward a bourgeois-liberal position than toward a doctrinaire proletarian one; and Arthur Schlesinger Jr., points out that the Kennedy Administration policy *vis à vis* Guyana "was based on the assumption that Forbes Burnham was, as the British described him, an opportunist racist and demagogue intent only on personal power" (241). So Jagan's characterization can be regarded as succinct and not unreasonably coloured by personal animus.

"The dream of Federation" that Gordon Rohlehr believed to be "nearing centre" at this time was of necessity broached by Jagan in his Congress speech in 1956. Admittedly, some Guyanese Indians feared an influx of Blacks if there were a single West Indies citizenship, though the geography and society of Guyana would seem to have been a protection, and the Blacks feared aggravated economic conditions. Yet Jagan found a means of rationalizing the legitimate self-interest of his mainly Indian supporters with the internationalism of his proletarianism in advocacy of Federation on the basis of prior dominion status of the compacting members. Accordingly, the points that Jagan expresses in this speech are moderate, significant, adequately supported, and devoid of malice or petulance.

In the *Rhetoric*, Aristotle said that, of the three branches of speaking, he preferred "the deliberative branch, that of the statesman, which is nobler, since it deals with communal interests and affords less room for ... biasing the audience by playing on their emotions" (4). Corcoran takes up this point and is adamant that "affective speech in all the forms characteristic of oral culture finds itself relegated to its now more appropriate place outside the significant channels of public discourse.... Emotional language loses its authority in literate society" (48). Yet, in Jagan's speech at the opening of the Commonwealth Caribbean Governments Summit Conference in Jamaica in 1964, we find that (for what must surely be conceded to be a literate audience) the speaker makes far greater use of emotional proofs than in his Congress speech, which would have had a less literate audience. As if speaking for the Third World, Jagan says:

> The masses the world over are no longer contented to be exploited and humiliated. They are on the move. They are determined to abolish imperialist wage slavery as their forefathers abolished chattel slavery. Some of them will be shot, imprisoned, detained, tortured, brainwashed, and corrupted. They will neither be deflected nor defeated. And win they will. Their numbers are beyond reckoning. But for every one fallen, thousands will rise up. They have written the word *independence* on their breasts, and history and logic are on their side. They are armed with a superior ideology, superior to that based on greed and profit.

The opening sequence of simple, declarative sentences provides an enthymematic argument with an historical parallel that suggests historical inevitability. Following this the catalogue of punishments—vivid, yet factually justified—followed by the antithesis of falling/rising and the heraldic image prior to the dogmatic assertion, "history and logic are on their side," is surely effective prose style. Then the whole motif of inspired crusaders is successfully developed. The cliches of anti-colonial rhetoric have been supplanted by a more traditional and regionally meaningful metaphor: the analogy, because developed both literally and figuratively, acts as a quasi-logical form of proof as well as a means of clarification of context.

This speech is noteworthy for a number of attributes of style, particularly since Jagan is sometimes thought to be deficient in this canon of rhetoric. First, there are several antitheses (peace/war, buying cheap/selling dear, government debt/private profit), which clarify by simplification; and a number of implied causations (war/hunger; war/profits; neocolonialism/exploitation). There are correlatives (neither deflected/nor defeated), triads ("high interest rates ... high charges ... high profit margins") and slogans ("We do not want neocolonialist chains," and "Let it not be said that we have failed"). Likewise, there is commendable development by both example and comparison: in the body of the speech this becomes almost a litany of colonialist shortcomings and excesses that convinces by the devices of cumulation of grievances and elimination of justifications. Unfortunately, a number of trite expressions and allusions (Trojan horses, hard-won freedoms, and root causes) detract from the quality of the language, though it could be argued that these commonplaces would be found acceptable to the wider audience to whom the text of the speech was ultimately circulated. But they are few and are seldom conspicuous in context; the stylistic elements that enhance are certainly the more numerous.

It is apparent, then, that between 1948 (when he delivered his maiden speech in the House of Assembly) and 1964 Cheddi Jagan developed a mature prose style. The structure of his speeches improved markedly and most commonly utilized the topical, causal, or logical patterns of development. His developmental devices—though characteristically accumulation of example, illustration, or quotation—gradually became more varied, allusive, and vivid. Throughout his speeches run the leitmotifs of colonial economic oppression, long-suffering native peoples, and workers struggling for independence and self-realization in a peaceful world where cooperation and progress replace exploitation and despair. And nowhere are there signs of change of fundamental direction or diminution of enthusiasm: party hegemony in a polyglot society is the paramount goal.

Of Forbes Burnham as a speaker, the editors of *A Destiny to Mould* write:

> His skill as an orator and his dedication to the struggle for independence of his own country and of all colonial peoples led him to the presidency of the West Indian Students' Union.... He also became an active member and vociferous spokesman for the original League of Coloured People.... Jagan placed heavy reliance on him as spokesman and advocate for the party's cause during their trip to London and subsequently in Europe and India.... His advocacy at the Bar frequently jammed the courtroom with spectators. (xvii-xx)

Yet he waited six weeks before making his maiden speech in the Guiana Assembly on moving the repeal of the Undesirable Publications Bill, a most repressive piece of legislation. Even the archbishop of the West Indies had objected to the original bill, saying in style reminiscent of eighteenth-century liberals: "With all my heart I have revolted against this Ordinance.... This is an infringement of the liberty of the individual. This is not just restraint ... this is tyranny." Unfortunately, Burnham was not similarly moved, and it is to be regretted that he did not see fit to exhibit his oratorical skills.

From 1960 Burnham had constantly been arguing in favour of election to the Assembly by proportional representation rather than by constituency. This method, devised in the nineteenth-century to protect minorities, has never been widely adopted, and its endorsement by Burnham now seems to have been tactical: to polarize voters along racial rather than ideological lines. *Hansard* reveals several occasions when he affects the vernacular in comments such as "Me only blackman, but ..." and "You, blackman, why you sitting with all those coolies?" in contexts that do not suggest levity. The editors of his speeches state, "Burnham's pragmatism is political and not philosophical" (185), but at times the two are inseparable.

The 1964 election was held on the basis of proportional representation. The "black" P.N.C. received 40% of the vote (down .5%) and the "Indian" P. P. P. received 46% (up 3.2%). Supported by the United Front, Burnham became premier of a coalition government. Peter Simms later commented that

Burnham's greatest problem was "to win the trust and participation of the Indian community."

As premier, Burnham's first major speech was given over the radio on 19 December 1964. It is an interesting speech. He does not claim victory; rather, he evasively says that "On the results, the P.N.C., in the interests of peace and stability in Guiana, has agreed with the support of the U[nited] F[ront] to form a government." He then gives as his immediate priority "the attainment of independence"—adding that horrendous phrase, "at the earliest point in time." Next, he refers to racial strife as "an apparent cleavage" brought about by "colonialism and seven years of mismanagement and misrule" (an interesting conjunction of scapegoats) and alludes to the "opportunist propaganda" of the P.P.P. (which presumably meant the *Apan jhaat*, "Vote for your own" slogan), stressing that his government, in contrast, is determined to overcome "racial antagonism and distrust":

> The reduction of tension, which is already apparent, and which will become more pronounced with every passing day, when it is realised that not only are we intent on being fair and just, but also that we have at our disposal the means to carry out our intention, is merely the first fruits of our attainment of office.... We will dispel the fears of the apprehensive and confound the hopes of those who seek the destruction of this country.

Here, of course, are the traditional elements of self-congratulation and intimidation of opposition; there is self-identification with community virtues, such as fairness and moderation, reduction of tension, elimination of fears, and implacable hostility to the enemies of these goals; there is the inchoate threat of force in the deliberately non-specific phrase," we have ... the means to carry out our intention." And there is the veiled subsequent identification of the largely-Indian P.P.P. as the "would-be destroyers of this country" and of the Jagan government as "the evil machinations of those bent upon the establishment of a totalitarian dictatorship founded on hatred, violence, and mutual distrust." The stylistics of these sections of the speech are disquieting: moderation and compromise are submerged by bombast and fustian that reveal a deep-seated and barely controlled animosity that verges on vindictiveness unbecoming a democratic statesman and spokesman.

Throughout the speech the diatribe continues, largely developed by means of comparison and contrast or antithesis and disjunction. The P.P.P.'s sins are copiously catalogued: nepotism, corruption, deliberate delay of independence, and a plan, "under the tutelage of their foreign totalitarian masters, to introduce the form of tyranny and slavery that is their conception of freedom." In fact, the speech is noteworthy for its emphasis upon the shortcomings and dangers of the defeated government rather than upon the strengths and policies of the new one. In his only reference to economic policy, Burnham states that "This government is not bent on the confiscation of property," yet the subsequent nationalization of the bauxite industry amounted to just that, in some critics' views.

This first major speech of Forbes Burnham is therefore disappointing: it is too intemperate for its occasion, too loosely organized, and too vapid in substance. Here, Corcoran's observation on contemporary political rhetoric is of interest, for he says that it is used "not to stimulate thought, but to prevent it; not to convey information, but to conceal and distort it; not to draw public attention, but to divert or suppress it. In short, ... the reverse role from that classically conceived" (xv). And this reversal, according to Corcoran, is normally to be found only in post-literate societies.

Most major statements of government policy are made at the annual delegates' congresses of the P.N.C.: "On this occasion the prime minister seeks to identify and rationalise, in economic and social terms, the ideological thrust of the party for the developing nation," according to C. A. Nascimento. The 1970 Congress was held just two months after the inauguration of the Cooperative Republic of Guyana, and hence Burnham's speech on this occasion (entitled "Planning for a New Era") was at once an explication of the cooperative philosophy and a major address.

The speech begins with an assertion that unemployment has been reduced (though Burnham provides no statistical evidence) but then describes in embarrassing detail the sad circumstances of a major sector of the work force: "Many are employed who are mere wage slaves and disinterested automatons ... they merely exist, with little hope for the future ... theirs are the jackal's pickings.... We who live here know the poverty that is rampant and the despair and destitution of the poor." And, acknowledging that Guyana's per capita income "places us high among the underdeveloped nations"—he cites figures that show it to be three times India's average—he suggests that the figure is skewed artificially by the earnings of "a few millionaires and highly paid executives." Apparently the implications of this candour escaped Burnham: in six years of unchallenged authority the government had not introduced income taxes of sufficient effect as to correct gross abuses of earning and profiteering, nor had it had any discernible effect on widespread under- and unemployment. The recital of shortcomings amounts to a self-indictment.

Then, after castigating both the International Monetary Fund and foreign private investors (collectively "international aristocrats"), Burnham unrealistically calls for national development of Guyana through savings from what he has already declared to be inadequate incomes. The means of "giving the masses economic power" he identifies as the nineteenth-century phenomenon the cooperative. Through this, he claims, "the small man's economic power must be in direct proportion to his political power," thus reversing the accepted tenet of capitalistic societies.

As an example of national development, Burnham alludes to his 1961 proposal to found a Hinterland city and announces the appointment of a committee to study its feasibility. Once again, the proposal appears counterproductive, as far as speech support is concerned. If the plan has merit, why is its feasibility only now being studied? Why has it been dormant almost a decade if its great merit is that it will employ large numbers of idle workers in an essential national project? Then, almost inadvertently, Burnham states clearly what had been only implicit earlier: "I have been referring to the social and economic revolutions, the national ownership and control of Guyana's resources, and their development by and for Guyanese. That is what Black Power is about." Thereupon, he quotes at length from his 1969 Congress speech, reiterating such statements as "In Guyana [the government's] role, therefore, without descending into racial fascism, is to seek to strengthen and support the social and economic revolution that is taking place here. In Guyana, there is an opportunity of the black man being a real human being." The concern in the speeches of earlier years for the well-being of the "six races" of the polyglot society, for equal opportunity, for racial harmony, and cooperation is absent: the new concern is unabashedly for the welfare of the black segment of Guyana's society. And this is made more poignant by the inclusion of lines from Claude McKay's poem "Enslaved," which condemns "The white man's world of wonders" and ends with the vow "To liberate my people from its yoke." Thus multiethnicity has become Black Nationalism.

In his several speeches Burnham uses the conversational mode with skill, constantly resorts to emotional proofs to stimulate the audience, tends to advance only such ideas as are assured of ready audience assent, and offers reassurance of improvement in personal and national affairs—though frequently risking his credibility by the exclusion of statistical supports and by the inclusion of specific, detailed examples to the contrary. He makes use of mainly European cultural allusions (Pandora, Cerberus, Rochdale Movement, Esau, Wolsey, and Cromwell), though there are also regional ones (Cuffy, Kaituma, Venezuela, and Essequibo River) in the consideration of less philosophical and more immediate matters in the 1970 Congress speech, for instance. Latinisms and polysyllabics are sprinkled throughout his speeches, so that they frequently exhibit an incantatory style resembling that of Chaucer's Pardoner. While low-frequency vocabulary normally contributes to the elevation of style, one wonders how many of Burnham's immediate audiences appreciated the niceties conveyed by such legalisms as *pari passu, en passant, mutatis mutandis, raison d'être, fait accompli,* and *ex mero moto.* Sentence structure is varied, and occasionally rhetorical questions are used effectively—though seldom for development of a yes-response. But in the most recent speeches there is no sign of the wit and humour that formerly flourished and added a fillip to rather lackluster content. The cliches of socialist propaganda remain everpresent, as do those of Black Nationalism and anti-colonialism.

Like their distinguished predecessors in the anti-colonialist movement within the erstwhile British Empire (the great Indian orator-statesmen B. G. Tilak and G. K. Gokhale) the Guyanese politicians Cheddi Jagan and Forbes Burnham are without doubt capable and effective public speakers who are able equally to convince and actuate audiences both literate and formally unschooled. Their appeals have been effective among all sections of the Guyanese electorate, though they have tended, understandably, to appeal to their particular ethnic constituencies—the one Indian, the other African in origin. Yet it can be concluded that Jagan's own speeches have uniformly sought general support, have attempted to minimize the "two cultures" realities of Guyanan society, while Burnham—particularly in more recent times, has discarded even the convention of adapting to a heterogeneous audience and has explicitly advocated a policy predicated on black power and advancement.

Their ideological differences, at first sight, have become more pronounced, though they are perhaps not as substantial as some observers would propose; but their "politics and prose," their programs and speeches have not wrought those great and necessary improvements in their national society that Derek Walcott hoped to witness in all Caribbean nation-states.

It is, of course, doubtful whether Jagan's idealism, dogmatism, and doctrinaire Marxist socialism could be more effective than Burnham's tauted realism, pragmatism, and cooperative socialism as a means of mollifying the social antagonisms of their country or ameliorating its sad legacy of centuries of rapacious colonialism in a short period; but the speeches of both men indicate that these were long their special goals.

Times have changed, and mere-anticolonialism no longer suffices as either national policy or the theme of countless speeches: beyond the rhetoric that justifiably reminds the people of the basic causes of their problems must be sound policy and effective administration to achieve "One people, one nation, one destiny."

NOTES

[1] *Hansard* commenced in British Guiana in 1880. Before that time only minutes of governmental meetings were kept; however, major speeches by officials and parliamentarians were often reported verbatim in the local journals and newspapers, most of which are available in the National Library in Georgetown. See Allan Young, "On Writing History." *Kyk-over-al*, 8.23 (1958): 47-48.

WORKS CITED

Aristotle. *The Rhetoric*. Trans. Lane Cooper. New York: Appleton, 1922.

Burnham, Forbes. *A Destiny to Mould: Selected Discourses by the Prime Minister of Guyana, Forbes Burnham*. Ed. C. A. Nascimento and R. A. Burrowes. Kingston: Longman Caribbean, 1970.

Bustamante, Lady. Letter to the author, 23 August 1971.

Corcoran, Paul E. *Political Language and Rhetoric*. St. Lucia: U of Queensland P, 1979.

Jagan, Cheddi. *The West on Trial*. New York: International, 1966.

Nascimento, C. A. Letter to the author, 29 July 1971.

Rohlehr, Gordon. "The Creative Writer and West Indian Society." *Kaie: The Literary Vision of Carifesta 72*. Ed. Celeste Dolphin. Georgetown: National History and Arts Council of Guyana, 1973. 55-65.

Schlesinger, Arthur M. Jr. *A Thousand Days: John F. Kennedy in the White House*. Boston: Houghton, 1965.

Seymour, A. J. "The Creation of Quality in the West Indies." *Kyk-over-al* 6.18 (1954): 52-55.

Simms, Peter. *Trouble in Guyana*. London: Allen and Unwin, 1966.

Williams, Denis. "Art and Society." *Kaie: The Literary Vision of Carifesta 72.* Ed. Celeste Dolphin. Georgetown: National History and Arts Council of Guyana, 1973. 100-110.

1982

10. Race and Colour in Caribbean Protestant Sermons

From the time of British entry into the Caribbean the Christian church has played an important role. As an institution of the white settlers' culture, the church initially remained largely apart from the native and slave populations in which it found itself. Interaction with these non-white groups was not undertaken until 1700, when the Anglican church formed the Society for the Propagation of the Gospel in Foreign Parts; however, these early efforts produced only meagre results until the latter half of the eighteenth century, when England felt the effects of the evangelical revival, with its emphasis on the worthwhileness of the individual and the expectation that God would act powerfully on and through the convert. With the popularization of the great ideas of the Reformation, missionary efforts gained new impetus and independence: Wilberforce saw missionary work as an essential counterbalance to the secular influence of England's expansion and concomitant exploitation.

The sermon was key to the work of Protestant missionaries in the Caribbean, as it provided the preacher with a means of interpreting the Bible to potential converts who could not read and of exhorting them to accept Christ. An examination of sermons given from 1671 until 1825 discloses the literary and rhetorical methods used by preachers in their ministry to their parishioners and their attempts to win converts to Christianity: the preachers' adaptation of Biblical themes and church doctrines to these audiences will be considered.

Of the Protestant churches represented in the Caribbean, the Church of England has had the longest association, having been established officially in Jamaica in 1662 by Sir Charles Lyttleton, the deputy governor. Before that date Oliver Cromwell had sent an expedition in 1655 to Jamaica and Santo Domingo to drive out the Spanish and establish Christianity and commerce. In a letter to the Dutch ambassador, Cromwell recommended "Such enterprise as shall be for the encircling of both states and for the propagation of true religion," and stipulated that "teachers, men gifted with knowledge of Jesus Christ, shall be sent by both states respectively unto all people and nations to inform and enlarge the gospel and the ways of Jesus Christ." Milton shared Cromwell's conviction of the success of the expedition, and wrote of "opportunities of promoting the glory of God, and enlarging the bounds of Christ's kingdom, which we do not doubt will appear to be the chief end of our late expedition to the West Indies" (qtd. in Ellis 25). Here we see expressed the conviction, widely held during the colonial period, that imperial expansion was beneficial and that commerce and Christianity should co-exist.

The church that was planted in the Caribbean, however, did not embark on any missionary activities; it ministered to the white population of the islands, in keeping with the intention of a 1634 Order of the King in Council, extending the jurisdiction of the Bishop of London to all English congregations and clergy abroad. A sufficiently numerous white population soon existed in Jamaica to warrant the services of the clergy, for in 1655 under an Order in Council "one thousand Irish girls and as many youths of fourteen or under" were exiled to Jamaica, and the King permitted certain dissenters to be "transplanted" to Jamaica with oaths of supremacy and allegiance to be lifted. The accession of William and Mary assured the continued flow of white émigrés, through either individual voluntary effort or transportation of felons and dissenters.

Records of this early period indicate that in Jamaica by the close of the seventeenth century there were barely enough clergymen to serve the needs of the population of 4,000 white colonists, officials, servants, and slaves—to say nothing of the

40,000 Africans who by this time had been brought in to work on plantations. Little information is to be had concerning the ministry of the clergymen in Jamaica; however, some insight may be gained by examination of a sermon delivered on 1 February 1671 to the first meeting of the governor, council, and assembly by Mr Henry Houser, a native of Switzerland who served the parish of St. Katherine. The sermon clearly shows that the Anglican Church was primarily engaged in a ministry to the free white citizens of the islands; we may also conclude that the published sermon owes its survival in large measure to the political importance of the occasion.

The sermon title, "An Exact Model or Platform of Good Magistracy: or a Sermon," states the preacher's purpose and indicates the explanatory, advisory tone that he takes. In a dedicatory preface the Reverend Mr Houser expresses his disbelief that, "being conscious of my own Private Weakness, that this poor Sermon should gain Acceptance with You, as to judge it worthy either of your Thanks or of Publick View." Quoting from the speech of Ruth (2.10), he confesses his consternation at having been chosen to address such an august body: "Why have I found grace in your Eyes, that you should take knowledge of me, seeing I am a Stranger." But he ascribes his good fortune "unto God's infinite Mercy, and your own Goodness," thereby attempting to cast himself in an appropriate light of becoming modesty. He closes his dedication and thanks by reiterating the main points of the sermon: urging the officials to show themselves to be "Men of Ability, fearing God, men of Truth, hating Covetousness."

The sermon is organized into the two processes of discussion and application common to the period. After drawing a fulsome likeness of the present meeting to a "great Conjunction of Heavenly Bodies ... attended with great and notable changes," he avers that such change will come about when his listeners take up the advice of Jethro (Exodus 18:21): "Moreover thou shalt provide out of all the people able men, such as fear God, men of truth, hating covetousness." He then divides the text into two parts, giving an exegesis of each through citations of key words in Hebrew and in Greek; in fact, throughout the sermon there is evidence of his extensive knowledge of Scripture. His approach tends toward dry admonition and scholasticism, but he connects his sermon directly to his audience, as when he expounds on the "four essential Characters, or Properties of good Magistrates." His discussion of "ability" as a "prime and first Character" illustrates his closeness to his listeners and his method of using biblical material for exposition:

> This Ability includeth strength of body.... It includeth greatness of Estate and Descent, of Riches and Wealth, of Birth and Blood ... Understanding and Wisdom: Therefore Solomon prayed to God for an understanding heart..... Give thy Servant an understanding heart to judge thy People, that I may discern between good and bad.... Moderation of mind, which enables him to Rule and Govern his Passion and Affection.... *Fortior qui sese, quam qui fortissima vincit Moenia*.... Such an one is stronger than he that subdues and conquers the strong Cittadel.

His method of explanation is appropriate to his listeners; they are presumably intelligent, educated, and cultivated, so he is not indoctrinating but giving advice based on biblical allusion and quotation (often in Hebrew and Latin) on how they should fit themselves to carry out their duties. His audience are men of importance and culture, and he adapts his message to them.

There is no evidence of literary elevation in the sermon, no striking use of metaphor or analogy; but there is an outspoken directness that recommends the sermon in the absence of literary polish. In view of the catastrophic earthquake which destroyed Port Royal on 7 June 1692, Houser seems almost prophetic when he rails against the wickedness that "reigns in every state, in every condition ... as if he would defie God to his Face, and call upon him to hasten his Judgments upon our Land, upon our Families and Persons."

Houser does not hesitate to call upon his listeners to show courage in carrying out the charge given to the first governor of Jamaica and reiterated in similar form to each successive leader "to discourage vice and debauchery and to encourage ministers that Christianity and the Protestant religion, according to the Church of England, might have due reverence and exercise" (Ellis 30). In this regard, his listeners are to be especially diligent against

> those proud *phanatick* Emissaries, who under pretence of New Discoveries, and New Revelations of the Spirit wander from place to place ... and in opposition to the true Light of the Gospel cry out New Light ... whereby they Seduce, Deceive, and Delude the Hearts of the Poor, Simple and Ignorant People.... You must be a living law, and be an Example to all Good.

In thus urging his listeners to be zealous guardians of the established church, Houser gives them a specific charge and enhances his own appearance as a vigilant watchdog of the official religion. And it would have been vital for him to assume such a stance, since the Anglican Church in the islands, although entrenched, was by no means notable for exemplary clergymen.

Reports of the Anglican Church in Jamaica during the eighteenth century indicate that it reached a very low ebb, reflecting the torpor and disinterestedness which pervaded the church at home. While the Bishop of London had jurisdiction over the colonial church (extending later even to India and Australia), it was an authority unsupported by any underlying diocesan organization to enforce discipline or to see that the work of the church was carried out. Henry C. Wilkinson writes that the supervision of the bishop "proved to be only an embarrassing and meaningless adjunct of his duties," with the real authority devolving on the governor of each colony (265). Lowell J. Ragatz reports that the lax supervision thereby produced gave rise to "irregular services and a tendency to fill livings with mean individuals" (19); and writing on the state of the Church of England in the Caribbean, Alfred Caldecott quotes the historian Long to the effect that, while

> there have seldom been wanting some who were equally respectable for their learning, piety and exemplary good behaviour others have been detestable for their addiction to lewdness, drinking, gambling, and iniquity; having no control but their own sense of the dignity of their function, and the censures of the Governor.... Some were much better qualified to be retailers of salt-fish or boatswains to privateers than ministers of the Gospel. (59)

J. B. Ellis, a historian of the Anglican Church, reported that his investigation of the available records led him to conclude that in Jamaica "the Church itself was regarded as little more than a respectable and ornamental adjunct of the State, the survival of a harmless home institution which would cease to be tolerated if it showed any signs of energy or activity outside its own particular groove" (40-41).

As to the religious condition of the slaves, whose numbers were increasing rapidly, in 1790 a Commons Committee inquiring into the existence in Jamaica of religious institutions for slaves was told that none existed (Smith 10). The eighteenth-century Church of England saw no contradiction between slavery and Christianity: the Society for the Propagation of the Gospel in Foreign Parts owned and managed its own slave plantation, Codrington, on Barbados, but had little success in Christianizing the Negroes (Klingsberg 11) Of the Society's apparent indifference to the condition of slavery, Ellis explained that

> S.P.G., as its full name implies, had for its object to establish and conduct missions in foreign parts. Jamaica was not foreign; it was a British colony. The probability is that the Bishops of London, in sending out clergy gave no instructions as to missionary work among Negroes, about whom they cared little or nothing.... The Church represented the religion of the white settlers and planters and officials; but it cannot claim to have been in any sense a missionary Church to the black labourers. (12)

Slavery was a spiritual advantage, according to Bishop William Fleetwood, who wrote in 1711 that "it was better to be sold as a slave than to die in sin" (qtd. in Klingsberg 101). And Bishop Isaac Maddox indicated that if the slaves suffered hardships, it was the responsibility of the planter to "alleviate that Distress, by furnishing their Minds with good Principles."

Attitudes such as these modified slowly, and then only toward the end of the century, as humanitarian feeling began to increase throughout England. Without a doubt, much of the impetus for the humanitarian movement came from the nonconformist churches (Moravian, Methodist, and Baptist), which were responsible for making the first serious missionary attempts in the Caribbean later in the century. We know that Anglican congregations did not exclude Blacks: in *The Church in Bermuda* John Waters Stow, Archdeacon of Bermuda, reported that a Rev. Alexander Richardson, rector of St. George's from 1755 to 1805, ministered "to the coloured folk, old and young, bond and free ... baptized ... white and black" (8). But black worshippers did not form a significant part of the Anglican congregations and there is no indication, apart from the sermons, of the approach a clergyman might have taken with a mixed audience.

Robert W. Smith described the plight of an exceptional minister, the Rev. Charles Peters, who in 1800 urged his planter communicants in Dominica not to use their slaves harshly, for "true religion required masters to consider the health and welfare of their slaves" (172). In the vituperative controversy that ensued Peters returned to England to join the cause of the abolitionists.

Some of the disinterestedness of the eighteenth century and its lack of engagement with social concerns is reflected in a sermon by the Rev. John Alexander Moore, Anglican rector in the western parishes of Barbados. The sermon, "Be Not Conformed to this World," was first preached at Somers Island on 30 November 1766 and subsequently delivered on seven other occasions. There is no hint in the sermon of any association of the church with the slave population, although we could assume that some slaves and mulattoes may have attended the services.

Moore analyzes the character and motivational problems of the Anglican communicant who would be upright in the midst of a sinful world; he directs his words to personal, not social, concerns and assumes that his listeners have a firm grounding in the Bible and Christian principles. Just how meaningful the sermon would have been to any slaves who heard it is problematical, for there are no specific references to them or to the unique problems deriving from their condition of slavery.

This sermon is largely undistinguished in either content or organization. Beyond the opening statement, which gains attention because of the seeming paradox it poses of authority as "one of the greatest supporters of absurdity, and of immorality," the sermon fails to command attention because it lacks focus. Moore enunciates his text, "Be not conformed to this world" (Romans 12:2), and indicates that he intends to follow the customary pattern of discussion and application; however, the parts of the sermon are not clearly set out, and it is easy to become lost in a repetitive flow. Although Moore is capable of a pithy statement: "more examples of ill living than of ill thinking," and "a well-moralized conversation is a greater rarity than an orthodox head," his style is generally fulsome, as in this passage where he thunders against the dearth of godliness to be found:

> And how much more rare is it to see one that's truly serious and considerate, circumspect and recollected, that considers thoroughly and effectually the end of his coming into the world, the shortness and uncertainty of his staying in it, and what shall become of him when he goes out of it; and accordingly lives under a constant and lively sense of God and of his duty to him; walks with him, and gives himself wholly to him; makes religion and the care of his soul the main business and concern of his life; works with all his might while 'tis day, and is utterly resolved, whatever it costs him, to mind and secure the one thing necessary!

Moore can be drawn into ellipsis, which spoils the focus of his message, as during this tirade against the wickedness of the world: "For not to mention the particular vices of the perverse and unleadable people, the Jews; their superstition, their idolatry, their infidelity, their rebelliousness, their lust and luxury."

Again, Moore punctuates his over-abundant treatment with numerous rhetorical questions, which help to command the listeners' attention; but his sermon ultimately lacks vividness because the images he portrays remain on a fairly simple and stereotyped level:

> Does not the present age abound with a sort of men who are crafty and designing, false and treacherous, rotten and hypocritical; men that seem to have their eye fixed upon and terminated with the honours of the world, that make gain their godliness and interest

their measure, that will betray the church or preferment, sell their religion and their souls for money, and will depart from the way of truth for the wages of unrighteousness, and be damned hereafter to be rich and great here.

His presentation of human motivations and behaviour is not far off the mark, as when he invites his listeners to "imagine what private insinuations, what sly contrivances, what spiteful whisperings, what treacherous arts there are daily used even among those that profess decency and kindness to one another, to undermine one another's interests and blast one another's honours and reputations?"

In this passage he seems to appreciate the personal, subtle, but very real problems his listeners would encounter in human relationships, and he seems to speak with sound insight into the workings of the human mind and will.

Counselling his listeners to resist conforming to the world, Moore admonishes them that "the precepts and rewards of our religion require a very different method of life from what is ordinarily practised; the precepts are strict and severe.... Our religion obliges us to great strictness and singularity." He repeatedly urges them "to undertake that religious singularity" which Christianity demands and supports his exhortations with Biblical and classical illustrations: the lives of Socrates, Lot, and Noah are used to inspire his hearers to "converse ... like an angel of light among fiends and evil spirits ... surrounded with the works of darkness, but [having] no fellowship with them."

In one instance, Moore seems to be addressing both black and white, slave and free, among his congregation:

> We Christians have one more peculiar reason not to be conformed to the world. We have renounced it in our baptism, with all its pimps and vanities. By which are meant not only the heathen games and spectacles, their vain shows and loose festivities, their lewd bacchanals and Saturnals, which we renounce absolutely, and the wealth and glory and grandeur even of the Christian world, as often as they prove inconsistent with the ends of our holy institution.

This is the application of his text, and Moore vigorously enjoins all his listeners to "forsake the multitudes and ascend up to the mount of solitude and holy separation."

Moore sustains to the end his attacks on wickedness, his injunctions to avoid the "polluted streams and torrents of the age," and his exhortations to be courageous in the face of "the censure of preciseness and singularity which the men of the world commonly charge against good men." This is a sermon that is direct and personal, and in the Reformation tradition of placing responsibility on the individual for his own salvation. The preacher makes no exceptions for the special difficulties of slaves, whose problems arose from bondage, not heathenism, and whose efforts to practice Christianity were severely hampered in most cases by the harassment of their masters. With religious passion he seeks the moral regeneration of black and white alike; if he seems too censorious, too ready to find fault, he is also quick to point the way to salvation. His method of preaching is in the evangelical tradition, which sets great store by the sermon "that leaves a lively searching sting behind it" (Brastow 44).

The evangelical fervour which swept through England in the latter half of the eighteenth century provoked public outrage at the condition of West Indian slaves and inspired the missionary efforts of zealous nonconformist ministers in the Caribbean, who carried out the most successful attempts to Christianize the slaves.

Of Anglican efforts, Ellis conceded that although there were "men of zeal, perseverance and devotion in the ranks of the Establishment ... the lion's share of the honours of persecution belonged to the Nonconformist Churches." These dissenting ministers, he conceded, may have been rash, but

> the heedless indiscretion of Wesleyan or Baptist compares favourably with the apathetic indifference which characterised many of the ministrations of the Established Church.... No one can deny that these efforts were in the direction of justice to the black population. Honour to whom honour is due. Those who provoked the hostility of the Church and of the planters earned the gratitude of the poor and the oppressed.... The Government was a negrophobic Plantocracy and the Established clergy sympathized with the Government. (56)

Given the heated opposition of the planters and the indifference (if not open corruption) of the official church, the work of Christianizing the slaves was painfully slow. In 1823 a member of Parliament, Sir George H. Rose, struck by the failure of that body to investigate the state of religion of the West Indian slaves, during debate on abolition published a lengthy pamphlet in which he touched on the extent to which Christianity had been achieved, the difficulties encountered in spreading the Gospel, and the benefits to be gained from vigorous missionary efforts. His comments, supported by numerous letters from clergymen, are valuable not only because they give first-hand accounts of problems encountered in this special ministry, but also because they reveal the attitudes of the clergy to the slaves.

It is obvious that the clergyman faced linguistic and cultural barriers to his ministry; in letters from clergy to their governors, which Rose appended to his pamphlet, slaves were described as "unenlightened, unguided, unrestrained by moral or religious obligations, or feeling," suffering from "stupid ignorance, thoughtlessness, and superstition, their minds are totally destitute of all cultivation." In the opinion of the Rev. W. Chaderton of Antigua,

> to crowd them into a church therefore without some previous preparation, would be a procedure equally useless and absurd. Our liturgy would be wholly unintelligible to them; and the addresses from the pulpit, which surely must be adapted, in some degree, to the superior information of our more enlightened hearers, would be to them as unedifying as if they were preached in a foreign tongue.

The same difficulty was reported by the Rev. William Nash of Grenada:

> Our excellent liturgy is totally beyond their comprehension; and were we to address our congregations in language which the Negroes could only imperfectly conceive, there is no person of any erudition, or even of a moderate understanding, who, unless his patience were supported by his piety, would bear to hear us.

And the Rev. John West in Jamaica reported the same problem, but he also saw the situation from the slaves' point of view:

The fact is, in respect to slaves in general, that their knowledge of the English language is so very limited, that they can derive little or no advantage from their attendance in church. They are so conscious of this defect, that when I go to church for the express purpose of catechising them, very few will attend, and not one of these will utter a word but what has been put in his mouth.

In the records examined (with the exception of the Rev. Thomas Williams of Jamaica, who reported that more slaves were attending divine worship and that "their desire of religious instruction is great"), the Anglican clergy appeared to despair of success. Rose felt that Anglican difficulties—apart from the great hostility of the planters—lay not in church doctrines, which had been maintained "in universal vigour and integrity," but in part in the Church's "temporal circumstances," and the scattered slave population. But he cited the chief impediment to progress as the education of the clergy, which often omitted instruction in homiletics and

> which could by no possibility have been conducted with a view to qualify them to convert Negroes. We cannot quarrel with them for having the education of English gentlemen ... raised too far above the level of the comprehension and reasoning of the heathen negro, for it to be practicable for them to lower themselves to the standards of such mental instruction of a being so unenlightened, and so little capable of thought and reflection as the uninstructed slave is found to be.

Nor did Rose feel that the Anglican clergy possessed the necessary attitude and outlook, for they lacked

> that ardent spirit of solicitude for the propagation of the Gospel; of that zeal for heavenly things; and of disregard of human things, which is properly termed religious enthusiasm, and which can be engendered in no old establishments, without some alteration in their principles.... As a body, they are not pervaded by that spirit.

The Rev. Mr Chaderton suggested the nature of the change which must take place if the Anglican clergy were to be successful as missionaries:

> We must first undergo a thorough metamorphosis; we must entirely alter our present habits and manners, and assimilate ourselves to the Negroes. We must give a complete turn to the train of our ideas, and

bring them down to a level with those of the slave. We must acquire new methods of thinking, or reasoning, and of expressing ourselves: and when we have effected this change, to make any progress in our work, we must go in continual and painful pursuit of reasonable opportunities to address these people.

It is clear that the established clergy were aware of the great gulf which separated them from their potential converts and were able to assess the situation candidly, both in terms of their own attitudes and of the readiness of the slaves for Christianity. Because the Baptist and Methodist preachers were drawn mainly from the lower classes and were popular, Rose was of the opinion that the established church should give full support to the missionaries of dissenting churches to carry out the work, for,

> The very habits of life, and the education of the missionary of the sects, give him a marked advantage over our ecclesiastics in matters of conversion where those, who are to be the subjects of it, are of the description of the heathen Negroes. He is used to deal with ignorant men, of coarse habits, and whose minds comprehend slowly: he knows how to understand them; how to unravel their half-intelligible jargon; and how to descry and aid the first glimmerings of their reason and conviction. None of these things can be expected from the graduated member of an English University.

Dissenting clergy did receive instruction designed to help them minister to all types of men. Adam Clarke, in a preacher's manual prepared in 1820 for the instruction of Wesleyan missionaries, considered the "spirit" in which the minister did his work as second only to his acquaintance with the Scriptures. The minister was enjoined to cultivate "simplicity of spirit ... gentleness of conversation and conduct toward others." At least two of the numerous injunctions seem particularly designed to keep the minister from the pitfalls of false pride and affectation, thus presumably aiding him in making the right approach to potential slave converts:

> Do not *affect the gentleman*.... A preacher of the gospel should be *the servant of all*.... [Be not] above serving yourself or others, even in the meanest offices of life.... Be *ashamed* of nothing but *sin*: not of fetching wood or drawing water ... of cleaning your own shoes, nor those of your neighbour. (80-81)

Presumably, the dissenters' stress in right "spirit" accounted at least in part for the discernible sympathy in their treatment of slave congregations: Smith wrote that the Negroes preferred the sectarian chapel to the Anglican churches,

> for their service with its greater emphasis on group participation and singing of hymns was more interesting.... The attitude of the dissenting missionary, too, was different from that of a typical Anglican West Indian churchman. To hear a white man conversing with him freely, addressing both bondsmen and free blacks as brethren and sisters filled the slave with elation. When inside the Methodist or Baptist chapel, the slave had a momentary feeling of independence both of thinking and acting. Within the chapel there was no reminder of slavery. (174)

While the missionaries may have accorded the slave sympathy and equal treatment in terms of his religious life, they had no notion of addressing the politics of his bondage. Dissenting preachers were adjured to "shun all controversies about politics: and especially that disgrace of the pulpit, political preaching" (Clark 100). The London Missionary Society in 1816 instructed its ministers not to carelessly inflame the slaves, and thus endanger public peace and safety: in pastoral work and in preaching

> Not a word must escape you, in public or private, which might render the Slaves displeased with their Masters, or dissatisfied with their Station. You are not sent to relieve them from their servile condition, but to afford them the consolations of religion, and to enforce upon them the necessity for being subject 'not only for wrath but for conscience sake' (Rom. 13:5, and Peter 2:19).
>
> The Holy Gospel you preach will render the Slaves who receive it the more diligent, faithful, patient and useful Servants, will render severe discipline unnecessary, and make them the most valuable Slaves on the Estates, and thus you will recommend yourself and your Ministry even to those Gentlemen who may have been averse to the religious instruction of the Negroes. We are well assured that this happy effect has already been produced in many instances, and we trust you will be the honoured instrument of producing many more. (qtd. in Wallbridge v).

Rose concluded his inquiry into the religious condition of the slaves by arguing that the most important purpose of missions was to spread the benefits of British institutions, especially Christian marriage, which alone, he insisted, was able to provide the stability necessary for healthy economic conditions on the plantations. Pointing out that West Indian property had suffered a serious decline, he stressed the importance by bringing the "idle, debauched, and thoughtless labourers on these estates to such a frame of mind, as shall ensure their honesty, frugality and industry" (40).

Although Rose stated his conviction that the "hideous institution" of slavery must eventually die, his main concern was to convince Parliament and planters not to interfere in the spread of Christianity, but to use it to prompt social good. He did not use the Bible or Christianity to justify slavery; his arguments were designed to justify Christianity to the planters.

An Act of the Barbados assembly in 1676 expressly forbade religions instruction of slaves on grounds of "leading to notions of equality," and Caldecott cited the testimony of a Barbados planter as to the incompatibility of Christianity and slavery: "Being once a Christian, he could no more account him a slave; and so lose the hold they had on them as slaves, by making them Christians" (65). The planters' strong opposition seriously hindered the preaching and work of Christian missionaries and, in the opinion of Smith, "helps to explain the relative harshness of slavery there as compared to Latin America" (186).

An examination of two sermons delivered in 1825 to slave congregations in Barbados by the Wesleyan missionary William J. Shrewsbury shows how he attempted to accommodate his message both to his immediate slave audience and to the larger politico-legal situation dominated by planter opposition. They are entitled "The Gospel Command," and "Christ, Our Saviour, Example, and Judge."

Both sermons have a careful, didactic tone, as if Shrewsbury realizes that he must give instruction before his listeners can fully understand. The Wesleyans recommended that the minister should "endeavour to gain the attention of the congregation before embarking on the sermon," and Shrewsbury does that in "The Gospel Command" by first stating his text, then providing a short background wherein he draws a lesson for his hearers. Using short sentences, simple language, and explanatory asides, Shrewsbury seems to be gently and patiently guiding his flock:

> These words were spoken by a very great preacher of God's word. His name was Paul. This Paul was once an enemy to the religion of Jesus Christ, and a persecutor of all that were called Christians. But that was in 'the times of his ignorance;' as he himself confessed afterwards, that he did it 'ignorantly and in unbelief.' You see what a sad thing it is to be ignorant, for it leads people to call evil, *good*; and to think they are doing what is right, when, according to God's word, they are doing what is *wrong*.

And he tries to win his listeners' approval by showing his good intentions to them. He tells them that he is a missionary,

> that is, one who leaves his own country, and, from love to the souls of the Heathen, goes to preach the gospel unto them. In this respect, we, that are called *missionaries*, strive to be like him, and are come to preach unto you. In our own country, England—that good country—we heard that you knew not Jesus Christ our Saviour: We loved you, though we had never seen you: And because we wish you to be good and happy in this world, and after you die, we have left our parents, and brethren, and sisters, and are come to teach you the way to heaven. May the Lord help you to understand what we say, that your souls may be saved.

He draws numerous moral lessons, emphasizing good conduct and relating it to the everyday duties of life. His address is both direct and challenging, as when he assures his audience in "The Gospel Command" that God takes account of everything: "Ought you not to fear this Almighty God? And whenever you are tempted to steal, or to do any bad thing, instead of saying to your heart, *No one sees me*, you should say, 'Thou God, seest me! How can I do this wickedness and sin against God!'"

And, later on in the same sermon he calls up his listeners' own experiences, confronting them with their personal sinfulness: "Now you all know what it is to feel sorrow. If any trouble befalls you, you cry; if your wife or your children die, you weep, and some of you cry out, and make a great noise when you follow them to the grave. But did you never weep on account of your sins?"

And, in another appeal to right conduct: "O let me exhort you to repent! You that get drunk, you that curse, you that tell lies, you that steal, you that have two wives, you that are lazy, you that are always quarreling, repent, repent, I beseech you; for 'if you die in your sins, where God is you can never come.'"

There is nothing striking or dramatic in this imagery; it is down to earth and it helps to carry his point.

Shrewsbury reveals that he is willing to meet his audience on their own ground, and remonstrates with them vigorously to change their ways: "Some of you Africans think, that you go to your own country; or to some place where you will meet with your countrymen and friends. This is one of the devil's delusions to keep you from seeking that heaven where all good people dwell."

In some passages he refers directly to his listeners' servitude, with a view to helping them find consolation in their troubles. He is expressing the view of religion common to the period when he says,

> To repent is God's command, not mine.... You would not repent in your own country. God has, therefore by bringing you to this land, punished you for worshipping devils, and trusting to gree-grees.... But mercy is mixed with the punishment, for he has brought you hither for good, that you may repent and be saved.

The preacher continues in this vein until the end of the sermon, stressing the universal condition of sin and the need for repentance: "Jesus Christ will not ask you, *What country did you come from? Were you rich or poor, slave or free, white or black? But, Did you repent?*" And, in another section he insists, "it does not matter where a man lives, whether in his own country, or amongst strangers, if he only fear and serve God."

Shrewsbury's sermon "Christ, Our Saviour, Example, and Judge," exhibits the same methods and arguments. On this occasion, he gives brief sketches of several important Biblical figures, drawing moral lessons from their experiences. Of Joseph being sold into slavery, he says, "But Joseph was one of the best of men, and never ran away from his master, never stole from him, was always industrious and faithful; and though very well used without deserving it, he never once said anything bad of his master, nor yet reviled his mistress, though she was a very wicked woman."

Once again, we see the evangelical plea to face the hardships of life unflinchingly, to persevere, and to prevail.

The theme of submission and forbearance is a fruitful one for Shrewsbury's invention, and he pursues it didactically through a long passage which illustrates his penchant for giving instruction to his audience: exhorting his listeners to look to Jesus as their example, he reminds them that Christ's example was one of "universal goodness.... He hath shewed men how to do good, and *How to suffer ill.*" As Christ set an example of obedience to parents, so Shrewsbury's listeners should do likewise: "A Christian slave will endeavour to be industrious in working his grounds, that, beside honestly maintaining his wife and children, he may have something to give his poor old father or mother, to comfort them in their last days." And he tells them to follow Christ's example of obedience to rulers:

> You must do nothing that Christ would not do, if he were in your place. You must obey your masters, and all magistrates and governors, not to get the praise of men, but that you may bring glory to Christ. Some people will say, 'A poor slave can do no good in the world!' But I think a Christian slave can do a great deal of good. He cannot preach, he cannot make a book, and get fame as a wise and learned man: But his very station in life gives him an opportunity of setting such an example of Christian submission and obedience, as shall not only benefit his fellow-slaves, but also cause his Redeemer to be glorified in countries that he has never seen, and amongst people that he has never known. O be Christians; be Christians, and you will be everything that is good.

The congregation are to endure suffering, as Christ did: "Strive not then with your fellow slaves, nor with any man, but invariably bear, forbear, and forgive.... Despise not thou the chastening of the Lord, nor faint when thou are rebuked of him. For whom the Lord loveth he chasteneth, and scourgeth every son whom he receiveth."

The themes which Shrewsbury develops are highly reflective of the attitudes of his time, as they were set out in Rose's pamphlet: personal responsibility for right conduct, perseverance in overcoming worldly obstacles, submission to earthly authority, aspiration to the rewards of heaven—all are presented to the Christian slave as obligatory and within his reach, even though he remains in bondage.

During the period immediately leading up to Emancipation the missionaries acknowledged the civil authority of the slave system and concerned themselves exclusively in their sermons with the religious state of the slaves, insofar as they could overcome heathen ways and become Christians; Christianity was equated not with any fundamental rights of man but with his duty to God. But there was a growing awareness of the inconsistency of preaching submission to the master while extolling the brotherhood of man; as this conflict forced itself more clearly into the consciousness of the missionaries abroad and the English public at home, it was inevitable that resolution in the form of emancipation would come; when it did, the Baptist preachers became the most popular.

If we agree with Arthur Pollard that "the sermon was the product not only of its author's own qualities, his religion, temperament and general outlook, but also of his environment, and of the modifying effects which particular audiences exerted" (7), we are not surprised to discover in the sermons examined a close affiliation between official and clerical attitudes to the slave.

The sermons examined for the period 1671-1825 all bear the mark of the age in which they were given. Anglican sermons of the seventeenth and eighteenth centuries show concern for the continuation of the traditional role of the church as ministering to congregations grounded in Christian principles. Those directly addressed were persons of substance in the community with an official or important civic role to play. To a considerable degree both sermons from that period have a reactionist tone, turning toward the past, endeavouring to uphold past forms and truths.

The two early nineteenth-century sermons addressed by dissenting ministers to slave congregations reveal a thorough grounding in prevailing thought, but with a marked attempt to engage new problems and to enlarge the scope of the church through an application of the truths of evangelical Christianity. None of the sermons is prophetic or ahead of its time, but all reveal the interplay of the great social polities—family, church, state, and all forms of social organization—and the efforts of the ministers to adjust themselves to time and audience.

WORKS CITED

Brastow, Lewis O. *The Modern Pulpit: A Study of Homiletic Sources and Characteristics*. New York: Macmillan, 1906.

Caldecott, Alfred. *The Church in the West Indies*. London: Society for Promoting Christian Knowledge, 1898.

Clarke, Adam. "A Letter to a Methodist Preacher." (1800). *The Preacher's Manual*. New York: Carlton, 1855.

Ellis, J. B. *The Diocese of Jamaica: A Short Account of Its History, Growth and Organisation*. London: Society for Promoting Christian Knowledge, 1913.

Houser, Henry. *An Exact Model or Platform of Good Magistracy: or a Sermon*. London: Francis Tyson, 1673.

Klingsberg, Frank Joseph. *Codrington Chronicle: An Experiment in Anglican Altruism on a Barbados Plantation, 1710-1834*. Berkeley: University of California Press, 1949.

Moore, John Alexander. *Be Not Conformed to This World: A Sermon Preached First in Somers Island. Bermuda, Nov. 30, 1766*. London: n.p.

Pollard, Arthur. *English Sermons*. London: Longmans, Green for the British Council and the National Book League, 1963.

Ragatz, Lowell J. *The Fall of the Planter Class in the British Caribbean, 1763-1833*. New York: Century for the American Historical Association, 1928.

Rose, G. H. *A Letter on the Means and Importance of Converting the Slaves in the West Indies to Christianity*. London: Murray, 1823.

Shrewsbury, William J. "The Gospel Command: A Sermon Delivered to a Congregation of Slaves"; "Christ, Our Saviour, Example, and Judge: A Second Sermon Delivered to a Congregation of Slaves." *Sermons Preached on Several Occasions in the Island of Barbados.* London: Butterworth, 1825.

Smith, Robert W. "Slavery and Christianity in the British West Indies." *Church History*, September 1950: 165-78.

Stow, John Waters. *The Church in Bermuda.* Toronto: Canadian Church Historical Society, 1957.

Wallbridge, Angel. 'The Demerara Martyr: Memoirs of the Rev. John Smith, Missionary to Demerara.' Georgetown, British Guiana : *Daily Chronicle*, 1945.

Wilkinson, Henry Campbell. *Bermuda and the Old Empire.* London: OUP, 1950.

1983

11. Thomas P. Callender: Presbyterian Preacher in Jamaica

From the moment of Columbus's penetration of the Caribbean, the Roman Catholic church maintained an unassailed position as proprietor of Christianity in the region until Cromwell's despatch of an expedition to Jamaica and Santo Domingo in 1655 with the dual commissions of "encircling of both states and the propagation of true religion." This second goal was to be achieved by "teachers, men gifted in knowledge of Jesus Christ," who were to be sent "unto all people and nations to inform and enlarge the Gospel and the ways of Jesus Christ." And, given Cromwell's personal religious beliefs and attitudes, it is probable that he fully intended activist missionaries rather than functionary celebrants to undertake catechetical and proselytizing work quite literally among "all people"—African, European, Caribbean, bond and free—by means of the traditional Protestant instruments, education and homiletic (if not exegetical) preaching.

But Cromwell's Commonwealth collapsed before his intentions for the West Indies were effected; and on the Restoration, Presbyterianism (which Charles decried as "a religion not fit for a gentleman") almost instantly became ineffectual in English life. Ironically, had it not been for the interminably disputatious Westminster Assembly (which held 1163 meetings between 1 July 1643 and 31 December 1648), Presbyterianism might well have remained the established denomination in Britain. Cromwell concurred with Milton that

"New presbyter is but old priest writ large" and, dismissing Parliament, provided the Dissenters with sufficient national mission work to render similar work abroad almost superfluous. However, since "one thousand Irish girls and as many youths of fourteen or under" were exiled to Jamaica by Order in Council in 1655, one might assume that some provision was made for their religious instruction and salvation.

By the end of the seventeenth century there were upwards of 4000 whites in Jamaica and some 40,000 Africans, whom they were officially enjoined to convert to Christianity; the labours of the clergy were seemingly devoted entirely to the spiritual well-being of the whites of the administrative and commercial superstructure, as is suggested by the title of the earliest extant printed Jamaican sermon, that delivered by the Rev. Henry Houser on 1 February 1671, entitled "An Exact Model or Platform of Good Magistracy." In this, Houser calls upon his audience of officials, including the governor, Sir Thomas Lynch, "to oppose the violent stream of all Lewdness, and Wickedness, and Profaneness, and be a lively Example to the Practise of Piety, of Holiness and Godliness, since ... Sin is grown to such an height that our Island had been made a second Sodom and Gomorrah" (16-17).

Yet accounts of the Church of England in Jamaica during the eighteenth century indicate that it was characterised by the same torpor and disinterest that pervaded the metropolitan sees. Church offices and services were irregularly observed, benefices were awarded to mean individuals, and as Alfred Caldecott notes, many of the vicars and curates "were much better qualified to be retailers of salt-fish or boatswains to privateers than ministers of the gospel" (59). In effect, the Church of England in Jamaica was little more than a distant parish of the diocese of London and a formal appendage of the State. As late as 1790 a House of Commons committee was advised that there were no religious institutions for blacks or slaves; the Church of England acknowledged no disparity between Christian belief and slavery; and the Society for the Propagation of the Gospel in Foreign Parts even owned its own slave plantation,

Codrington, on Barbados, where it had little success in Christianizing its labour force.

Episcopal statements indicated the official position: in 1711 Bishop William Fleetwood wrote, "it is better to be sold as a slave than to die in sin," and shortly thereafter his colleague, Bishop Isaac Maddox, cautioned that if slaves suffered physical hardships, it was the responsibility of planters "to alleviate that distress by furnishing their minds with good principles" (qtd. in Klingberg 114). As church historian J. B. Ellis has written: "The church represented the religion of the white settlers and planters and officials; but it cannot claim to have been in any sense a missionary church to the black labourers" (41).

The task of providing outreach to the black, slave, and white labouring and exile groups was therefore relegated, by default, to the dissenting Protestants. First were the Moravians (1754), then the Wesleyan Methodists (1789), the Baptists (1813), and finally the Presbyterians (1824). Because they were so late and so few in number (as well as because they laboured principally outside the larger population centres), the Presbyterians in Jamaica remained without significant denominational following or influence; notwithstanding, certain missionaries, such as the Rev. Thomas P. Callender, exerted noteworthy personal influence and achieved widespread attention and audience.

But the dissenting clergy were generally unwelcomed by the Establishment and especially the plantocracy, for they almost alone advocated emancipation. In the wake of the 1831-32 slave uprisings that resulted from accounts of deferral of emancipation, so-called Colonial Church Unions were founded and harassed and hounded both blacks and dissenting pastors. Examples of the horrendous actions of the Colonial Unions are legion; suffice just one or two by way of illustration. The Rev. Mr Murray, a Baptist at Montego Bay, was arrested and imprisoned on 25 March 1833 for "preaching to his very respectable congregation, composed chiefly of coloured persons"; Robert Lamont, described as "a leader of one of the Falmouth church classes, on account of his intelligence, prudence, and piety," was seized by the militia and sentenced to 500 lashes and work in chains for the term of his natural life for preaching to blacks after sundown without a license; and Henry Williams, a slave, received 450 lashes on 19 January 1832 after having been discovered praying in his house (Samuel 102-03, 181).

The post-emancipation decline in status of the established church in Jamaica is thus easily understood, though the historian William Green attributed this also to the resurgence of native African religions and of novel Afro-Christian hybrids, promulgated by self-appointed or poorly prepared black enthusiasts. William P. Green reported that Obeah and myalism had not been eliminated by the nonconformist missionaries, but were in fact still flourishing: emancipated Blacks, he claimed, had not renounced "their African spiritual heritage, [which] legacy lay barely concealed beneath a thin layer of catechetical Christianity" (344). The slaves' ready conversion to Christianity in some areas probably had less to do with religiosity *per se* than with social and material expectations.

Post-emancipation nonconformist preachers, trained in the evangelical tradition and hardened by their humiliation at the hands of planters and colonial administrators, maintained themselves almost wholly apart from the white communities and demonstrated by their endurance of persecution their determination to preach and convert. It is, therefore, not hard to understand the frequent inclusion in sermons of allusions to the suffering of early Christians (especially in reference to their defiance of Roman authority) even when the text of the sermon would not seem to warrant such allusion. In Callender's sermon on "The Fulness of Christ," for example, he speaks of Christ as redeeming us "from the curse of the law, being made a curse for us; there he made peace even for the rebellious"; which in modern terms would be referred to as "code words"— expressions that convey to the initiates a more specific and meaningful message than the language itself apparently justifies.

The Rev. Thomas P. Callender, a graduate of the University of Edinburgh and the Divinity Hall of the United Secession Church and sometime pastor of congregations in both Glasgow and Edinburgh, arrived in Jamaica in 1846, following the suggestion of his physician that the West Indian climate might be conducive to his recovery from tuberculosis, and he became *locum tenens* for the Rev. Mr Watson at Lucea for a year. And although the Presbyterian mission had by then been maintained for over twenty years, his ministry was not without its difficulties. Almost a generation later, the United Presbyterian commissioners who visited Jamaica and Trinidad reported that

> the wealthy and middle classes ... are almost entirely unrepresented in the Jamaica church. With only an occasional exception, the membership of the country congregations is composed of small settlers, whose settlements ... are in the vast majority of cases from half an acre to three acres; and of day labourers, whose wages do not exceed five shillings a week.
>
> It must be remembered that our Jamaica mission was in its origin exclusively a mission to the slaves; and that even since the Emancipation it has been our policy to confine our labours almost entirely to the negro population. We have followed the emancipated slaves to their retreats among the mountains and have furnished them with the means of grace in the neighbourhood of the whites where they labour. (qtd. in Carlisle 77-78)

Callender preached his first sermon in Jamaica to "a black and coloured audience," as he described it, at Hampden, Trelawney, on 3 January 1847, "with mixed feelings of delight, and bewilderment, and trembling" (22), and on 14 February he had, he wrote,

> an opportunity of conversing with, and catechising, the old people of the congregation—all native Africans. One or two of the leading doctrines of the Gospel they understood; still, with them superstition is mixed with faith and requires long labour to get it weeded out of their mind. It is a false idea many entertain that missionary work is more rapid than home work. The same slow progress is made and the same hard heart of unbelief opposes the missionary as the minister.... The operation of the spirit of God is every where similar, and the African must be dealt with the same fashion as the European, the Indian as the Englishman.
>
> Slavery has indeed proved most debasing to the blacks. It will be the work of long and weary years to elevate them from the kind of idiocy into which they have been sunk. Even the best among them read but imperfectly and indistinctly. Still, the gospel has done much for them, and elevated not a few to the liberty of Christ's people.

What is especially noteworthy here is Callender's clear statement of belief, after even so brief an experience, that the Blacks of Jamaica should be treated by missionaries (and, presumably, others) in exactly the same fashion as Europeans— and particularly Englishmen. His other observation, that the so-called lack of civilized traits in the West Indian black population ("the kind of idiocy" that he alludes to and which was doubtless the very same characteristic that Oliver Goldsmith termed "the vulgar") has been imposed ("into which they have been sunk," as he puts it) is most salutary, for it reveals him as far more enlightened than many of his compeers of the established church. For example, Sir George Rose, M.P., commented in his *Letter on the Means and Importance of Converting the Slaves in the West Indies to Christianity* (1823) that the chief impediment to Anglican success among the Jamaican blacks was the education of the clergy, which raised them "too far above the level of comprehension and reasoning of the heathen negro ... a being so unenlightened, and so little capable of thought and reflection as the uninstructed slave is found to be" (23). But another Presbyterian missionary, Warrand Carlisle, suggested that it was not *incapability* that caused the slaves to seem inferior in ability; rather, he wrote, "In all valuable knowledge the people were little superior to the beasts, [for] almost the only power used to control them was that which is used to govern horses, mules, and asses—the fear of the lash" (45). And in that same year, 1847, Lord Macauley, in a speech to the House of Commons, reminded his auditors that even Adam Smith, that great advocate of *laissez faire*, argued the necessity of government provision of basic education for the masses as an act of enlightened self-interest in a commercial nation; he then concluded: "It seems to me that no proposition can be more strange than this, that the State ought to have the power to punish and is bound to punish its subjects for not knowing their duty, but at the same time is to take no step to let them know what their duty is" (qtd. in Cubberley 528-9). And even today the Committee for Adult Literacy reminds us that there are twenty-five million illiterates in the United States. Clearly, then, Callender was a trifle too critical of his slave congregation.

Notwithstanding the near-impossibility of the Jamaican plantation and country folk obtaining even the most rudimentary schooling, their achievement was a constant pleasure for Callender. After examining 150 children at the Hampden missionary school on 11 March 1847, he noted in his *Journal*: "The whole proceedings were exceedingly interesting and would bear comparison with many of our home schools. Where is the much-talked-of theory of the inferiority of the negro intellect? Certainly here there was abundant evidence of the very contrary: of complete mental parity in the negro with the white (31)."

Few missionaries could have been more active than the consumptive Mr Callender. In an entry in his *Journal*, made at Lucea on 3 July 1847, he noted:

> By calculation, the other day, to my no little amazement, I found that, during the last twelve weeks I have preached more than sixty different times and fifty different sermons, of which forty, or rather thirty-six, were composed and written carefully out, just as I would have required to have done at home; for this being a town congregation, it does not do to give them anything that may come to hand; nor do I consider that it would be faithful on my part to serve our great master "with that which cost me nothing." (50)

When the Rev. Mr Goldie, the Church of Scotland minister in Kingston, died at the end of 1847, Callender received the call, which he accepted for one year only; but as a Dissenter, he declined to accept the government stipend. "The gospel," he wrote, not "denominational distinctions" or "Presbyterian predilections" was what the people wanted to hear, so he determined not to "preach Presbytery"; instead, he continued, "I'll practise it and preach Christ as far as I can." And his preaching was apparently both acceptable and effective, to judge from the contents of his own *Journal*.

From the several sermons that he published (and occasional paraphrases, abstracts, and summaries) much of what Callender preached accorded with the Scottish common-sense school of philosophy and was well adapted to his congregations, whether in Kingston itself or in the parishes. Unfortunately, his apparent modesty restrained him from publishing all but a few of his many sermons and addresses, even though (as he states) they were all written out carefully—as was the custom of the time. This modesty, combined with a humanitarian motivation and a pragmatic philosophy, apparently assured Calender and his fellow Presbyterian missionaries of success that largely eluded their Anglican counterparts, though Sir George Rose offered a somewhat different explanation. His view was that

> The very habits of life, and the education of the missionary of the sects give him a marked advantage over our ecclesiastics in matters of conversion where those, who are to be the subjects of it, are of the description of the heathen Negroes. He is used to deal with ignorant men, and whose minds comprehend slowly; he knows how to unravel their half-intelligible jargon; and how to descry and aid the first glimmerings of their reason and conviction. None of these things can be expected from the graduated members of an English University. (15)

Another explanation of Callender's personal success as a preacher may be found in his systematic analysis of need and his orderly approach:

> Moral preaching has been so much the fashion here, that I am constrained to take for a little the other extreme and keep Christ *alone* before their eyes, both in the pulpit and the school, in meetings and in private. In public, on Sabbath forenoons, I am dwelling on the Messianic Psalms; in the afternoons, on Christ's parables. On Mondays, the evangelical prophets, and on Thursdays, the evangelists lead us to Him who is and ever must be the centre and sum of our preaching. (84)

Evidence suggests that Callender's ministerial addresses ranged from the briefest post-communion remarks to long, formal expositions and homilies that accorded with the nineteenth-century concept of the sermon as a literary genre proper. Occasionally he offered his listeners what he himself termed "travelling maxims," or a brief series of tags, in response to a direct or hypothetical question. On one occasion, in answer to the question, How should we prepare ourselves to enter the world? he advised his communicants in four heads: Advance, be alert; be hopeful, and be strong.

Elsewhere, he was far more traditional, and his sermons reflect, to a limited extent, some of the changes that the moderatism of the Secession movement had produced within the Calvinist Scottish church. He used familiar and frequent Biblical quotation and sometimes included references to the major poets (for example, he quotes Coleridge's impressions of the beauties of tropical landscape). But he does not really escape from the Calvinist concept of Christianity as a doctrinal religion; and in the distinctively educative tone of his sermons he follows the established tradition of the Scottish pulpit.

He was firm on the need to establish a clear understanding as the basis on which to build a sound Christian faith. Wesleyans and Baptists, he thought, tolerated their slave converts to act "on the impulse of feeling, not the dictate of Christian principle, or the decision of a well-judging knowledge"; and in consequence, he proposed that "their people, ignorant of Christian truth, and unguided by Christian principles, have fallen and are falling back from them." And there is a discernible self-conscious superiority in his conclusion that

> The principle on which Presbyterians, and they alone, are patiently acting is 'Impart knowledge before you expect faith—enlarge knowledge, that you may reap larger fruits of faith.' 'Tis nonsense to harangue an audience from the pulpit on a subject they do not understand, in a language with which they are but imperfectly acquainted. Every Presbyterian testifies that their preaching is useless to them to whose minds they have had no previous access in the Sabbath or weekday classes. Their testimony accords with the natural deductions of reason. (27-28).

Callender had very firm ideas on what his own approach to the audience should be. In the first place, since "the operation of the Spirit of God is everywhere similar," it followed that the black and white members should be dealt with alike, and that whether in ministry or mission, "the groundwork has to be laid, ere faith can live and actuate; viz., of that knowledge without which conversion is impossible, faith a delusion, Christianity nothing but a name." Of his black and slave congregants, Callender held high regard—some indications of this having already been provided; but after his move to Kingston, he found

Thomas P. Callender: Presbyterian Preacher in Jamaica 179

the "godless behaviour of the merchants and planters" to be "saddening," and he resolved to "try and lead their minds in a right direction ... to preach plainly and pointedly on the subject from Jeremiah 8:16, 'Give glory to the Lord,' and Amos 3:6, 'Shall there be evil in a city and the Lord hath not done it?'" He found, he said, that "the great majority of the Scotch are ungodly, and it may be the Spirit of Truth may point an arrow to the souls of some." For this audience he delivered a sermon (which he judged to be "appropriate") based on the two texts just mentioned and entitled "A Call to Immediate Repentance." In many ways it is representative of his straightforward, fervent, evangelical preaching.

After announcing his text, Callender briefly expounds on the intent of the Biblical author, quickly drawing his immediate audience with the question, "How does the thoughtless, perverse sinner still feel and speak when pressed with the message of the gospel and warned of the danger of neglect?" Then he moves boldly ahead, announcing his intention to speak candidly and directly:

> Convinced, as we are, that there are those before us that are still careless about the one thing needful, still unhumbled beneath the mighty hand of God, still deaf to the gospel call, we would seek to enter into the prophet's spirit, and whether ye will hear or whether ye will forbear, declare unto you the whole counsel of God and urge on your attention the importance of the necessity of giving honour to whom honour is due, even glory to that God from whom we are by nature alienated.

The divisions of the sermon are easy to follow: the preacher systematically subdivides his discussion of the text into five headings wherein he gives the correct means of glorifying God; next, he carries out the application of his text by presenting "the solemn motives" by which God enforces his ordinances. While "the sinner fancies he has an antidote," Callender says, by seeking pardon in a death-bed repentance, this is a "soul-ruining delusion," for God has said, "My spirit shall not always strive with man," and the sinner may find his experience to be that of Saul, who "found at length that God, from whom he had erred, had departed from him." Then, with frequent and pointed rhetorical questions the missionary relentlessly harangues his listeners to repent:

> What security have you, sinner, that God will not at any time—say tomorrow or tonight—in his anger at our present impenitence, seal up every fountain and shut you up to your hardness of heart? Where, then, your future repentance? Farewell every thought of it and every hope of light when God thus causes darkness.

The sermon continues in the same vain of urgent exhortation and provides two vignettes of notable detail that have the very characteristics that mark the seventeenth-century charactery of Overbury, Hall, and Earle. The first of these two florid word-pictures of "the foolish pilgrims to eternity" depicts "the giddy youth released from parental control." He

> walks in the delusive paths of sinful indulgence; following the heated guidance of his carnal appetites, his unhallowed lusts ... drinks sweetened poison and runs to riot with the noisy and the sensual.... In the haunts of vice, at the gaming table, or in the tavern ... he has fallen into disease and emaciation; and, horror-stricken, he would not repent; but, alas! he is on the dark mountains—he has erred. There is no friendly voice from on high.... Ah strange is the ease of a shattered constitution, a fevered, frenzied, dissipated intellect. Ease! Mark it in the bloated form, the laboured breathing, the glazed eye, the death-cold sweat, the awakened conscience, the clouded mind. Ease, alas! His is only the ease of the maniac, wandering ever in the madness of his thoughts over the items of a misspent life and visiting in his delirium even those regions to which he is doomed.

The second is a description of "the giddy daughter of vanity and fashion":

> She trips along so vauntingly in her tinsel and her beauty ... keeps in her room with her pleasant novel or her idle thoughts ... goes from her mirror, that altar of her self-idolatry to the round of her fashionable friends ... enters her favourite ballroom and exults in the feverish excitement of the dance; lounges in reckless frivolity amid the impurity and impiety of the theatre.... How is it possible for one accustomed only to frivolities, when at length frightened into involuntary, unchosen, sudden piety, to find the inclination or ease to believe and live! Heaven is not to be so easily purchased ... it is strange such a vain thought should delude a single soul.

Now, while the description of "the giddy youth released from parental control" might be rather cautionary, its excesses place it in the tradition of the melodramatic stereotype, notwithstanding its faint resemblance to life in contemporary reggae-saturated West Kingston; and the first half of the description of "the giddy daughter of vanity and fashion" could well have provided the inspiration for those sections of Claude McKay's *Home to Harlem* (1928) that drew condemnation from W. E. B. DuBois for catering to "prurient interests" and praise from others for picturing the realities of poverty-stricken black urban life.

But apart from these excesses, the remainder of the sermon progresses in an appropriately formal, though strong, tone. It is often punctuated by doubled elements, though seldom as pointed as in another sermon, "The Fulness of Christ," which contains the expression, "the strange scene of suffering and sadness, of darkness and death, where life and immortality opened up to human view." Even in the conclusion of the sermon there is further use of sustained rhetorical questioning, pithy and aphoristic summary, and metaphorical word-pictures, as the following lines illustrate:

> How would that which cost the Son of God his life be so lightly attained as by a deathbed sigh? ... Sowing the flesh, they can never reap the fruits of the Spirit; living to the world, they cannot die to God.... In the morning of life the business of giving glory to God is easy; then the heavenly penitential dews descend and dwell in the soul; but when the day is far spent and the heat of temptation has dried them up and they are gone, and the soil of the soul is parched and dry, if the business be begun at all, it will be severe labour; for every tear a struggle, for every desire a writhing; and even if the blessing be given, can the fruit to the praise of divine glory be other than stunted and poor?.... Prepare to meet thy God.

The achievement of the nonconformist missionaries in Jamaica is not readily to be assessed: contemporary records often overstate their successes, either from vanity or from ignorance of backsliding, or else understate them because of the prevalence of non-European cultural appurtenances and practices. But two tests were widely used: the extent of Christian marriage and the strength of African religious practice.

Many retired missionaries wrote in their reminiscences of life in Jamaica of their constant inveighing against what they interpreted as concubinage (though it was generally tolerated in the British noble class) and of their pleasure in officiating at Christian marriages; yet the circumstances of plantation life had militated against it, and emancipation made little change in a well-established way of life in which the substance of marriage was seen to be more important than the ceremony. Green reports that by the mid-1850's "stipendiary magistrates in Jamaica uniformly regretted that marriage ties were thoroughly disregarded by the peasants" (345), so that in this one respect Christian ministrations must be regarded as having been essentially ineffectual.[1] On the other hand, Ellis, the historian of the Episcopal Diocese of Jamaica, points out that the nonconformist missionaries' efforts had been "sufficient to prevent Obeahism from becoming a religion or a creed like Voudouism" (220), and hence their efficacy could be clearly established.

Yet it must be remembered that the nonconformists were few in number and widely scattered throughout Jamaica, so that what "progress" they might claim was often disputed or deprecated by other churchmen. In a sermon delivered in Kingston in April 1858, just a decade after Callender's own ministry began in that city, Bishop Courtenay commented:

> We are in Jamaica in a land but partially reclaimed from heathenism—from heathen superstition and licentiousness ... those we would convert in understanding are children, while in malice they are men. Unable to read and write—without books, without instruction, without external control, unintellectual, immoral—the baser impulses of human nature are indulged without restraint either from a sense of shame or of religious obligation. (4)

But the reverend gentleman apparently saw nothing inconsistent in his not having welcomed just those whom he castigated into the fellowship of his communion, or having observed proscriptions against providing the Blacks with instruction and mission schools. At least Callender and his associates understood the nature of the problem and attempted to solve it, and hence must, by comparison, be adjudged liberal, pragmatic, and even enlightened.

If, as Lewis O. Brastow, an early professor of practical theology at Yale University believed, "the best missionaries are those who are interested in the presentation of Christianity to the actual needs of men and to the conditions of life as they find them" (85), Callender could justly be included in their number as also in any pantheon of Presbyterian clergy ministering in the interests of Christendom, for he amply meets the criteria established by Voltaire and paraphrased by Oliver Goldsmith in his essay "On Eloquence" that appeared in the *Bee* in 1759:

> The good preacher should adopt no model, write no sermons, study no periods; let him but understand his subject, the language he speaks, and be convinced of the truths he delivers. It is amazing to what heights eloquence of this kind may reach! This is that eloquence the ancients represented as lightning, baring down every opponent; this the power which has turned whole assemblies into astonishment, admiration, and awe ... eloquence is the gift of nature.

NOTES

[1] At the 1971 meeting of the Association for Commonwealth Language and Literature conference held at the University of the West Indies in Kingston, Jamaica, Professor Edward Kamau Brathwaite made the point, in a plenary session, that at the time some 80 per cent of Jamaicans were born out of wedlock (in the Western sense). Sociologists nowadays recognise the existence of a quite responsible extended family system in Jamaica and the West Indies as well as in most other non-European-based black communities. However, sociologists and family-welfare professionals in the United States inveigh against out-of-wedlock births as the cause of multifarious social problems.

WORKS CITED

Brastow, Lewis O. *The Modern Pulpit*. New York: Macmillan, 1906.

Caldecott, Alfred. *The Church in the West Indies*. London: Society for Promoting Christian Knowledge, 1898.

Callender, Thomas P. *Memoirs of the Late Rev. Thomas P. Callender, Missionary to Jamaica. With Selections from His Pulpit*

Discourses and Communion Addresses. Edinburgh: Oliphant, 1850.

Carlisle, Warrand. *Twenty-Eight Years' Mission Life in Jamaica: A Brief Sketch.* London: Nisbet, 1884.

Cubberley, Ellwood P. *Readings in the History of Education.* Boston: Houghton, 1948.

Ellis, J. B. *The Diocese of Jamaica: A Short Account of Its History, Growth, and Organisation.* London: Society for Promoting Christian Knowledge, 1913.

Green, William. *British Slave Emancipation.* Oxford: Clarendon P, 1976.

Houser, Henry. *An Exact Model or Platform of Good Magistracy: or a Sermon.* London: Francis Tyson, 1673.

Klingberg, Frank Joseph. *Codrington Chronicle: An Experiment in Anglican Altruism on a Barbados Plantation, 1710-1834.* Berkeley: University of California P, 1949.

Rose, G. H. *A Letter on the Means and Importance of Converting the Slaves in the West Indies to Christianity.* London: Murray, 1823.

Samuel, Peter. *The Wesleyan-Methodist Missions in Jamaica, and Honduras, Delineated.* London: Partridge, 1850.

12. Public Address and Commonwealth Literature

Melvil Dewey, in compiling his decimal system for library classification, assigned 815 to American oratory and 825 to English oratory (including the English-language oratory of all countries outside the United States), thereby acknowledging that public address, or public discourse (as oratory is sometimes referred to nowadays) constitutes one of the principal genres of literature—in his scheme, subordinate only to poetry, drama, fiction, and the essay, and taking precedence over letters, satire and humour, and miscellaneous writings, and presumably also over biography and autobiography, since they were relegated to historical studies.

But in Commonwealth literary studies, for the recent past, research and criticism have been increasingly restricted to poetry and prose fiction. The explanations are generally tenable: poetry abounds, either in journals or in small volumes—often privately published—and is readily evaluated in even a short article; the substantial financial investment in publishing a collection of short stories or a novel indicates that there has been some sort of literary judgment that the work merits the capital expenditure involved, and the public in general is keen to read *about* fictions, even if it is not prepared to read them.

Furthermore, there has developed a belief that the Great Tradition in English literature has continued in the present century in only a severely attenuated form: great poetry presumably ended with W. B. Yeats and T. S. Eliot, major essays with J. B. Priestley and George Orwell, and drama with G. B. Shaw, Sean O'Casey, and John Galsworthy. Satire has, of course, done well as a mode: John Betjeman, A. D. Hope, V. S. Naipaul, and others have continued the tradition of humorous, critical, sardonic writing perhaps best represented in English by Swift, Pope, Wilde, and Dickens. The literary letter—and even agreeable personal correspondence—has apparently passed on. But despite oversight, the great tradition of public address in English did not disappear at the end of the eighteenth century: it has been continued in large measure in the new nations of the Commonwealth, which are coming to grips with the same issues that evoked the heated debates and memorable speeches of the older countries in time now long distant.

Admittedly, the proper consideration for Commonwealth oratory has been hampered by the general unavailability of the texts of even major colonial and national speeches; but this impediment is now finally being overcome. Already there are a few collections of speeches, such as *Australia Speaks* (1969) and *Representative South African Speeches: The Rhetoric of Race and Religion* (1980), which include examples of speeches from parliament, pulpit, platform, and bar that illustrate the rhetorical forms of deliberative, forensic, and epideictic speeches. Yet what has been done for Australia and South Africa will have to be done also for the remaining countries of the Commonwealth if public address is to regain the place it once enjoyed in the study of literature in English.

Few students of English literature would feel adequately trained without some appreciation of Donne's sermons or the parliamentary speeches of Sheridan, Fox, Burke, Disraeli, and Churchill; few students of American literature would consider themselves fully acquainted with their subject unless they had read the sermons of John Witherspoon, Henry Ward Beecher, and Jonathan Edwards or the political speeches of Patrick Henry, Benjamin Franklin, Abraham Lincoln, and Franklin D. Roosevelt. Likewise, students of Commonwealth literature should feel obliged to become acquainted with the great speakers and speeches of their chosen field of study: and important practitioners of the rhetorical art are to be found in each of the Commonwealth countries, for all have experienced social, political, or economic crises of sufficient magnitude to call forth the best in their leaders' thoughts, organization, and style and resulted in speeches of at least national importance—and in some instances of international and lasting significance.

Canadian public address has, somehow, almost totally evaded academic study; yet there are, of course, great issues and great speakers in Canadian history. Perhaps the most outstanding figures in the period immediately after the American Revolution were William Lyon Mackenzie, a fiery, tempestuous, eloquent advocate of an elected legislature after the American style; Robert Gourlay, a dynamic speaker who was eventually expelled from Upper Canada in 1819 for having tried to arouse the farmers against government land-settlement policy; Robert Baldwin, leader of the faction that advocated moderate reform and the adoption of the British form of responsible self-government; and Egerton Ryerson, who persuaded the strong Methodist wing of the Reform Party to endorse and then espouse the Tory platform. In Lower Canada the reform movement was led by the speaker of the Assembly, Louis Joseph Papineau, who sought control of revenue and thereby of government policy. Later, Papineau moved beyond his reformist position and began to speak darkly of revolution and advocacy of an America-style constitution, his violent words inflaming his supporters to the extent that they formed groups known as Sons of Liberty (in imitation of American revolutionary brigades). Tension rose, and Papineau was ultimately forced to flee to the United States. Clearly, his persuasive speeches would be worthy of study, and particularly as precursors of the speeches of the Quebec Separatists.

Although there was less unrest in the Maritimes, the movement for reform in an orderly fashion was led by Joseph Howe, editor of *The Nova Scotian* and (in speeches in his own defense against a charge of libel) one of the important early orators. Howe's *Poems and Essays* (1874) established him as a competent belle-lettrist, potential short-story writer, provincial poet, and (in his essay "Eloquence") advocate of a dignified, vigorous, allusive, and didactic style. Of Howe's own style Fred

Cogswell has observed that it is well adapted to his audiences and "does credit to the intelligence of the working man in the Maritimes during the nineteenth century" (116).

Howe's sponsorship of Thomas Chandler Haliburton resulted in the development of one of the most original talents of the first era of Canadian literature. As barrister, parliamentarian, and judge, Haliburton was a vigorous, indefatigable speaker, representing the more aristocratic, conservative school of thought.

Practically every speaker in the Confederation debates of 1865 appears to have spoken in logical terms: Joseph Royal represented the main rational approach by emphasising defense against the United States. Virtually the only emotional voice was that of Thomas D'Arcy McGee, "the chief orator and literary man among the 'Founding Fathers of Confederation,' who brought Ontario, Quebec, New Brunswick, and Nova Scotia into a national union," as Carl Klinck has written (155). McGee's speeches are splendid, moving orations, and his phrases have become a part of the Canadian idiom. On numerous occasions his Irish gift for language and speech visibly and effectively moved his audiences, whether workingmen or "an enchanted legislature," as Arthur Meighan once described it.

However, Sir John A. Macdonald, the first prime minister of Canada, a respected Conservative, was highly regarded for his unflagging speaking for national unity and independence—independent of the United States yet tied firmly to "the sovereignty of Her Majesty," so that "The executive authority of government shall be vested in the sovereign of the United Kingdom of Great Britain and Ireland, and be administered according to the well-understood principles of the British constitution, "as he said in his crucial speech to parliament in 1865. This impressive oration richly deserves its place in *The World's Great Speeches* (1942).

A generation after Macdonald, Sir Wilfrid Laurier became prime minister, leading a Liberal government. Not surprisingly, he was a stalwart supporter of Great Britain in World War I, but he opposed conscription, and he delivered many memorable speeches against it. One of Laurier's best speeches is "Canada,

England, and the United States," which he delivered in Chicago on 9 October 1899, in which he said, in part,

> There was a civil war in the last century. There was a civil war between England and her American colonies, and their relations were severed ... through no fault of your fathers; the fault was altogether the fault of the British government of that day. If the British government of that day had treated the American colonies as the British government of the last twenty or fifty years has treated its colonies; if Great Britain had given you then the same degree of liberty which it gives to Canada, my country; if it had given you, as it has given us, legislative independence absolute, the result would have been different—the course of victory, the course of history, would have been different. But what has been done cannot be undone.

Laurier makes extensive use of the hypothetical syllogism, of repetition, and of propositions of common ground before concluding with a rhetorical question that invites cooperation "in the defense of the oppressed, for the enfranchisement of the downtrodden, and for the advancement of liberty, progress, and civilization." Here he effectively touches American national aspirations through allusions to traditional slogans and simultaneously raises Canadian, British, and American goals from the regional to the universal level.

Like his predecessors as prime minister, Sir Robert Borden was a stolid Conservative and advocate of Canadian cooperation with Britain—especially in World War I. His chauvinism was unquestioned, and is well seen in his speech to a patriotic meeting in London in August 1915, "The Voice of the Empire," which—predictably—is replete with emotional proofs.

But following the Great War fashions changed in politics as in all else, and political speeches soon took on a somewhat different content and tone. Depression, European rearmament, then another war became the focus of public address worldwide.

In his essay "The Writer and His Public, 1920-1960," a chapter in the *Literary History of Canada: Canadian Literature in English*, Desmond Pacey points out that

> The First World War effectually obliterated in Canada whatever traces of "high colonialism" had survived the boom of the first decade

of the twentieth century and the bitter debates over Reciprocity with the United States and the Navy Bill for Empire defence. The War shattered the core of common beliefs and attitudes suggested by the adjective "high": the mood of Canada in 1918 and 1919 was angry, skeptical, and restless. And if Canadians were not yet sure what role they wished their country to play in the world, they were virtually all agreed that it should not be that of a colony.

Change was everywhere. The Easter riots of 1918 in Quebec over conscription, the angry demonstrations of the United Farmers of Ontario in May 1918, the break of western labour with the Trades and Labour Congress and the formation of the One Big Union, the Winnipeg strike in 1919 ... the death of Sir Wilfrid Laurier and the retirement of Sir Robert Borden: these events combined to transform the traditional image of Canadian society beyond recognition. The new Canada had new leaders—William Lyon Mackenzie King of the Liberals, Arthur Meighen of the Conservatives, T. A. Crerar and J. S. Woodsworth of the Progressives—and there was general hopefulness that they might find new solutions to the old problems. For the old problems did remain: the problems of the relations between French and English Canada, between the provinces and the federal government, between Canada and the British Empire. (477)

This environment would normally call forth oratory of memorable content and admirable style, but it seems to have been largely unproductive—perhaps because of the Canadian predisposition to moderation, amelioration, and compromise. And Mackenzie King, who was to dominate Canadian political life for almost thirty years, was respected for his palliation rather than for his being a dogmatist, a demagogue. Nonetheless, his speeches deserve more detailed study than they have so far received, since they demonstrate that political life can accommodate a paraclete as well as a firebrand.

Likewise, Louis St. Laurent (1882-1973), Canadian prime minister from 1948 to 1957, when his Liberal Party government was defeated by the Progressive Conservative Party, led by John Diefenbaker, was a quiet yet effective speaker and leader. Both before and after his parliamentary career, St. Laurent was a successful lawyer, generally acknowledged as a formidable opponent. (He was a Laval University law graduate and had declined a Rhodes Scholarship as well as positions on the bench.) He led the fight for construction of the Saint Lawrence Seaway and first proposed the formation of N.A.T.O.; and with Lester B. Pearson, he attempted to resolve the Suez Canal crisis in 1956.

Prime Minister Pierre Elliott Trudeau was a great pragmatist and a fluent speaker in both English and French, so that he was able to mollify the Quebecois and satisfy the remainder of Canada with his policies that tried to steer an "independent" Canada between the Scylla and Charybdis of Cold War foes. Even within the Commonwealth he was noted as a calm and honest mediator, a broker of fidelity and character. As he said in the speech to the Commonwealth Heads of Government meeting in Ottawa on 2 August 1973,

> Since men and women first gained the gift of speech, they have been aware of the importance of wise counsel and of the value of communicating honestly and fully with their neighbours. Today ... the need to understand one another has become critical.
>
> None of us in the Commonwealth is so powerful or so self-sufficient that he is able to act independently of the opinion or the assistance of others.... The Commonwealth is for many of us our window on the world. Over the years its importance will deepen largely because it has no specific role, but emphasizes instead the value of the human relationship.

When he addressed a joint session of the United States Congress on 22 February 1977, Trudeau stressed that the separatist movement in Quebec was bound to fail, and that "Canada's unity will not be fractured." He cited the need for "repatriation" of Canada's constitution through abrogation of the British North America Act; and he stressed that though there were occasional differences between the two countries, Canada and the United States were closely allied. His twenty-minute speech was twice applauded.

It would be of considerable interest to have a collection of speeches by Canadian-Indian speakers, for there were many influential leaders of the several Indian nations during the Seven Years' War, especially. In the United States Tecumseh, the Shawnee, and Red Jacket, of the Six Nations, were accomplished orators; they undoubtedly had their equivalents north of the forty-second parallel.

Towards the end of the nineteenth century Canadian cities and towns supported their series of lectures after the fashion of the Lyceum and Chautauqua movements in the United States or of the Schools of Arts and Mechanics' Institutes in Australia and the United Kingdom, but there seems to have been no study of the speakers involved in them. In all probability their style of presentation was not remarkably different from that found in America and the subject matter but little changed. With few exceptions, it seems that the common-sense tone and style prevailed over the florid and lofty—except in the Presbyterian sermons of the Maritime preachers.

In more recent times, Mackenzie King, Lester Pearson, Louis St. Laurent, John Diefenbaker and Pierre Elliott Trudeau have achieved some renown as speakers, and it would be well to have their best speeches collected and subjected to rigorous literary or rhetorical criticism. As Gordon Thomas noted some years ago,

> Although Canadian history has not been as richly productive of historical events in which public speaking has played a central and crucial part as has been true in the history of the United States, it is nonetheless true that it is far from being devoid of such moments. Canada's history has often been exciting and frequently controversial. (7)

Confederation and separatism are undoubtedly major national subjects that could be expected to produce major national speeches, but even greater is that of world peace in a nuclear age—the theme of most of the mature discourses of both Pearson and Trudeau, who have also been seen as voices of the nonaligned and small nations (if not necessarily of the underdeveloped ones).

"In New Zealand, any fine elusion of a fine mind stands out like a pretty deed in a dark world, an outward and audible sign of an inner and cultural grace" according to Professor Kenneth Melvin, author of numerous studies of the national educational and cultural scene (130-31). Notwithstanding, there have been many effective speakers in church, legislature, and courtroom, if not so obviously on the platform. The main subjects have been native policy, representative government, land policy, socialist legislation, and—most recently—adaptation to the European common market.

The great tradition of Bishop G. A. Selwyn, outspoken critic of Earl Grey's native and land policies and indefatigable missionary, was carried on for a while by similar clerics: Dr. Rutherford Waddell of Dunedin might be considered one of his intellectual descendants, though his *The Voyage of Life: Four Addresses on Certain Aspects of It* (1907) is somewhat more literary in its style (quoting Stevenson, W. E. Henley, and Matthew Arnold, "the most characteristic poet of our age").

Political oratory in New Zealand has produced some speeches worth reading. Sir George Grey's *The Policy of the Future: Not Class Against Class* (1877), delivered in the House of Representatives is a thoughtful analysis of the subject phrased in deliberate and sedate language. Scobie Mackenzie has been described as "perhaps the best public speaker" of the turn of the century, his speeches being considered "excellent, showing careful thought and great ability ... they have a real rhetorical force and genuine humour. They have, moreover, a literary charm about them, a feature the more pleasing because it is not common," in the opinion of the early critic William Gisborne (306).

Since the beginning of this century, speakers worthy of some study might include John A. Lee, who was expelled from the Labour Party; W. B. Seetch, whose major statements are included in *Colony or Nation: Addresses and Papers* (1966); Walter Savage; Julius Vogel; John R. Marshall; Prime Minister Muldoon; and—by association—Lord Cabham, whose speeches given during his term as governor-general (1957-62) were edited by O. S. Hintz.

Yet for the student of literature the greatest interest may attach to the speeches of W. Pember Reeves and James Edward FitzGerald, the associate and correspondent of John Ruskin, William Ewart Gladstone, and Charles Kingsley, and one-time undersecretary at the British Museum. Reproached by Grey for "striving to transport the old world in portions to the new," he nonetheless exerted a considerable influence on the development of the "small utopia": "In political assemblies noted for their oratory he won fame as a speaker—fluent, eloquent, though to the modern taste sometimes over-rhetorical," in the judgment of E. H. McCormick, author of *New Zealand Literature: A Survey* (19).

The West Indies seem to have provided great opportunity for sermons, more slight for political speeches until recently, and almost none for the expository or entertaining speech of the platform. (Of the most celebrated courtroom speeches, such as those in the trial of Paul Bogle and similar early leaders of opposition to slavery—like George Gordon—there are only paraphrases and summaries.) As Arthur Pollard observes in *English Sermons*, "Through the centuries the tradition of great preaching has developed, and it continues in our time ... but today the sermon is not noticed as it used to be.... Nor do people read sermons as they used to do" (53). In the Anglophone Caribbean, perhaps because of the rather special role of the clergy in society, the sermon continues to be published and read, studied and quoted.

The special place of the sermon in West Indian society can be assumed to have derived from Oliver Cromwell's injunction to the leaders of his expedition to Santo Domingo in 1655 to assure "the propagation of true religion" of "teachers, men gifted in the knowledge of Jesus Christ" who would "inform and enlarge the gospel." But most of the sermons of the period were clearly designed for the semi-literate white settlers and their administrative superiors rather than the more numerous slave population, as is suggested by both the content and title of the earliest extant published sermon from Jamaica, one preached on 1 February 1671 by the Rev. Henry Houser, entitled *An Exact Model or Platform of Good Magistracy*.

Because the West Indian church was little more than an extension of the State, sermons in the Caribbean colonies were rather like those in Britain itself: "The circumstances under which they were preached, as well as the character of the preachers" made them "examples, par excellence, of propagandist literature. They were not counsels of perfection or dogmatic expositions" (Kirby 528).[1] The Church of England saw no disparity between Christian doctrine and the institution of slavery, and the Society for the Propagation of the Gospel in Foreign Parts even operated its own plantation, Codrington, on Barbados, with slave labour.

In the eighteenth century Nonconformist missionaries started preaching in the West Indies, and their sermons are clearly more emotional and energetic than those of the Episcopalian clergy—and more successful. This success was laid by Sir George Rose to the Nonconformists' ability to adapt to the inferior intellects of blacks and indentured servants and to the disadvantage of logical and classical education suffered by Established Church missionaries and ministers. The Rev. G. Nash of Grenada thought that most Anglican sermons seemed to slaves and workingmen "as if delivered in a foreign tongue," but perhaps as significant was their constant opposition to singing, dancing, "vain shows and loose festivals," and their unrelenting support for the planter aristocracy and of slavery itself.

Ultimately, the Nonconformists (Baptists, Moravians, Wesleyans, and Presbyterians) built up respectable congregations who attended to sermons as means of obtaining knowledge that was otherwise rigorously proscribed. And with the passage of years the Church of England clergy have attempted to regain communication with the people, especially in Jamaica, where Lena Kent, the poet, published two volumes of sermons (*Seed for the Sower*, 1960), designed to be read privately or by small groups or used as models for untrained preachers. In a foreword to *Goodness and Mercy* (1969), a similar compendium by the Rev. K. D. Carnegie, this bishop of Jamaica alluded to Lena Kent's books as the first contemporary collections of sermons. That a second collection by Mr Carnegie (*The House of the Lord*, 1971) was published could attest to the vitality of the sermon as a literary form in Jamaica, where charismatic Baptist congregations abound.

Yet political oratory has surely dominated Caribbean public discourses. And this raises problems for the serious student, for until very recent times West Indian politicians spoke extemporaneously or impromptu and kept neither notes nor manuscript copies of speeches. As a result, we have almost none of the major addresses by such speakers as Albert Gomes, Captain Cipriani, Sir Alexander Bustamante, and even the mercurial Sir Eric Gairy that were not delivered in parliamentary situations. Many speeches of Cheddi Jagan and the major political figures of the newer, smaller island nations are to be obtained in the form of mimeographed leaflets only: but they are often rare publications and unavailable even in the libraries of the University of the West Indies or the several national libraries and archival repositories. Clearly, then, there is great need for rhetorical research and anthologies to support the scholarly investigation of early West Indian public speaking, including preaching.

In recent years, a number of the Caribbean nations have started to provide for future students of West Indian public address by issuing collections of their leaders' speeches. Noteworthy among them are the following volumes: *A Collection of Addresses* (1968), by Sir Hugh Wooding, Chief Justice of Trinidad and Tobago; *Forged From the Love of Liberty: Selected Speeches of Dr. Eric Williams*, edited by Paul K. Sutton (1981), which includes most of the major speeches issued earlier in pamphlet form; *A Destiny to Mould: Selected Discourses by the Prime Minister of Guyana* (1970), which covers the early and less controversial period of Forbes Burnham's premiership; *Forward Ever!: Three Years of the Grenadian Revolution. Speeches of Maurice Bishop* (1982); *The Faith that Moved the Mountain* (1979), speeches and essays by Randolph Fawkes of Bahamas; and *Manley and the New Jamaica: Selected Speeches and Writings, 1938-1968*, skilfully edited and introduced by Professor Rex Nettleford. To these must, in time, be added the speeches of the eastern Caribbean leaders who advocated and then defended the United States intervention in Grenada during 1983—especially those of Mrs Eugenia Charles of Dominica—and of Prime Minister George Price of Belize (a poet of some achievement) and his outspoken critic, Evan X. Hyde, essayist, dramatist, poet, and journalist.

Perhaps no area of Commonwealth public address has been more carefully considered than that from South Asia; the importance of public speeches in the political and social movements of the past century have indubitably given the illiterate masses a keen appreciation of effective oratory and given the socially conscious intelligentsia a special awareness for well-argued cases, sound evidence, practicality in problem-solving, and the development of style. Although, in general terms, Indian public address may be said to have commenced in the eighteenth century with the great courtroom dramas of the trial of Warren Hastings and the tribulations of the begums of Oudh, the tradition of Indian eloquence antedates these, and has long been closely associated with both the drama and religion.

S. C. De, author of *Public Speeches in Ancient and Medieval India*, after noting the development of rhetoric and public address in Greece and Rome, reminds his readers that long arguments composed in characteristic and even prescribed style and accompanied with cogent argumentation and development are to be found in the traditional Sanskrit and Prakrit literatures of India; and he further observes that

> Though forensic oratory and eloquent appeal to the masses are rare in the literature of ancient and medieval India, it may be stated that carefully prepared speeches addressed to select audiences are to be found specially in the epics, where good speaking is highly lauded and where Rama, for example, is described as expert in speaking, Bharata as the greatest of orators, Hunaman as skillful in speech, and Krishna as the greatest of speakers and most skillful in elocution. (6)

Then, from an examination of numerous speeches from Indian traditional literature and of such works as the *Alankara-Kaustubha* (a rhetorical treatise) of the dramatist-rhetorician Kavikarnapura (born 1524 in Kanchanapalli), he infers that analogy, metaphor, antithesis, interrogation, sarcasm, and hyperbole are the favoured tropes; Sanskrit authors and speakers regarded "hyperbole as the best of the figures of speech" (98), and so idealization and exaggeration became the almost universal marks of Indian public address.

At the end of the nineteenth century, with the burgeoning of the movement for Indian independence, the great nationalist orators Mohandas K. Gandhi, B. C. Tilak, and G. K. Gokhale established themselves as pre-eminent speakers, and their printed speeches exerted a persuasive influence far beyond their immediate audiences and at the same time influenced the formation of a characteristically Indian and Hindu rhetorical method, one that amalgamated Brahmin analytic philosophy, *satyagraha,* and incredible patience that results from an emphasis rather on the spiritual than on the material, immediate, and visible.

Professor K. R. S. Iyengar, in his *Indian Writing in English,* devotes several pages to a discussion of the major Indian speakers and notes that just before World War I "A good English speech ... attracted only a few hundreds, perhaps a thousand or two; but it was a fit intellectual audience." (358). And the adaptation to great masses by Gandhiji and Jawaharlal Nehru never seemed to eliminate the intellectual content of their speeches—a point made in a Ph.D. dissertation by Professor Agnes G. Doody of the University of Rhode Island on the speeches of Nehru, and by C. D. Narasimhaiah of the University of Mysore, editor of selected Nehru speeches. Whereas most Western speakers appear to choose between simplistic statements for mass audiences or reasonably erudite and intellectually demanding ones for select, small groups, Indian speakers have somehow managed to address both audiences in the one discourse.

Of the great stature of Tilak there is no dispute: whether in Marathi or English he seemed equally at ease, and Sri Aurobindo (himself a distinguished speaker) declared Tilak's speeches "straightforward, lucid ... like a series of self-evident propositions," even if it was his celebrated twenty-one-hour courtroom speech in self-defense (1908). Lord Minto declared that there were, in England in 1906, few speakers of the stature of Gokhale or of his unusual gift of parliamentary advocacy and persuasion. And Gokhale's protégé, Srinivasa Sastri, who was categorized by competent critics as "the Empire's silver-tongued orator," "an artist in words," "the greatest Indian orator of his day," and (in Tagore's words) "like a stream speaking," was truly a gifted speaker—and writer—who repays thoughtful reading.

Fortunately, the modern Indian interest in printed speeches has equalled the interest in oral, delivered ones; as a consequence, we have accurate texts available. Some can be recommended: *Speeches and Writings of Gopal Krishna Gokhale* (1966), *The Select Gokhale* (1968), *Speeches of President V. V. Giri* (1974), *Selected Speeches of Lal Bahadur Shastri* (1974), *President Zakir Husain's Speeches* (1973), *Speeches of President Rajendra Prasad* (1972), *President Radhakrishnan's Speeches and Writings* (1969), and both *The Years of Challenge* and *The Years of Endeavour* (1975), selected speeches of Indira Gandhi. To these should, of course, be added the collected speeches of Gandhi, Nehru, and Bal Gangadhar Tilak at least, and some would add to the list speeches by Swami Vivekananda, Ramaswami Aiyar (Dewan of Travancore), Lajpat Rai, and even Subhas Chandra Bose. The list could be extended, for public speaking in India is a major genre of literature, and it has been developed to an extraordinary degree of excellence just at a time when it has declined in the older democracies.

The Muslim politicians of British India could be said to have worked within a somewhat different oratorical tradition,[2] and because their leadership roles (except in Bengal, Hyderabad, and Punjab) were generally less significant than those of Hindus, their speeches received more regional and parochial than national attention and influence. Notwithstanding, some of the early speeches of Mahomed Ali Jinnah have merit as oratorical literature, though those in *Speeches as Governor-General of Pakistan, 1947-1948* (1949) are rather insipid, pedestrian statements—perhaps the result of his new role. On the other hand, *Bangladesh, My Bangladesh: Selected Speeches and Statements* (1972), a collection of thirty speeches by Mujibur Rahman, and the speeches of Zulfikar Ali Bhutto evince enthusiasm, vitality, and at times a frenetic quality that is wholly absent in the staid discourses of Yahya Khan, Liaquat Ali Khan, Mohammed Ali Zia, and Ayub Khan. Doubtless the long absence of democratic conditions in Pakistan and Bangladesh accounts for the absence of confrontational or reformist-revolutionary rhetoric there, but one might expect that the leadership would use occasions of public communication to exhort, inveigle, or inspire.

Speeches in English appear to have been uncommon and undistinguished in Ceylon, at least until the recent past, when

Prime Minister Mrs Bandaranaike delivered several of some merit during periods of internecine disturbances. Prior to these speeches, perhaps the only ones to merit recognition are some by James Alwis (1823-78), who achieved considerable renown as parliamentarian, lawyer, lecturer, and general savant. Well-read in British legal and political speeches, Alwis developed a style that was indebted to the long phrases and scholarly elaboration of the eighteenth-century parliamentarians, even though he was a noted defender of the integrity of Sinhalese. In general, writes Professor Yasmine Gooneratne, of Macquarie University, Alwis's literary activities "extended from the literary essay and the public lecture to the political speech; his practice of invoking established custom in the aid of reform [and] his concern that his speeches should be accurately reported stemmed in part from his awareness that the smooth sentences were the product of years of labour" (137-38). Unfortunately, a collection of his speeches has yet to be published.

African speakers in English have been legion for a century now, and many of them are represented by printed collections: D. D. T. Jabavu, Sir Abubakar Tafewa Balewa, Edward Blyden, Casely Hayford, Kwame Nkrumah, Nnamdi Azikiwi, Obafemi Awolowo, Tom Mboya, Milton Obote, Julius Nyerere, Jomo Kenyatta, and Kenneth Kaunda, for example. But I have already commented on these elsewhere.[3]

The magnitude of the task of reading and evaluating the speeches of the Commonwealth is perhaps now apparent; and since Hong Kong, Malaysia, Brunei, Malta, Seychelles, Mauritius, Papua New Guinea, and similar less-familiar nations have not even been included in this brief conspectus, there is clearly material for as many as are interested in studying public address as a branch of Commonwealth literature.

NOTES

[1] Alfred Caldecott, in *The Church in the West Indies* (London: Society for the Propagation of Christian Knowledge, 1898), states quite categorically that "Many were much better qualified to be retailers of salt fish or boatswains to privateers than ministers of the Gospel" (59).

[2] A convenient brief introduction to the Muslim rhetorical tradition is to be found in H. Samuel Hamod, "Arab and Moslem Rhetorical Theory and Practice," *Central States Speech Journal* 14.2 (May 1963): 88-99.

[3] Marian B. McLeod, "The Development of African Oratory in English," *African Literature in English: Development and Identity*, ed. A. L. McLeod. Philadelphia: African Studies Association, 1991, 29-47. See also Arthur L. Smith, "Markings of an African Concept of Rhetoric," *Today's Speech* 19.2 (Spring 1971): 13-18.

WORKS CITED

Cogswell, Fred. "Literary Activity in the Maritime Provinces (1815-1880)." *Literary History of Canada: Canadian Literature in English*. Ed. Carl F. Klinck. Toronto: University of Toronto P, 1967. 102-24.

De, S. C. *Public Speeches in Ancient and Medieval India: Based on Sanskrit and Prakrit Literature*. Delhi: Ajanta, 1932, rpt. 1976.

Doody, Agnes G. "Spokesman for India: A Rhetorical Study of the Speeches of Jawaharlal Nehru." Diss. Pennsylvania State U. 1958.

Gisborne, William. *New Zealand Rulers and Statesmen: From 1840 to 1897*. London: Sampson, 1897.

Gooneratne, M. Y. *English Literature in Ceylon, 1815-1878*. Dehiwala: Tisara Prakasakayo, 1968.

Iyengar, K. R. Srinivasa. *Indian Writing in English*. New York: Asia, 1962.

Klinck, Carl F. "Literary Activity in Canada East and West (1841-1880)." *Literary History of Canada: Canadian Literature in English*. Ed. Carl F. Klinck. Toronto: University of Toronto P, 1967. 145-62.

McCormick, E. H. *New Zealand Literature: A Survey*. London: OUP, 1959.

Melvin, Kenneth. "Education." *The Pattern of New Zealand Culture*. Ed. A. L. McLeod. Melbourne: OUP, 1968. 98-131.

Pollard, Arthur. *English Sermons*. London: Longmans, for the British Council and the National Book League, 1963.

Thomas, Gordon. "Canadian Public Address." Paper delivered at the Speech Association of the Central States convention, 15 April 1962.

13. Maurice Bishop: The Voice of the Grenada Revolution

The events of 13 March 1979 in Grenada, though startling to many extra-Caribbean observers, were really the culmination of an inexorable logic to others: they were the inevitable consequences of the long, personal, and eccentric administration of Sir Eric Gairy, who (the *New York Times* reported) frequently made the anachronistic claim that he ruled by divine right and with direct instructions from God (sometimes referred to as "the Great Supreme Architect," at others as "the Great Supreme Divine Master"). These events were more than a simple rebellion, which does not bring structural change, or a political revolution, which does not transform the social structure: they amounted to a social revolution. And such social revolutions, Theda Skocpol notes,

> are rapid, basic transformations of a society's state and class structures; and they are accompanied and in part carried through by class-based revolts from below. Social revolutions are set apart from other sorts of conflicts and transformative processes above all by the combination of two coincidences: the coincidence of societal structural change with class upheaval, and the coincidence of political with social transformation. (4)

Such social revolutions depend, in large measure, on intellectual, articulate leadership skilled in the practice of political rhetoric. The French revolution had its Danton and its Robespierre; the Russian revolution had its Lenin and its Trotsky; and the Grenada revolution had its Jacqueline Creft and Maurice Bishop. Perhaps they had heard of Mirabeau's famous speech of 1789 to the Etats de Provence in which he railed against the greed and intransigence of the established government, saying, "Privileges shall have an end, but the people is eternal." The intransigence of the French resulted in lasting change in their social structure; now in Grenada the people had reached the limits of their toleration and looked to Bishop and his colleagues for redress.

In a speech to literacy workers on 14 June 1982, Minister of Education Jacqueline Creft said,

> We cannot stress enough the need to master language. Our process, as you know, is a very *oral* one, through which we expect our people always to speak out, to suggest, to criticise, and to overcome the timidity and passivity forced upon us....
>
> Since our revolution is a revolution in ways of communicating, consulting, organising, criticising, and planning, the language arts that we learn must give us the capacity to master all those aspects. (qtd. in Searle 70)

Fortunately, Maurice Bishop was able to provide in himself a paradigm of the revolution's goal. In 1956 he won a scholarship to Presentation College, Grenada's Roman Catholic secondary school, where he eventually became president of the student council, editor of the school newspaper, and president of the historical and debating societies; subsequently, he and Bernard Coard, who attended the Grenada Boys Secondary School, founded the Grenada Assembly of Youth After Truth, "an organization designed to bridge the confessional differences between the two secondary schools and to enable the students of both institutions to address the important questions of the day" (Schoenhals and Melanson 22). When Bishop graduated from high school, he went to London and read for his LL.B., graduating in 1969. But while in England he continued his social activism as president of the West Indian Students' Union, director of the Standing Conference of West Indian Organizations, and co-founder of a legal aid committee in Notting Hill Gate: in all of these activities his deliberative, forensic, and epideictic speaking skills were practised as he refined his understanding of the rhetorical implications of political and social situations. As one of the board of governors of the West Indian Student Centre observed, "He was a persuasive speaker. The Grenadian inflections in his speech had been sobered by the demands of the Inn where he was reading his law, to articulate clearly ... the ardent young man, eloquent, and with manners that were almost courtly, had lived up to expectations" (qtd. in Carew 221).

By virtue of his academic successes, humanitarian interests, and leadership positions, it is clear that even before he left London Bishop had gained recognition as an effective, persuasive speaker and master of dialectic. While it is always difficult to assess the limits of altruism, he seems to have been motivated not just by self-interest; accordingly, he gained a high degree of what Aristotle, in the *Rhetoric*, termed ethical proof—the persuasion that inheres in the speaker himself through public perception of his knowledge, character, and goodwill (and what is nowadays often called credibility). Without ethical proof, Quintilian reminds us, all other forms of proof are ineffectual; so Bishop's speaking appears to have had the enviable strength of unimpaired credibility.

Many writers have, in fact, gone further and asserted that Bishop at about this time developed an unusual charisma as a speaker. Jan Carew notes his "eloquence and his charisma" (228); Lorna McDaniel, a Howard University ethnomusicologist who did research on Carriacou and who was particularly interested in the spiritual elements of Grenadian culture, noted that "This spiritualism promoted the 'personal rule' of Maurice Bishop that was clothed in a humanistic frame and supported by a loving following: his charisma and individual leadership offended the other figures in the New Jewel movement" (4). And Millette and Gosine, clearly less sympathetic writers, qualify this trait by alluding to Bishop's "alleged charismatic leadership," (1) and then state that both Gairy and Bishop "knew that in societies that are both colonial and agrarian, the leader must possess a certain tint of charisma" (50). Subsequently, they acknowledge that "Grenadians were caught up in the rhetoric and charismatic leadership of Maurice Bishop.... He used his charisma as a revolutionary force" (55-56); that is, he was perceived as something of a religious figure who inspired individuals and crowds to follow him and absorb and repeat his words uncritically with the enthusiasm of the newly converted.

Grenada, like most of the Caribbean island-nations, has long enjoyed a tradition of orality, which Jacqueline Creft frequently alluded to and which the People's Revolutionary Government sought to redevelop after the long era of national quiescence under the Gairy government. And among the small group of national heroes in the pantheon of the revolution were three speakers of outstanding effectiveness: Theophilus Albert Marryshow (1887-1958), the greatest spokesperson for the rising middle class and for the devolution of political power to Grenadians; Tubal Uriah ("Buzz") Butler (1897-1973), founder of the Representative Government Association and organizer of the Trinidad trade union movement; and McGodden Karensky ("Cacademo") Grant (1917-1982), a pioneer militant of the New Jewel party. All three, in the words of Chris Searle, demonstrated "not only literacy, but also competence and eloquence" (xxii).

Marryshow, editor of the *West Indian* for twenty years and parliamentarian for thirty, indefatigably pursued his journal's policy-motto, "The West Indies Must Be West Indian" in editorials, essays, speeches, and a series of articles published as *Cycles of Civilization* (1917), in which he took issue with Jan Christian Smuts's disguised policy of *apartheid*. The intensity of Marryshow's feelings about the future of both African and West Indian society can be judged from his statement that Blacks throughout the world must unite to emancipate Africa from "the murderous highwaymen of Europe who have plundered her, raped her, and left her naked in the broad light of the boasted European civilization" (4). With similar intensity he advocated the federation of the West Indies (despising "parish pump politics"), opposed official censorship of even radical political programs such as Marcus Garvey's black separatism, and melioration of the hardships of the working and unemployed classes during the Depression. Yet he was *petit bourgeois* in many respects and opposed universal suffrage and trade unionism. But his sustained nationalism, undisputed personal proof, and mastery of rhetorical techniques are creditable. A life-long Methodist, Marryshow drew heavily upon the King James Bible for allusions, quotations, illustrations, and proofs in both his writing and his speeches, so that at times his pronouncements have a certain oracular quality, his predictions an almost divine certitude.

Butler, pastor of the Moravian Baptist Church in Fyzabad, Trinidad (a town largely populated by expatriate Grenadians) also drew heavily on biblical language in his secular addresses to open-air mass meetings. In addition, however, he displayed a more-than-casual acquaintance with the canon of Victorian literature; and he was clearly a master of the elements of prose (including repetition, parallel construction, and triadic expressions) that distinguish the sermons and essays of the great English eighteenth-century stylists such as Addison, Wesley, and Johnson. Here is an example from his speech of 9 December 1937:

> When you remember others, you are bound to have a feeling to make sacrifices, as I feel where I am standing. Yes, I can die, I can suffer pain, I can suffer anything in this fight for justice for the oppressed people of beautiful Trinidad. Make no mistake about it. This is a cause that demands real men as leaders. Yes, a time like this demands real men as followers. A time like this demands real men, men of opinion, men of will, men whom the lust of office cannot kill. Yes, men with the soul of the Master, the mind of the Master, to make sacrifices that others might enjoy a better and a brighter day. Where I am standing I am in a position to tell you that I have sworn to serve you loyally, faithfully, and well unto the end. There is no power in Heaven (or in Hell, for that matter) to make me turn. There is no power, no bribe, to make me turn aside from the paths of truth and beauty and freedom. Beauty and freedom and all that these contain fall not like ripened fruit about our feet. We climb to them through years of sweat and pain; without life's struggles none do you attain. (Jacobs 8-9)

As the *Sunday Guardian* (Trinidad) reporter commented in the 10 April 1945 issue on this great speech before sentencing (comparable to those of Sacco and Vanzetti and John Brown), "He speaks with the full weight of his being.... That intense, consuming, passionate quality.... I have never witnessed before. Speaker and audience were organic and indivisible" (qtd. in Searle 9).

Chris Searle, in *Words Unchained: Language and Revolution in Grenada*, proposes that

> This tradition of Butlerian eloquence is still alive in Trinidad and Grenada.... The language of the Grenada Revolution partly arises from this great tradition of Butlerian oratory: 'justice shall come to the poor and the meek shall inherit the earth!' has often been heard at public rallies since 13 March 1979. Allusions to the liberating aspect of biblical language often come spontaneously from the lips of the revolutionary leaders and calypsonians. (9)

Grant, like Marryshow and Butler unschooled beyond the elementary grades, added to biblical cadences and allusiveness an earthy humour, anecdotes from the daily life of the people, and folk maxims and aphorisms. Further, he often clarified a point by analogies and metaphors drawn from the everyday occurrences of working-class life and from cricket ("hitting imperialism for six," for example), and appropriately conjoined Creole vernacular with standard English for clarity and effectiveness.

Unfortunately, Grenadian public address did not develop in an uninterrupted, linear fashion. There was the aberration of the bizarre rhetoric of Eric Gairy, who (apart from using a triad in describing the New Jewel Movement leaders as "socialists, communists, and misfits") seems not to have mastered many of the elements of advanced composition—except for an occasional memorable phrase, such as his depiction of the opposition leaders as "masters in the art of political provocation." But most of Gairy's phrases were trite: a list of his cliches could be extended, but here are some from a single speech: "the small man's leader," "the people's leader," "town and country," "God's servant," and "the rich and the poor" and "big shots." On 3 May 1970, in a radio address, he noted that " 'A stitch in time saves nine' is indeed a wise maxim," and then announced the formation of a supplementary secret police force.

Gairy did convene numerous community meetings, but at them he was the undisputed main speaker. His disdain of the electorate could be demonstrated in many ways, but it is clearly shown in his boast that "Grenadians would vote for a *crapoo* [a frog] if I say so" (qtd. in Millette and Gosine 31). At the same time, his egotism is constantly revealed in solipsistic statements and his general lack of sophistication becomes apparent in his rambling—even incoherent—musings. In a radio address on 15 March 1951 (when he was twenty-nine) Gairy said:

> Yes, folks, this is your leader, Uncle Gairy, speaking to you. My dear, fellow Grenadians, you know that I am deeply concerned over the present state of affairs in this our dear little island. As head of Grenada's two largest organizations—the Grenada People's Party and the Grenada Manual and Mental Workers Union—I feel obligated morally and spiritually to do something to alleviate, to stop (and when I say stop I mean stop) the burning of buildings and fields, interfering with people who are breaking your strikes! Stop taking things away from the estates that are not belonging to you, particularly cocoa and nutmeg.
>
> And now we take another matter—the going back to work. When I lifted my finger on the nineteenth of February and said "Strike!", several thousands went on strike; that is because you have confidence in me and know very well that Uncle Gairy knows his whereabouts. (qtd. in Schoenhals and Melanson 14)

This avuncular (rather than egalitarian) approach to the populace degenerated into a travesty of political-social relationships as time passed. On 20 October 1972, for example, in a broadcast to the nation, the prime minister said:

> I call upon my mystic brothers and sisters, Fratres and Sorores of the Rosicrucian Order—and certainly all other mystic and spiritual bodies—to join in meditative and other metaphysical exercises at this time. We must remove the enemies from our paths of progress.... I believe in the philosophy that God helps those that help themselves. And so while we pray, we shall work. (17)

Then, in an address to the General Assembly of the United Nations on 7 October 1975, he advocated research into unidentified flying objects and psychic phenomena and lamented "the bountiful human talents that go to waste because of man's ignorance of certain aspects of his immediate environs—most certainly of his esoteric or inner self." Some psychoanalysis, self-analysis, and consideration of the state of affairs in Grenada itself (which shortly led to the revolution) might have been more to the point.

It was against this background and this rhetorical tradition that Maurice Bishop rose to the leadership of the New Jewel Movement and the People's Revolutionary Government. His basic tenets were that colonialism had emasculated Grenada, that neocolonialism augured ill for the future, and that only radical change (sometimes involving a reversion to earlier and discarded patterns of social involvement) could effect a fundamental restructuring of the body politic in the interests of the masses. Quite clearly his reading of the past was diametrically opposed to that of Robert Millette and Mahin Gosine, who write in *The Grenada Revolution: Why It Failed*, "Despite its alleged inhibitions, plantation society was very much an open system that advocated democratic ideals, one that Grenadians had grown accustomed to over the years" (137).

In his Address to the Nation on 13 March 1979, Maurice Bishop gave a brief summary of events of the previous few hours, offered amnesty to all who did not offer resistance to the new government, and stated the goals of his colleagues succinctly and straightforwardly:

> People of Grenada: this revolution is for work, for food, for decent housing and health services, and for a bright future for our children and great-grandchildren.
>
> The benefits of the revolution will be given to everyone, regardless of political opinion or which political party they support.
>
> Let us all unite as one.

There was, of course, almost no dissent: not because of fear of the new leaders, but because, as Millette and Gosine point out, during the previous decade "Bishop had replaced Gairy as the leader of the crowd. Maurice Bishop, with his charismatic abilities and organizational skills, was able to provide the political release and discharge" that the occasion demanded (54). The immediate means was a program of daily meetings with all sectors of the people, so that "Their rhetoric offered Grenadians hope and a longing for a new beginning" (55).

Many of Bishop's speeches have been published separately (such as "Fight Unemployment with Production!" and "Address to the Caribbean Conference of Intellectual Workers"—both in 1982), and there are extensive selections in the books of Chris Searle, *Grenada: The Struggle Against Destabilization* (1983) and *Words Unchained: Language and Revolution* (1984); but the principal texts are to be found in *Forward Ever!: Three Years of the Grenadian Revolution* (1982) and *Maurice Bishop Speaks: The Grenada Revolution, 1979-83* (1983), both substantial collections of speeches on a wide range of topics and occasions (and with some inevitable duplication). And from reading these speeches, what conclusions are we able to draw?

Those sympathetic to the People's Revolutionary Government are, predictably, laudatory. A reviewer in *Cuba Times* wrote:

> One cannot complete a review of the words of Maurice Bishop, no matter how brief, without commenting on the quality of the man that comes through all the speeches, interviews, and addresses.... His natural intelligence and commitment of principle (though not to formula) abound in these reminders of the person. His great commitment to and practical achievements towards nationalism, regionalism, and internationalism throughout the entire course of his political life is reflected.... The reader is moved by the clarity and simplicity of Bishop's presentation. When addressing his own people he educates, though he is never condescending or paternalistic. Instead, his genuine respect for the intelligence of the people, his sincerity, integrity, and humility—combined with a sense of historical responsibility—are self-evident. (5)

And Jan Carew, who heard Bishop speak on several occasions, also notes the educational intent of many of Bishop's speeches to mass audiences, in which he would "heighten the level of their consciousness and take them into his confidence," and concludes that he was, in a phrase, "a magnificent orator." (210)

Kai Schoenhals, a more objective writer, indicates that he was disturbed by Bishop's (and the leadership's) "provocative rhetoric" (x). On the other hand, Millette and Gosine conclude that there was a growing tendency to have recourse to slogans, "phrases that had become part of the NJM's vocabulary," and an increasingly apparent "weakness of leadership capabilities" (68, 130). It could be argued that Bishop's leadership capabilities were never impaired, but that colleague jealousy and intra-party disagreement on policy diminished the leadership that was still perceived by the people.

In *Political Change and Public Opinion in Grenada, 1979-84*, an occasional paper of the University of the West Indies, we are told that under 14 per cent of Grenadians held an unfavourable view of Bishop's performance, and that no other political leader fared as well. The public perception of Bishop was of "a man who loved the people and was loved by them, that he was devoted to improving their welfare, that he educated Grenadians with his all-round ability as a leader and a variety of other worthwhile qualities people saw in him, including honesty and egalitarianism." Some 41 per cent stressed Bishop's relations with the masses as the trait that they most admired; 32 per cent responded that Bishop's development policies meant most to them; 9 per cent were most impressed by his speeches (Emmanuel et al. 24).

But that slogans increasingly assumed an important part of speeches is readily apparent. The major one (one introduced by Bishop himself), was "Forward Ever, Backwards Never!" Others were: "Each One Teach One"; "If You Know, Teach; If You Don't, Learn"; "We Are One People"; "No Liberation Without Education"; and "Education Is a Right, Not a Privilege." Some, like "The Revolution Is the People and the People Are the Revolution," bear a resemblance to Cuban slogans; but in the chiasmic form the slogan has long been a part of Western culture, as in the "I like cucumbers, but..." expression and in John F. Kennedy's "Don't ask what your country can do" speech.

The slogans, chants, refrains, and repetitions that appear in many of Bishop's speeches are, after all, characteristic of religious gatherings and are therefore appropriate to Grenadian as well as to many other cultures. They are to be observed, also, in American political conventions, popular gatherings, and athletic arenas—so their use may be regarded as a sophisticated rather than as an unsophisticated rhetorical technique. In fact,

Paul E. Corcoran, in his study *Political Language and Rhetoric*, says that contemporary (or what he terms post-literate) political language

> is a display of style with no meaningful content. Thus an oratorical performance, such as a campaign speech, offers the broadcast audience perfunctory, congratulatory cliches which are little more than a survival of formulaic tropes.... Rhetorical devices such as slogans ... strongly reinforce the formulaic, ritual-like stylization of political language. (197)

Yet if the slogans of the Grenadian revolutionary spokesmen are too formulaic, they are certainly not as offensive as the slogan inscribed on a wall in St. George's by a member of the 82nd Airborne Division: "Eat shit, commie faggot!" (qtd. in Searle xix).

The characteristics of the three important Grenadian speakers whose achievements have been alluded to are, as has been noted, also to be seen in the rhetoric of Maurice Bishop, but his range is much greater. He is master of the demotic ("If I wrong, tell me..... Any time you not feeling so well, and they jook your finger...."), of the Creole-vernacular; yet he also commands Standard English and can write and speak in that and its more esoteric variants, diplomatic speech and courtroom presentation. He tends to be pedagogic in the best sense (he can explain the theory of allocation to a peasant by showing the analogy between household expenditure and a national budget), but he is never pontifical.

Without doubt, Maurice Bishop was an exceptionally able speaker who understood the principles of rhetoric and used them in his endeavour to lead his nation to a better future as he saw it.

WORKS CITED

Carew, Jan. *Grenada: The Hour Will Strike Again*. Prague: International Organization of Journalists, 1985.

Corcoran, Paul E. *Political Language and Rhetoric*. St. Lucia: University of Queensland P, 1979.

Cuba Times, May-June 1984.

Emmanuel, Patrick, Farley Brathwaite and Eudine Barriteau. *Political Change and Public Opinion of Grenada, 1979-1984*. Occasional Paper No. 19. Cave Hill: Institute of Social and Economic Research (Eastern Caribbean), University of the West Indies, 1986.

Gairy, Eric. *Premier's Address*. St. George's: Grenada Government Printer, 1969.

Jacobs, M. R., ed. *Butler v. King*. Port of Spain, Trinidad: n.p., n.d.

Marryshow, T. A. *Cycles of Civilisation*. New York: Pathway, 1973.

McDaniel, Lorna. "Report on the Grenada Conflict." Mimeographed. University of Atlanta, 10 March 1984.

Millette, Robert and Mahin Gosine. *The Grenada Revolution: Why It Failed*. New York Africana, 1985.

New York Times 14 March 1979, p. 2.

Rennie, Bukka. *A History of the Trinidad Working Class in the Twentieth Century*. Toronto: New Beginning Movement, 1974.

Schoenhals, Kai P. and Richard A. Melanson. *Revolution and Intervention in Grenada: The New Jewel Movement, the United States, and the Caribbean*. Boulder, CO: Westview, 1985.

Searle, Chris. *Word Unchained: Language and the Revolution in Grenada*. London: Zed, 1984.

Skocpol, Theda. *States and Social Revolutions*. Cambridge: University P, 1979.

14. Jessie Street and the Rhetoric of Australian Feminism

In *Australia Speaks: An Anthology of Australian Speeches* (1969), a compilation of some of the major speeches of twenty noted orators, not one woman is included, although there had, by that time, been several women who had played important roles in the development of the nation:[1] among these should be numbered Caroline Chisholm, the advocate of immigrants' rights; Mary Gilmore, the utopian socialist and (with William Lane) one of the founders of New Australia in Paraguay at the turn of the century; Representative Enid Lyons and Senator Dorothy Tangney (elected 1943); and Dame Pattie Menzies, wife of the celebrated and longtime prime minister Sir Robert Menzies, who was indefatigable in her activities on behalf of the Red Cross, the Country Women's Association, and similar groups interested in social service and the amelioration of the hardships of life in the Outback and areas removed for the amenities of city living. In fact, the citation accompanying Dame Pattie's award of the Grand Cross of the Order of the British Empire indicated that she was being honoured "in recognition of her addressing and encouraging many thousands of women in every state"; she thus became the first woman in Australia to be accorded public recognition for her effective, continuing commitment to public speaking as a means to the implementation of public policy.

But the scarcity of significant—and especially charismatic—women speakers in Australia is not unusual: in *Public Speaking*

Jessie Street and the Rhetoric of Australian Feminism 215

in the Shaping of Great Britain (1987), Robert T. Oliver devotes just 15 pages out of almost 250 to women, and then to Emmeline Pankhurst and the suffragettes, primarily; for, he notes, "Throughout history it has generally been taken for granted that women had no right to participate in government ... until the new idea of genderless equality was initiated in the French Revolution" (174) and that "It was taken for granted that their interests were 'included' in those of their fathers and husbands.... Although women were clearly abjectly subjected to the control of men and were often ruthlessly exploited, they could not speak for themselves and few men felt induced to speak up for them" (175).

The nineteenth-century view that women's interests were included in those of men seems to have survived even to the present, though there have been a few dissidents in the last generation; Indira Gandhi, Margaret Thatcher, Eleanor Roosevelt, and Helen Suzman (in South Africa, where she was, for thirty years, a true *vox clamantis in deserto*), however, stand out from the mass of women activist-speakers by virtue of their irrepressible enthusiasm, the high seriousness of their goals, and the lasting effects of their principled discourses. After them, it was no longer defensible to speak of "the invisible and unheard sex," and in Australia—as well as in the auditoriums and councils of the world—Jessie Street became a visible and much-attended-to speaker and writer in the fight for women's rights.

Jessie Mary Gray was born on 18 April 1889 in Chota Nagpur (now Bihar), India; her father was a member of the Forest Service. At age three she moved to Darjeeling, but until age six she spoke what was then called Hindustani almost exclusively: this late introduction to spoken and written English might well account for her subsequent characteristic use of the plain style, one free of rhetorical flourishes; the more sophisticated, rarer tropes, and stylistic embellishments. Her *Truth or Repose* (1966), a long autobiography, presents her style exquisitely: it is conversational and even demotic, repetitive, factual, and modest—though always stressing the importance of the subjects, positions, and justifications discussed.

In fact, in many ways Jessie Street might seem to have exemplified the rhetorical teaching of Baruch Mendelssohn, the socialist scholar in Christina Stead's novel *Seven Poor Men of Sydney* (1934), who, in a discussion with another character, Joseph, commented, "These glib, rhetorical speakers sometimes fire the men, but more often they betray them," and men advised him,

> Follow the interest of your class. Become your own tactitian, your own Caesar. Don't be afraid to criticise the speaker. Don't become refined.... You must think for yourself. For preference, listen to those of your class who speak simply, without the flowers of rhetoric, without jokes, without cleverness. (178)

And she certainly agreed with fellow-socialist George Bernard Shaw, who (in commenting on *Cymbeline*) counselled that one should not waste criticism "upon unresisting imbecility, upon faults too evident for detection, and too gross for aggravation."

That her early life in India affected her is pellucidly apparent from the opening pages of *Truth and Repose* and subsequent allusions to her formative adolescent years.

> As I got into my teens, I realized that the reasons given by my father for the discrimination practised against coloured people were all the same, and had the same basis, as the discriminations practised against women. I saw plainly that the reason for these discriminations was to protect the status, rights, and privileges of the white man *vis à vis* women and the coloured races. (2)

On a year-long leave of absence in England, the Gray family met Robert Browning, and Jessie grew to resent the restrictions that were placed on her because of her gender; she earnestly prayed to be changed into a boy but "pledged ... in the future to exert all my efforts to remove discriminations against women" (14). Back in Australia, she enrolled at the University of Sydney in Professor Francis Anderson's course in the history of religion; there she became acquainted with Mrs Maybanke Wolstenholme "who had taken a prominent part in women's struggle for equal rights" (36). Upon graduation, Jessie visited England again and stayed with a cousin, Winifred Mason, "one of the followers of Emmeline and Christabel Pankhurst, and joined in processions and sold copies of *Votes for Women* on street corners; she came out in favour of Egyptian independence and for closing down whore houses established in Cairo for British troops. As a consequence of her radical stances, she was anathematised in certain social circles because, she later wrote, "To be called a suffragette then carried a greater stigma in certain circles than to be called a 'communist' in capitalist countries after the cold war started" (45). She married in 1916.

A major influence in Jessie Street's life was the International Conference of Women's Organisations in Geneva in 1914, sponsored by Mrs Carrie Chapman Cott (U.S.A.) and Lady Nunburnham (U.K.): "I came away more of a feminist than ever," she later commented, adding, "women whose self-confidence has been undermined can make no contribution of importance" (75). On her return to Sydney she established the Women's Club, the Feminist Club, and the House Service Company, which hired, insured, and trained domestic workers (at one time employing some 300 girls and women) for over thirty years. "One of the objects was to raise the status of domestic workers and to gain recognition of domestic work as a skilled occupation.... The unique feature of domestic work is that it is one of the remaining vestiges from feudal times—she alone works only for her keep" (85).

Almost immediately, Street started the United Associations of Women, which offered classes in public speaking and debating and periodically held open meetings at which equal rights (including status, opportunities, and pay for women) were fully discussed. Then she organised the Nurses' Union, which managed to raise salaries from five shillings to fifteen shillings a week and reduced hours from 72 to 52 a week. She visited Margaret Sanger in the United States, to learn more about her movement to establish birth-control clinics, and admired the parliamentary efforts of Lady Nancy Astor, the first woman member of the British parliament.[2] She decided that women ought to seek membership in the Australian parliaments also.

In what may have seemed an odd position, Jessie Street opposed the introduction of the basic wage in Australia—

because it "placed an almost insurmountable obstacle in the campaign for equal pay for women" by declaring that the wage was intended to provide an adequate standard of living for a *family*, which was defined as a man, wife, and one child—although a third of male workers were unmarried and many single women had parents as dependents. (Contemporary legislation provided that women receive 54 percent of the male wage; forty years later, the proposition has not changed materially.) Throughout these years, Jessie Street was an indefatigable speaker and writer for the women's movement and advocate for progressive social legislation. She advocated a General Social Insurance Scheme (denounced by Prime Minister Joseph Lyons as "impractical" yet implemented at the end of World War II); she established a school for women to learn agricultural occupations; she opposed the dismissal of married women teachers during the Depression (to provide work for men); she opposed laws that made it mandatory for women to take the nationality of their husbands; she advocated the ordination of women in the several churches; she supported the League of Nations and the United Nations (in which she served as a member of the Australian delegation at the San Francisco Conference); and she became a frequent speaker for the Society for Cultural Relations with the U.S.S.R.

With the enthusiasm of the convert but the knowledge and wisdom of the long-time stalwart, Jessie Street spoke on a remarkably extensive range of liberal and progressive subjects for half a century; and always, she notes, "I prepared these lectures with great care" (179). She continued to encourage and train other women to speak in public, for "most of them said that they would never be able to address meetings." This was still the age of the public meeting, and elections were often decided by a few well-attended gatherings and the newspaper (or radio) reports of the speeches delivered at them. Jessie Street's speeches were customarily brief: they were to the point but not closely argued or exhaustively developed; logical and adequately supported by both factual and anecdotal evidence; and void of bombast, the florid phrase, and the purple passage. To some they might seem colourless and unmemorable—quite different from the speeches of some of her political contemporaries such as Arthur Calwell, William Charles Wentworth, and R. G. Menzies. She was more in harmony with her Australian Labor Party colleagues Ben Chifley, John Curtin, and Bill Heffron, whom she had associated with following her joining the party in 1939, and none of whom could be included in the speakers to be found on Sunday afternoons in the Sydney Domain or on midweek lunchtimes in several city locations such as are described by R. D. Fitzgerald in his poem "Macquarie Place":

> I will go out and hear the strain
>
> of rat-bag orators at large.
>
> There is a battery in my brain
>
> which just that fever might recharge.
>
> The blends of curious craziness
>
> which crank and anarchist extol
>
> could fill with their electric stress
>
> the run-down fury of my soul.
>
> So I will cross Macquarie Place
>
> and covet zeal as crude as loud
>
> in lunch-hour lunatics who face
>
> amused indifference of the crowd.

Jessie Street was neither anarchist nor zealot, though she was dissatisfied with the status quo and was enthusiastic about her several causes; likewise, though some members of the press tried to paint her as such, she was neither rat-bag nor lunatic; and although she lacked "electric stress," she never faced an indifferent audience: all her listeners sensed her genuine commitment, her thorough understanding of major and minor issues, and her obvious honesty, even though her ideas might be challenging, novel, and contrary to the mainstream. And, in spite of her incessant public speaking, she constantly adapted speeches to new audiences, new information, and changed circumstances, so that in *Truth or Repose* she was able to write, "I never made the same speech twice" (245).

In 1943 Jessie Street ran as the endorsed Labor Party candidate for the electorate of Wentworth, in the Eastern Suburbs of Sydney, in the election for members of the House of Representatives in the national parliament. It was her first foray into elective politics, and it created quite a stir, for her husband, Mr Justice Street, to whom she had been married since 1916, was a longtime member of the Supreme Court of New South Wales, a political conservative, and member of the informal aristocracy of the nation. (In 1950 he became Chief Justice and Lieutenant Governor.) Her principal opponent was (Sir) Eric Harrison, scion of a clothing-manufacturing company and the incumbent, a member of the United Australia Party (conservative).

Wherever Street spoke—whether in Monash Hall in Rose Bay or at shopping centres in Vaucluse—she drew large, enthusiastic crowds. At Monash Hall she was joined by the *grand dame* of Australian poetry and feminist causes, Dame Mary Gilmore, a redoubtable speaker even in her advanced seventies. When the results were tabulated, Street had gained the plurality of votes (31,048 to Harrison's 23,619), but the distribution of preferences in the five-way contest gave the election again to Harrison.[3] Thereafter, Jessie Street retired from elective politics. At the same election Dame Enid Lyons of the U.A.P. was elected to the House and Dorothy Tangney of the A.L.P. was elected to the Senate: they long remained unique in their positions, and as late as 1973 there were only three women senators and no women representatives. But no election candidacy by a woman, to that date, had aroused such enthusiasm as that by Jessie Street—and perhaps none since. In 1945 her abilities were finally recognised officially, and Prime Minister John Curtin appointed her (over the objection of Harrison) as a member of the Australian delegation to the United Nations conference in San Francisco, led by Dr H. V. Evatt (who became first President of the General Assembly). This was perhaps the high point of her life.

When A. L. McLeod was compiling *Australia Speaks*, he asked Jessie Street whether she could provide complete texts of representative speeches from which a selection could be made, since only paraphrases, abstracts, and excerpts were available. At the time she was engaged in writing *Truth or Repose* and was away from her retirement home at Tweed Heads, N.S.W., but she asked her longtime secretary, Muriel M. Tribe, to select and send some. In an accompanying letter Mrs Tribe wrote:

> Probably, if she had been here, she may have chosen others, but I have enclosed three speeches she has made: Women's Role in the Equal Pay Struggle, Married Women's Struggle Towards Freedom, and Three Situations Threatening Peace. I thought you could perhaps choose one of these, as I think they are all very close to her heart.

All three speeches are brief: the typescripts run from 750 to 1000 words, and at the speaker's customary delivery rate should have taken about eight to ten minutes to present. "Women's Role" carries the notation "Women's Charter Conference, 1961," and "Three Situations" is dated simply 1961, while "Married Women's Struggle" is undated; however, from internal evidence ("This war has helped the movement....") and the condition of the paper, it is certainly a speech given towards the end of World War II.

"Married Women's Struggle Towards Freedom" begins with an exposition of "the bad old days" the period "not so long ago, within the memories of our grandmothers,"

> when married women were classified under the law with infants and lunatics and had practically no rights at all. Upon marriage, the property of a woman passed entirely into the hands of her husband; a married woman was not recognised as the parent or guardian of her child (although the unmarried mother was regarded as the sole parent or guardian of her child); while a man could divorce his wife for a single act of infidelity, she could not divorce him on any grounds; she was forced to accept his domicile nationality, though he might be a foreigner, and she might never move from her home town after marriage; and she could not open a bank account or make an investment without his consent—and in innumerable other ways a wife was nothing more than a husband's chattel with rights and privileges and rewards which differed little from those of a slave.

Then Street acknowledges that progress has been achieved by "liberty-loving and progressive women" *only* with the support of "liberal-minded and progressive men" who were "champions of democracy" and who, from within the legislative and administrative institutions, "would open the door from the inside." That is, she makes no claim for unassisted progress; rather, she stresses the need for all liberal-minded persons to cooperate in the extension of the democratic ideals and the ending of gender-specific restrictions, exclusions, and penalties.

By way of contrast, Street then offers a review of changes that have been effected: the right of women to retain and control their property and earnings; the legal recognition of the father of illegitimate children (with their right to inherit); reforms in divorce law; changes in the law regarding nationality that recognise women's interests. And, she acknowledges, "The franchise has been attained, but economic independence only partially. After the last war and before this war, women were admitted in paid employment in the lower-paid grades. In the main, they were excluded from positions of authority and control and from the higher-paid occupations and professions."

This last observation is the crux of Jessie Street's social and political philosophy and is succinctly stated, in almost aphoristic fashion, in *Truth or Repose* in these words: "As there can be no independence without economic independence, neither can there be economic independence without social security" (106). That is, a universal social security legislation is a prerequisite of that economic independence from which women will derive complete social independence—if that is desired. (In her own married life, Jessie Street enjoyed a remarkable degree of freedom—social and economic: her husband and she had four children, they lived both together in Sydney and independently, and they supported opposing political parties; however, she was not entirely comfortable in the deputy-vice-regal position that she was eventually called to fill.)

The great breadth of Street's vision of feminism can be gauged by her almost polymath interests: not for her the equation of feminism and abortion rights only. In fact, while she strove for equal employment opportunities (and equal pay), she also valued immensely the role of the homemaker: on this subject she could at times rise to her best uses of emotional proof:

> Public opinion is beginning to recognise that the married woman as homemaker and mother is rendering a tremendously valuable service to the State—an almost incalculable service. Without her, the State could not continue. She is Public Servant No. 1, and as such must be cared for and encouraged. She must be given not only economic independence but economic security: her health must be guarded and proper homes must be provided.

Her conclusion is brief and pointed: "Yes, we are progressing." And though "sometimes we get discouraged," we should remember the enormous strides that have been made and "the encouraging change in public opinion generally towards the more serious claims" of the feminist movement.

In 1943 Jessie Street had been instrumental in founding the Australian Women's Charter Committee, which was intent upon having eliminated all the restrictions on women's rights in society; she was elected first chairman. Her speech before the 1961 conference of the group therefore allowed her to offer a retrospective view and a current assessment of the situation, a compositional structure that became increasingly characteristic as she aged. In part, this was in accordance with long-established precedent and with audience expectations: the method indicates continuity and suggests progress in the attainment of organizational goals.

Again, the speaker reminds her audience that their aims have been successful in part because "they have always been assisted by just-minded, forward-looking men" (quite different from contemporary American Women's Movement speakers, who seem to wish to have nothing to do with men); and then she proposes that the exclusion of women from higher-paid positions of responsibility is a characteristic of capitalist societies: "In the socialist world discriminations against women do not exist," she suggests, but offers neither examples nor statistical evidence in support. (Many would be pressed to name women members of the Politburo or the Presidium of the U.S.S.R.—or even women socialist ambassadors, orchestra conductors, or research institute heads.)

Instead of pious self-congratulations on achievements, the speaker reminds her audience of shortcomings and failures: In 1918 the British parliament passed the Sex Disqualification Removals Act, but did not remove salary differentials for any women promoted to high positions. And, she points out, the women's organisations did not challenge that provision; and the trade union councils did nothing to challenge this pay inequity for 32 years! Likewise, in Australia the Equal Pay Campaign was started about 1950 and eventually received government agreement for incremental removal of pay differentials, so that by 1961 there would be equal pay for men and women doing the same job; however, the trade unions objected to women receiving larger annual increments—the only way to eliminate the long-established discrimination against women workers. She therefore concludes that there must be cooperation between the women's movement, the trade unions, and the government: "If the government wishes to give equal pay, it can do so without any Women's Bureau. Women don't want special treatment as women—they want equal conditions with other workers and equal pay and opportunity."

"Three Situations Threatening Peace" proposed that the United Nations recognise only the government of the People's Republic of China, so that the border situation between India and China could be resolved by the two member states, thus averting a possible threat of war; that United States military bases in Australia be closed, since any conflict between the U.S.A. and the U.S.S.R. would invite nuclear attacks on extraterritorial American bases; that the incorporation of North Borneo, Sarawak, and Brunei into Malaysia without plebiscites in the three territories was undemocratic and would provoke unrest. (Brunei opted out.)

As can be judged from the above, Jessie Street's speeches are typically brief, address the basic women's problems (economic), seek support from the established male seats of power, and depend on logical and historical support rather than personal and emotional proof—though her credibility may be questioned because of her generally uncritical approach to the socialist model.

Truth or Repose is a mine of information on the international women's movements, yet it went from publisher to publisher for some years. It is a record of "A rewarding, if unrewarded, life" and "the ample evidence of the mountain of work that this very able woman achieved in a lifetime of unrewarded public service," as April Hersey phrased it in a review in the Sydney *Bulletin*. A reviewer for the *Australian Book Review* thought the book "school-essayish ... strangely depersonalised and detached. It is as an historical record of progressivism that this book will be valued." But the Melbourne *Age* reviewer, H. V. Hewitt, characterised the book as a "long, intensely serious, politically conscious book [that] will become recognised as a major Australian autobiography"; and, he wrote:

> It is impossible to estimate how much versatility, constructive energy, and fine mentality have been lost to Australia through its complacent pride in being a 'man's world.' Of all the Australian women who have broken through the nation-cramping, manmade, largely women-sanctioned, ridiculous assumption that women are second-rate human beings, none has done it more forcefully than Lady Jessie Street, a mighty fighter for the rights of women.

Unfortunately, *Truth or Repose* does not provide complete texts for Jessie Street's many major speeches—just paraphrases and excerpts; nonetheless, the effect is to suggest that she is roughly the Australian equivalent of Eleanor Roosevelt, to whom she bore a remarkable resemblance in stature, mien, rhetorical style, and interests.

Regretably, Jessie Street was never able to capture a mass following for her many enlightened programs and causes; perhaps this was the result of her lack of flair, flamboyance, gladhanding, and extravagant claims, her predilection for the analytical, the logical, the principled. And she yet has her heirs, both in speaking and in prose advocacy and autobiography: one wonders whether Kath Walker (Oodgeroo Noonuccal) could have done so much for the Aboriginal people of Australia if Jessie Street had not preceded her down the road to equal rights for all women, speaking and writing (particularly in her *Australian Women's Digest*) persuasively and informatively even when ignored, ridiculed, or disdained. For fifty years Jessie Street was *the* voice of feminism in Australia.

NOTES

[1] Vance Palmer, in his *National Portraits* (1940; 1954) includes no women in his studies, even though he and his wife, Nettie Palmer, were well-known liberals; however, Flora Eldershaw, in *The Peaceful Army* (1938), devotes her book to women.

[2] The first woman member of the Australian House of Representatives was Enid Lyons (later Dame Enid), representing the electorate of Darwin, Tasmania, from 1943 to 1951. The first woman member of the Senate was Dorothy Tangney, from Western Australia (also elected on 21 August 1943), who served until 1968. As Martin Lumb, editor of *Parliamentary Handbook* observes, "Technically, Lyons was the first woman minister (upon her appointment as Vice-President of the Executive Council on 19 December 1949), but the first woman minister to have a portfolio was Dame Annabelle Rankin, who was Minister for Housing in the Holt, McEwan, and Gorton Ministries from 26 January 1966 to 22 March 1971" (letter, 31 August 1993). At present there are four women ministers, but only one is a member of the cabinet. In the State of New South Wales, the first woman member of the Legislative Assembly (the lower house) was Millicent Preston-Stanley, who represented the Eastern Suburbs electorate from 1925 to 1927; the first woman in the Legislative Council (the upper house) was Catherine Green, who served ten months between 1931 and 1932. The first woman to be made a minister in N.S.W. was Janice Crosio (1984). Women had been granted the vote in New Zealand in 1895, in Australia in 1901, in the U.S.S.R. in 1917, in the U.S.A. in 1920, and in the United Kingdom in 1928: their long wait for representation by women seems extraordinary.

[3] As Street has observed, "I knew from the first results I could not win, as W. C. Wentworth was 2 on the ballot, was born in the electorate; his 11,000 preferences of course went to H[arrison]." (Letter to A. L. McLeod, 14 May 1966.)

WORKS CITED

Australian Book Review. Brief Reviews: *Truth or Repose*. Apr. 1967: 5.

Fitzgerald, R. D. "Macquarie Place." *The Penguin Book of Australian Verse*, ed. Harry Heseltine. Sydney: Penguin, 1972, p. 177.

Hersey, April. "A Rewarding, if Unrewarded, Life." *Bulletin* (Sydney) 21 Jan. 1967: 23-24.

Hewitt, H. V. "A Great Australian." *Age* (Melbourne). Rev. of *Truth or Repose*. 20 May 1967: 16.

Lumb, Martin. Letter, 31 Aug. 1993.

Oliver, Robert T. *Public Speaking in the Reshaping of Great Britain*. Newark: University of Delaware P, 1987.

Stead, Christina. *Seven Poor Men of Sydney*. Sydney: Angus, 1934.

Street, Jessie M. G. *Truth or Repose*. Sydney: Australasian Book Society, 1966.

———. Letter to A. L. McLeod, 14 May 1966.

Tribe, Muriel M. Letter to A. L. McLeod, 17 May 1966.

1994

15. Establishing a Canon of Commonwealth Public Address

When Chauncey A. Goodrich, professor of rhetoric in Yale College, published his *Select British Eloquence: Embracing the Best Speeches Entire of the Most Eminent Orators of Great Britain for the Last Two Centuries* ... in 1852, after some thirty years of teaching classical rhetoric, he acknowledged that the study of the great speeches of Greece and Rome, while edifying and instructive, was not sufficient for the development of an educated contemporary citizenry. Accordingly, he introduced a second course, one on modern eloquence, "to show the leading characteristics of the great orators of our own language...." His object in both courses was "not to awaken ... that love of genuine eloquence, which is the surest pledge of success, but to aid [students] in catching the spirit of the authors read" (v).

From the plethora of speeches delivered and recorded between 1625 and 1825, Goodrich selected seventy-four, delivered by twenty speakers, many of whom are not likely to be familiar, even as names, to modern readers. Who, for example, recognizes William Pulteney (Lord Bath), Lord Belhaven, or Sir James Mackintosh? And of them all, the anthologist declares that "Chatham, Burke, Fox, and Pitt stand, by universal consent, at the head of our eloquence, and to these Erskine may be added as the greatest of our forensic orators.... Among the orators of the second class, the reader will find..."—and he enumerates Lord Mansfield, Richard Brinsley Sheridan, George Canning, and John Philpot Curran.

That is, if we were to endorse something akin to the criteria of F. R. Leavis in the establishment of a Great Tradition of oratory in English, we would be restricted to a short list of five or six speakers between 1625 and 1825.

And from that date to the present, who might Goodrich have considered worthy of inclusion? Benjamin Disraeli, William Ewart Gladstone, Ramsay MacDonald, Charles Stewart Parnell, Eamon de Valera—doubtful, because born in New York, of an Irish mother and a Spanish father. Winston Churchill, and Margaret Thatcher could well have been in a short list, with only Churchill guaranteed of inclusion and Disraeli worthy of reconsideration.

And when William Norwood Brigance's *A History and Criticism of American Public Address* was published in 1943, its contents were devoted to the speeches of just twenty-eight individuals—all men, despite the significant speeches of Margaret Sanger, Elizabeth Cady Stanton, Susan B. Anthony, and Eleanor Roosevelt that were instrumental in the movements that effected women's emancipation, suffrage, and advancement.

Predictably, American public address gave rise to innumerable effective local, and eventually regional, public speakers, because, as George V. Bohman has noted, "nearly every colonist directly participated in the activities of public speaking, either as speaker or as audience member, and because this means of social communication and expression was more readily available ... than the various written means of communication" (3). Of the one thousand publications in the United States before 1700, the bulk were sermons, governors' speeches, and proclamations. Speaking occasions afforded many of the popular public diversions; sermons, deliberative speeches, and forensic addresses offered education, edification, and entertainment.

Almost all social histories of the United States remark on the stature of Jonathan Edwards, Henry Ward Beecher, and Phillips Brooks as pulpit orators; of Robert G. Ingersoll, Booker T. Washington, and Ralph Waldo Emerson as proponents of social reform; of William Jennings Bryan, Clarence Darrow, and Daniel Webster as advocates in the courtroom. But pre-eminent as debaters on the crucial matters of national independence and cohesion are surely Patrick Henry, Abraham Lincoln, and Stephen A. Douglas.

That is, if we were to select about a dozen speakers who represent the best in American public address over the past 350 years, they would assuredly come from the names just mentioned and a few from the years after 1940: Douglas MacArthur; Dwight D. Eisenhower; Franklin Delano Roosevelt and Eleanor, his wife; and Martin Luther King Jr.

Since the administration of Franklin Delano Roosevelt, speeches by American presidents have largely become professionals' and committee compositions, as has been made clear by studies of the part played by Robert E. Sherwood in aiding the tired and ailing Roosevelt and by numerous aides and agencies in constructing President George W. Bush's celebrated speech after the terrorist attacks in the United States in September 2001.

Of course, we must recognize that the demands for speeches by prominent public figures have increased exponentially in recent years, and no individual could possibly carry out his other responsibilities and compose thoughtful, thought-provoking, eloquent speeches at the frequency demanded by modern politics. One side-effect of this situation is certainly the demise of the long speech: only Fidel Castro still regularly delivers the two-to-four-hour harangue to an apparently enthralled audience standing in the public plaza. Even the old-time hour-long sermon has been transformed into the fifteen-minute homily—except in certain Pentecostal and evangelical churches.

When Melvil Dewey constructed his decimal system for library classification, he assigned 815 to American oratory and 825 to British oratory (which included all English-language speeches other than American). This classification acknowledged that oratory (also called public address or public speeches) was a major genre of discourse, one comparable to poetry, drama, fiction, and the essay, and taking precedence over letters, satire, humour, and miscellania.

Yet, while most students of English literature in the Commonwealth have studied the speeches or sermons of John Donne, Lancelot Andrews, Richard Baxter, and Oliver Cromwell, they remain quite unfamiliar with the many significant—if not truly great—speeches from the Commonwealth itself.

Unfortunately, because the emphasis in Commonwealth literary studies has been on poetry, drama, and fiction, the other genres have been largely overlooked. So much so, in fact, that it is clear that there has never been a canon of Commonwealth public address, a collection of speeches generally regarded as the sine qua non.

As international communication becomes more swift and widespread, speeches—like all the other forms and genres of discourse—become more easily compared; what seem for a time like important statements are soon regarded as imitative, derivative, or picayune and become part of an undifferentiated mass of words, undistinguished by content, illustration, delivery, or effect. In this they are similar to the great number of plays and novels that are extravagantly hailed locally and on appearance but are wholly forgotten within a year or two.

Fortunately, the establishment of critical standards by which to assess Commonwealth speeches is being facilitated by the publication of collections of addresses of individual politicians and preachers and of national anthologies, most of which have been issued by commercial publishers, though in India the central government has published extensive compendiums of each prime minister's speeches. In addition, the publication by individual governments of their politicians' speeches to the United States Congress and to the United Nations permits ready comparisons. The consequence of this widespread publication is that we can reasonably suggest that the great tradition of public speaking continues in the English-speaking Commonwealth, although it is not always familiar to the critics and historians of Commonwealth literature. Accordingly, it is now possible and desirable to establish an appropriate canon that should replace national, dated ones.

Canadian public address has, somehow, almost totally evaded academic study; yet there are, of course. great issues and great speakers in Canadian history. Perhaps the most outstanding figures in the period immediately after the American Revolution were William Lyon Mackenzie, a fiery, tempestuous, eloquent advocate of an elected legislature after the American style; Robert Gourlay, a dynamic speaker who was eventually expelled from Upper Canada in 1819 for having tried to arouse the farmers against government land-settlement policy; Robert Baldwin, leader of the faction that advocated moderate reform and the adoption of the British form of responsible self-government; and Egerton Ryerson, who persuaded the strong Methodist wing of the Reform Party to endorse and then espouse the Tory platform. In Lower Canada the reform movement was led by the speaker of the assembly, Louis Joseph Papineau, who sought control of revenue and thereby of government policy. Later, Papineau moved beyond his reformist position and began to speak darkly of revolution and advocacy of an American-style constitution, his violent words inflaming his supporters to the extent that they formed groups known as Sons of Liberty (in imitation of American revolutionary brigades). Tension rose, and Papineau was ultimately forced to flee to the United States. Clearly, his persuasive speeches would be worthy of study, and particularly as precursors of the speeches of the Quebec Separatists.

Although there was less unrest in the Maritimes, the movement for reform in an orderly fashion was led by Joseph Howe, editor of the *Nova Scotian* and (in speeches in his own defense against a charge of libel) one of the important early orators. Howe's *Poems and Essays* (1874) established him as a competent belle-lettrist, potential short-story writer, provincial poet, and (in his essay "Eloquence") advocate of a dignified, vigorous, allusive, and didactic style. Of Howe's own style, Fred Cogswell has observed that it is well adapted to his audiences and "does credit to the intelligence of the working man in the Maritimes during the nineteenth century" (qtd. in Klinck 116).

Howe's sponsorship of Thomas Chandler Haliburton resulted in the development of one of the most original talents of the first era of Canadian literature. As barrister, parliamentarian, and judge, Haliburton was a vigorous, indefatigable speaker, representing the more aristocratic, conservative school of thought.

Practically every speaker in the Confederation debates of 1865 appears to have spoken in logical terms: Joseph Royal represented the main rational approach by emphasizing defense against the United States. Virtually the only emotional voice was that of Thomas D'Arcy McGee, "the chief orator and literary man among the 'Founding Fathers of Confederation,' who brought Ontario, Quebec, New Brunswick, and Nova Scotia into a national union," as Carl Klinck has written (155). McGee's speeches are splendid, moving orations. On numerous occasions his Irish gift for language and speech visibly and effectively moved his audiences, whether working men or legislators.

Towards the end of the nineteenth century Canadian cities and towns supported series of lectures after the fashion of the Lyceum and Chautauqua movements in the United States or of the Schools of Arts and Mechanics' Institutes in Australia and the United Kingdom; but there seems to have been no study of the speakers involved in them. In all probability their style of presentation was not remarkably different from that found in America, and the subject matter but little changed. With few exceptions, it seems that the common-sense tone and style prevailed over the florid and lofty—except in the Presbyterian sermons of the Maritime preachers.

In more recent times, Mackenzie King, Lester Pearson, Louis St. Laurent, John Diefenbaker, and Pierre Elliott Trudeau have achieved some renown as speakers, and it would be well to have their best speeches collected and subjected to rigorous rhetorical criticism. As Gordon Thomas noted some years ago,

> Although Canadian history has not been as richly productive of historical events in which public speaking has played a central and crucial part as has been true in the history of the United States, it is nonetheless true that it is far from being devoid of such moments.

Canada's history has often been exciting and frequently controversial. (7)

Confederation and separatism are undoubtedly major national subjects that could be expected to produce major national speeches, but even greater is that of world peace in a nuclear age—the theme of most of the mature discourses of both Pearson and Trudeau, who have also been seen as voices of the small "unaligned" nations (if not necessarily of the underdeveloped ones).

"In New Zealand, any fine elusion of a fine mind stands out like a pretty deed in a dark world, an outward and audible sign of an inner and cultural grace" (130-31), according to Professor Kenneth Melvin, author of numerous studies of the national cultural scene. Notwithstanding, there have been many effective speakers in church, legislature, and courtroom, if not so obviously on the platform. The main subjects have been native policy, representative government, land policy, socialist legislation, and—most recently—adaptation to the European common market, immigration, and the environment.

The great tradition of Bishop G. A. Selwyn, outspoken critic of Earl Grey's native and land policies and an indefatigable missionary, was carried on for a while by similar clerics: Dr. Rutherford Waddell of Dunedin might be considered one of his intellectual descendants, though his *The Voyage of Life: Four Addresses on Certain Aspects of It* (1907) is somewhat more literary in its style (quoting Robert Louis Stevenson, W. E. Henley, and Matthew Arnold).

Political oratory in New Zealand has produced some speeches worth reading. Sir George Grey's *The Policy of the Future: Not Class Against Class* (1877), delivered in the House of Representatives, is a thoughtful analysis of the subject phrased in deliberate and sedate language. According to William Gisborne, Scobie Mackenzie has been described as "perhaps the best public speaker" of the turn of the century, his speeches being considered "excellent, showing careful thought and great ability ... they have a real rhetorical force and genuine humour. They have, moreover, a literary charm about them, a feature the more pleasing because it is not common" (306).

Establishing a Canon of Commonwealth Public Address 235

Since 1900, speakers worthy of some study might include W. B. Seetch, whose major statements are included in *Colony or Nation: Addresses and Papers* (1966); Walter Savage; and Julius Vogel.

Yet for the student of literature the greatest interest may attach to the speeches of W. Pember Reeves and James Edward FitzGerald, the associate and correspondent of John Ruskin, W. E. Gladstone, and Charles Kingsley, and one-time undersecretary at the British Museum. Reproached by Grey for "striving to transport the old world in portions to the new," he nonetheless exerted a considerable influence on the development of the "small utopia": "In political assemblies noted for their oratory he won fame as a speaker—fluent, eloquent, though to the modern taste sometimes over-rhetorical," according to E. H. McCormick (19).

Of considerable interest would be a collection and rhetorical evaluation of speeches by Maori leaders both past and present, for Maori sociology gave priority to effective public address, the language itself containing many terms relating to oratory; for example, *whatatu*, to make a speech; *whakaronga*, to inform; and *whakataki*, the exordium or introduction to a speech. The speeches delivered on the occasion of the Treaty of Waitangi alone, even in translation, would be of interest.

Australia Speaks (1969), a collection of deliberative, forensic, and epideictic speeches from 1803 to 1964, was the first anthology of that nation's best public address. Some of the titles suggest the range of subject matter: Robert Knopwood spoke "On the Everpresent God"; William Charles Wentworth "For the University Bill"; Henry Parkes spoke in favour of Federation; Alfred Deakin for Federation and for the White Australia Policy; William Holman "Against Sending Troops to South Africa"; Archbishop Daniel Mannix provided "The Case Against Conscription." R. G. Menzies, an excellent deliberative but weak epideictic speaker, gave addresses over a thirty-year political career on such topics as "Greece and the Anzac Spirit" and "The Nationalization of the Suez Canal," and delivered, by invitation, his "Eulogy of Churchill" from the crypt of St. Paul's Cathedral. Most Australians today would probably be familiar with only two or three of their nation's orators: Parkes, Menzies, and perhaps the long-time jurist, Labor Party leader, and first president of the United Nations General Assembly, H. V. Evatt.

The West Indies seem to have provided many opportunities for sermons, few for political speeches (until recently), and almost none for the expository or entertaining speech of the platform. Of the most celebrated courtroom speeches, such as those in the trial of Paul Bogle and similar early leaders of opposition to slavery—like George William Gordon—there are principally only paraphrases and summaries. As Arthur Pollard observes in *English Sermons* (1963), "Through the centuries the tradition of great preaching has developed, and it continues in our time ... but today the sermon is not noticed as it used to be" (53). But in the Anglophone Caribbean, perhaps because of the rather special role of the clergy in society, the sermon continues to be published and read, studied and quoted.

The special place of the sermon in West Indian society can be assumed to have derived from Oliver Cromwell's injunction to the leaders of his expedition to Santo Domingo in 1655 to assure "the propagation of true religion" by "teachers, men gifted in the knowledge of Jesus Christ" who would "inform and enlarge the gospel." But most of the sermons of the period were clearly designed for the semi-literate white settlers and their administrative superiors rather than the more numerous slave population, as is suggested by both the content and title of the earliest extant sermon from Jamaica—one preached on 1 February 1671 by the Rev. Henry Houser—entitled "An Exact Model or Platform of Good Magistracy."

Because the West Indian church was little more than an extension of the State, sermons in the Caribbean colonies were rather like those in Britain itself: "The circumstances under which they were preached, as well as the character of the preachers" made them "examples, par excellence, of propagandist literature. They were not counsels of perfection or dogmatic expositions," writes Alfred Caldecott, who further observes (in his *The Church in the West Indies*) that many of the preachers "were much better qualified to be retailers of salt fish or boatswains to privateers than ministers of the Gospel" (59).

In the eighteenth century, Nonconformist missionaries started preaching in the West Indies; their sermons are clearly more emotional and energetic than those of the Episcopalian clergy—and more successful. This success was laid by Sir George Rose to the Nonconformists' ability, as he wrote, "to adapt to the inferior intellects of blacks and indentured servants and to the disadvantage of a logical and classical education suffered by Established Church missionaries and ministers" (qtd. in Caldecott 23). (The Rev. G. Nash of Grenada thought that most Anglican sermons seemed to slaves and working men "as if delivered in a foreign tongue.") Perhaps as significant was their constant opposition to singing, dancing, "vain shows and loose festivals," and their unrelenting support of the planter aristocracy and of slavery itself (24).

Ultimately, the Nonconformists (Baptists, Moravians, Wesleyans, and Presbyterians) built up respectable congregations who attended to sermons as means of obtaining knowledge that was otherwise rigorously proscribed. And with the passage of years, the Church of England clergy have attempted to regain communication with the people, especially in Jamaica, where Lena Kent (pseudonym of the poet Lena A. King) published two volumes of sermons (*Seed for the Sower*, 1960), designed to be read privately or by small groups or used as models for untrained preachers. In a foreword to *Goodness and Mercy* (1969), a similar compendium by the Rev. K. D. Carnegie, the bishop of Jamaica, he alluded to Lena Kent's books as the first contemporary collection of sermons. That a second collection by Mr Carnegie (*The House of the Lord*, 1971) was justified, attests to the continuing vitality of the sermon as a literary form in Jamaica.

Yet political oratory has surely dominated Caribbean public discourse. This raises problems for the serious student, for until very recent times, West Indian politicians spoke extemporaneously or impromptu and kept neither notes nor manuscript copies of speeches. As a result, we have almost none of the major addresses by such speakers as Albert Gomes, Captain Cipriani, Sir Alexander Bustamante, and the mercurial Sir Eric Gairy that were not delivered in parliamentary situations. Many speeches of Cheddi Jagan and the major political figures of the newer, smaller island nations are to be obtained in the form of mimeographed leaflets only: but they are often ephemeral publications and unavailable even in the libraries of the University of the West Indies or the national libraries and archival repositories. Clearly, then, there is great need for rhetorical research and anthologies to support the scholarly investigation of West Indian public address subsequent to the impassioned and effective speaking of Marcus Garvey.

In recent years, some of the Caribbean nations have started to provide for future students of West Indian public address by issuing collections of their leaders' speeches. Noteworthy among them are the following volumes: *A Collection of Addresses* (1968), by Sir Hugh Wooding, Chief Justice of Trinidad and Tobago; *Forged From the Love of Liberty: Selected Speeches of Dr Eric Williams*, prime minister of Trinidad and Tobago (1981); *A Destiny to Mould: Selected Discourses by the Prime Minister of Guyana* (1970), which covers the early and less controversial period of Forbes Burnham's premiership; *Forward Ever!: Three Years of the Grenadian Revolution. Speeches of Maurice Bishop* (1982); *The Faith that Moved the Mountain* (1979), speeches and essays by Randolph Fawkes of the Bahamas; and *Manley and the New Jamaica: Selected Speeches and Writings, 1938-1968*, skillfully edited and introduced by Professor Rex Nettleford. The speeches of Samuel Sharpe of Jamaica seem beyond recovery.

Perhaps no area of Commonwealth public address has been more carefully considered than that from South Asia. The importance of public speeches in the political and social movements of the past century have indubitably given the illiterate masses a keen appreciation of effective oratory and given the socially conscious intelligentsia a special awareness of well-argued cases, sound evidence, practicality in problem-solving, and the development of style.

S. C. De, author of *Public Speeches in Ancient and Medieval India*, after noting the development of rhetoric and public address in Greece and Rome, reminds his readers that long arguments composed in characteristic, and even prescribed, style and accompanied with cogent argumentation and development are to be found in the traditional Sanskrit and Prakrit literatures of India; and he further observes that

> Though forensic oratory and eloquent appeal to the masses are rare in the literature of ancient and medieval India, it may be stated that carefully prepared speeches addressed to select audiences are to be found specially in the epics, where good speaking is highly lauded and where Rama, for example, is described as expert in speaking, Bharata as the greatest of orators, Hanuman as skilful in speech, and Krishna as the greatest of speakers and most skilful in elocution. (6)

Then, from an examination of numerous speeches from Indian traditional literature, he infers that analogy, metaphor, antithesis, interrogation, sarcasm, and hyperbole are the favoured tropes; Sanskrit authors and speakers regarded "hyperbole as the best of the figures of speech" (98), and so idealization and exaggeration became the almost universal marks of Indian public address.

At the end of the nineteenth century, with the burgeoning of the movement for Indian independence, the great nationalist orators Mohandas K. Gandhi, B. G. Tilak, and G. K. Gokhale established themselves as pre-eminent speakers. Their printed speeches exerted a persuasive influence far beyond their immediate audiences and at the same time influenced the formation of a characteristically Indian and Hindu rhetorical method, one that amalgamated Brahmin analytic philosophy and incredible patience that results from an emphasis on the spiritual rather than on the material and visible.

Professor K. R. Srinivasa Iyengar, in his *Indian Writing in English*, devotes several pages to a discussion of the major Indian speakers and notes that just before World War I "A good English speech ... attracted only a few hundreds, perhaps a thousand or two; but it was a fit intellectual audience" (358). And the adaptation to great masses by Gandhiji and Jawaharlal Nehru never seemed to eliminate the intellectual content of their speeches. Whereas most Western speakers appear to choose between simplistic statements for mass audiences or reasonably erudite and intellectually demanding ones for select, small groups, Indian speakers have somehow managed to adapt to both audiences in the one discourse.

Of the great stature of Tilak there is no dispute: whether in Marathi or English he seemed equally at ease, and Sri Aurobindo (himself a distinguished speaker) declared Tilak's speeches "straightforward, lucid ... like a series of self-evident propositions," even if it was his celebrated twenty-one-hour courtroom speech in self-defence (1908). Lord Minto declared that there were, in England in 1906, few speakers of the stature of Gokhale or of his unusual gift of parliamentary advocacy and persuasion. And Gokhale's protégé, Srinivasa Sastri, who was categorized by competent critics as "the Empire's silver-tongued orator," "an artist in words," "the greatest Indian orator of his day," and (in Tagore's words) "like a stream speaking" was truly a gifted speaker.[1] Likewise, Sarojini Naidu, perhaps the first and finest Indian woman political orator, achieved great fame and success. Of her speech to the 1906 session of the Indian Social Conference in 1906 Gokhale wrote to her, "Your speech was more than an intellectual treat of the highest order. It was a perfect piece of art. We all felt for the moment to be lifted to a higher plane" (qtd. in Iyengar 181). Professor Amalendu Bose said of her perorations that they made the speaker "a resplendent personage of a magic world," while Iyengar himself observed succinctly that Naidu's speeches "seemed to soar above the humdrum ... a typical speech would be a flood of splendid improvisation endowed with an oceanic movement, wave upon wave of emotion and sentiment singing and subsiding,... shriller in tone and more overwhelming in effect." And of her delivery he noted that "as she warmed up, her eyes acquired a lustre and sparkled more and more ... she was audaciously, imperiously alive" (181). She was, in truth, the perfect example of the poet as popular politician. The list of effective orators could be extended, for public speaking in India is a major genre of literature, and it has been developed to an extraordinary degree of excellence just at a time when it has declined in the older democracies.

Establishing a Canon of Commonwealth Public Address 241

The Muslim politicians of British India could be said to have worked within a somewhat different oratorical tradition,[2] and because their leadership roles were generally less significant than those of Hindus, their speeches received more regional and parochial than national attention and influence. Notwithstanding, some of the speeches of Mahomed Ali Jinnah have merit as oratorical literature, though those in *Speeches as Governor-General of Pakistan, 1947-1948* (1949) are rather insipid, pedestrian statements—perhaps the result of his role.

The speeches of Zulfikar Ali Bhutto evince enthusiasm, vitality, and at times a frenetic quality that is wholly absent in the staid discourses of Yahya Khan, Liaquat Ali Khan, Mohammed Ali Zia, Ayub Khan, and even Harvard-educated Benazir Bhutto's speech to a joint session of the United States Congress on 7 June 1989. *Bangladesh, My Bangladesh: Selected Speeches and Statements* (1972), a collection of thirty speeches by Mujibur Rahman, has little merit. Doubtless the long absence of democratic conditions in Pakistan and Bangladesh accounts for the absence of confrontational or reformist-revolutionary rhetoric there, but one might expect that the leadership would use occasions for public communication to exhort, inveigle, or inspire.

Speeches in English appear to have been uncommon and undistinguished in Ceylon, at least until the recent past, when Prime Minister Mrs Bandaranaike delivered several of some merit during periods of internecine disturbances. Prior to these speeches, perhaps the only ones to merit recognition are some by James Alwis (1823-78), who achieved considerable renown as parliamentarian, lawyer, lecturer, and general savant. Well-read in British legal and political speeches, Alwis developed a style that was indebted to the long phrases and scholarly elaboration of the eighteenth-century imperial and colonial parliamentarians.

In general, he "extended from the literary essay and the public lecture to the political speech his practice of invoking established custom in the aid of reform ... his concern that his speeches should be accurately reported stemmed in part from this awareness that the smooth sentences were the product of years of labour" (Gooneratne 137). Unfortunately, no collection of his speeches has yet been published.

African speakers in English have been legion for a century now, and many of them are represented by printed collections: the best seem to be Kwame Nkrumah, Jomo Kenyatta, Jan Christian Smuts, Paul Kruger, Archbishop Desmond Tutu, and Nelson Mandela. But I have already commented on these elsewhere[3] and collected many in *Representative South African Speeches: The Rhetoric of Race and Religion* (1980).

The magnitude of the task of reading and evaluating the speeches of the Commonwealth is perhaps now apparent; and one must remember that Seychelles, Mauritius, Papua New Guinea, Malaysia, Singapore, and many new and unfamiliar nations have not been included in this brief conspectus.

Who, then, should constitute the canon of Commonwealth speakers now? I would propose the following—some for perhaps a single speech, others for many. Australia: R. G. Menzies, Henry Parkes, and Alfred Deakin; Canada: Joseph Howe, W. L. Mackenzie King, and Pierre Elliott Trudeau; West Indies: Marcus Garvey, Norman Manley, and Eric Williams; India: Mohandas K. Gandhi, Jawaharlal Nehru, G. K. Gokhale, and B. G. Tilak; Africa: Jomo Kenyatta, J. C. Smuts, and Nelson Mandela.

These sixteen speakers, addressing timeless issues of personal freedom, national identity, and universal responsibilities, merit the attention of all students of Commonwealth literature and culture. However, in the era of postmodernism, where few, if any, standards can be regarded as universally applicable, it is doubtful that the use of Aristotelian or even post-Aristotelian rhetorical principles would result in consensus. Notwithstanding, it is incontrovertible that Commonwealth public address should no longer be excluded from the canon of Commonwealth literary studies.

Almost every student of English literature can quote (or at least recognise) phrases from some of the great orations of British history, whether they are centuries old or more recent:

one brings to mind, for example, Queen Elizabeth I's "I have the heart of a king"; William Pitt's "I rejoice that America has resisted" and "You cannot conquer America"; Edward VIII's "The woman I love" abdication speech; and Winston Churchill's "Blood, sweat, and tears," "An iron curtain has descended," or "This was their finest hour" and other (particularly wartime) addresses.

In America, even school children are familiar with phrases from many of the memorable speeches in their nation's history, such as Patrick Henry's "Give me liberty or give me death"; Jonathan Edward's "Sinners in the hands of an angry God"; Abraham Lincoln's "With malice towards none"—and many can even quote in its entirety his Gettysburg Address; William Jennings Bryan's "You shall not crucify mankind on a cross of gold"; John F. Kennedy's "Ask not what your country can do for you"; and Martin Luther King's "I have a dream."

What a delight it would be if students of the Commonwealth could quote from (and hopefully restate the theses of) some of the great speeches that have been delivered by representative orators of even Australia, Canada, India, South Africa, and the West Indies, for they deserve to be remembered.

NOTES

[1] Fortunately, the modern Indian interest in printed speeches has equalled the interest in oral ones; as a consequence, we have comprehensive, accurate texts available. Some can be recommended: *Speeches and Writings of Gopal Krishna Gokhale* (1966), *The Select Gokhale* (1968), *Speeches of President V. V. Giri* (1974), *Selected Speeches of Lal Bahadur Shastri* (1974), *President Zakir Husain's Speeches* (1973), *Speeches of President Rajendra Prasad* (1972), *President Radhakrishnan's Speeches and Writings* (1969), and both *The Years of Challenge* and *The Years of Endeavour* (1975)—selected speeches of Indira Gandhi. To these should, of course, be added the collected speeches of Gandhi, Nehru, and Tilak at least—and perhaps even those of Krishna Menon, though he was generally demagogic.

[2] A convenient brief introduction to the Muslim speech tradition is to be found in H. Samuel Hamod, "Arab and Moslem Rhetorical Theory and Practice," *Central States Speech Journal*, 14.2 (May 1963): 88-99.

[3] "The Development of African Oratory in English," *African Literature in English: Development and Identity* (Philadelphia: African Studies Association, 1981), 29-47.

WORKS CITED

Bohman, George V. "The Colonial Period." *A History and Criticism of American Public Address.* Ed. William Norwood Brigance. New York: McGraw, 1943. 3-54.

Brigance, William Norwood, ed. *A History and Criticism of American Public Address.* New York: McGraw, 1943.

Caldecott, Alfred. *The Church in the West Indies.* London: Society for the Propagation of Christian Knowledge, 1898.

Cogswell, Fred. "Literary Activity in the Maritime Provinces (1815-1880)." *Literary History of Canada: Canadian Literature in English.* Ed. Carl F. Klinck. Toronto: U of Toronto P, 1967. 102-24.

De, S. C. *Public Speeches in Ancient and Medieval India: Based on Sanskrit and Prakrit Literature.* Delhi: Ajanta, 1932; rpt. 1976.

Gisborne, William. *New Zealand Rulers and Statesmen: From 1840 to 1897.* London: Sampson, 1897.

Goodrich, Chauncey A. *Select British Eloquence....* [1852] Indianapolis: Bobbs-Merrill, 1963.

Gooneratne, M. Y. *English Literature in Ceylon, 1815-1878.* Dehiwala: Tisara, 1968.

Iyengar, K. R. Srinivasa. *Indian Writing in English.* New York: Asia, 1962.

Klinck, Carl F., ed. *Literary History of Canada: Canadian Literature in English.* Toronto: University of Toronto P, 1967.

McCormick, E. H. *New Zealand Literature: A Survey.* London: OUP, 1959.

Melvin, Kenneth. "Education." *The Pattern of New Zealand Culture.* Ed. A. L. McLeod. Melbourne: OUP, 1968. 98-131.

Thomas, Gordon. "Canadian Public Address." Paper delivered at the Speech Association of the Central States Convention, 15 April 1962.